Information Technology in Educational Management

Edited by

Adrie J. Visscher

University of Twente,
Faculty of Educational Science and Technology,
Enschede, The Netherlands

Phil Wild

Loughborough University,
Department of Education,
Loughborough, United Kingdom

and

Alex C.W. Fung

Hong Kong Baptist University,
Hong Kong SAR, China

KLUWER ACADEMIC PUBLISHERS
DORDRECHT / BOSTON / LONDON

A C.I.P. Catalogue record for this book is available from the Library of Congress.

ISBN 0-7923-7074-0

Published by Kluwer Academic Publishers,
P.O. Box 17, 3300 AA Dordrecht, The Netherlands.

Sold and distributed in North, Central and South America
by Kluwer Academic Publishers,
101 Philip Drive, Norwell, MA 02061, U.S.A.

In all other countries, sold and distributed
by Kluwer Academic Publishers,
P.O. Box 322, 3300 AH Dordrecht, The Netherlands.

Printed on acid-free paper

Printed in the Netherlands.

CONTENTS

APPENDIX   **SAMS Questionnaire**
(Alex C.W. Fung, Adrie J. Visscher & Phil Wild)

PREFACE

The knowledge surrounding the development and implementation of computer-assisted school information systems has been growing in many corners of the world since the mid-1980s. This originated from a group of people with vision and enthusiasm. They saw the enormous potential of these information systems for enhancing the effectiveness of school staff and improving school performance. As with any innovation they faced problems which they tried to solve, sometimes successfully, sometimes not. Gradually, expertise has accumulated and those who have been active in this field feel that the time is now right to share and exchange the lessons learned and, in co-operation with colleagues, to try to find solutions for those problems that have persisted. From our labors newcomers can learn from the efforts, successes and mistakes of others.

In 1994 Ben-Zion Barta and Yaffa Gev from the Ministry of Education of Israel were aware of the growing need to share information and managed to obtain funding to organize a conference on the utilization of information technology for the administration and management of schools. Scientists, system developers, implementers and others active in this area travelled to Jerusalem where these practitioners and experts from around the globe were brought together for the first time to share their knowledge.

The paper presentations and workshops were so successful that it was decided to organize an ITEM conference every two years (Yaffa Gev invented the ITEM acronym which stands for Information Technology in Educational Management). Since Jerusalem these conferences have been held respectively in Hong Kong, Maine in the USA, and Auckland in New Zealand. In 2002 the ITEM conference will be held in Helsinki. The conferences have engendered a spirit of co-operation amongst people around the world: they have resulted in papers and special issues for scientific journals, obtained research funding, carried out research projects and organized research fellowships. As a group we successfully applied in 1996 for the establishment of IFIP (International Federation for Information Processing) Working Group 3.7 to promote the effective and efficient use of information technology for the management of educational institutions in all respects (for more information, please refer to http://ifip-item.hkbu.edu.hk). International co-operation and exchange of information on the state of the art of the research, development, and implementation of ITEM will help us to achieve this overall goal.

Six years after the Jerusalem conference we are proud to be able to publish the results of activities in this field. Research into the design and implementation of computer-assisted school information systems worldwide has highlighted numerous pitfalls and many wasted resources. The lack of a vehicle to integrate the know-how gained has meant that there has been no way of capitalizing on these experiences. We considered it important to synthesize our experience and that of others into a publication providing practical and substantiated information on the design and introduction of computer-mediated school information systems for those who plan to start or extend the usage of these systems. However, just as importantly, we propose a vision of future developments in the application of IT in school administration and management based on our accumulated knowledge and projected advances in technology.

This book seeks to fill the significant gap in the body of literature on school information systems and related school management and thereby to promote the more successful design and implementation of computer-assisted school information systems in the 21st century.

The book has been written for an international audience in developing as well as in developed countries consisting of students, researchers, system designers and implementers, practitioners, policy-makers, and more generally, professionals in the field of school administration and management. We hope they find that we have been successful in providing valuable information and guidance to support the effective development, installation and usage of powerful school information systems that are continually growing in sophistication.

Book structure

The book is organized into three sections.

The first section is of an introductory nature. Chapter 1 starts with an introduction to 'school information system' and related concepts. Thereafter, Visscher analyzes the forms of support from which school staff can benefit when computer-supported school information systems. Finally, the author analyzes the reasons for improved school efficiency and school effectiveness and describes the developmental stages of SISs.

Chapters 2, 3 and 4 present examples of automated school information systems that are used extensively today in the United Kingdom (SIMS), Hong Kong (SAMS) and New Zealand (MUSAC). The descriptions all address similar topics thus enabling the comparison of the systems as well as a consideration of the pros and cons of alternative design and implementation strategies. The following topics are addressed by Wild and Walker (chapter 2), Fung and Ledesma (chapter 3), and Nolan, Brown and Graves (chapter 4):

- The political, educational and cultural context of the design ands introduction of SISs in their country;
- The history of SISs in their country;
- The strategy followed in the design of the information system;
- The structure and contents of the information system including the types of administrative and managerial support it provides;
- The implementation process (e.g., training and support) that has been followed to promote system utilization;

- Evaluations of the design and implementation strategy as well as of the quality of the resulting school information system;
- Evidence on information system utilization and its impact;
- The plans for the future development of the information system;
- The lessons learned and recommended strategies for system design and implementation.

The second section of the book collates research and development work on computer-assisted school information systems and draws up guidelines for further development and implementation.

In chapter 5 Fung & Visscher present an overview of the factors influencing the usage and impact of school information systems. This is done in two steps. First, a socio-technical, holistic approach to school information systems as an innovation is presented. This is followed by a more detailed presentation of the variables (and their interrelationships) that are significant in system design and implementation. This chapter serves as a basis for the chapters that follow.

Tatnall in the sixth chapter focuses on one of the important factors discussed in chapter five, that is, preferable strategies in the design of sophisticated school information systems.

In chapter seven, Visscher & Fung enlarge on two further influential factors affecting school information systems:

- the nature of the implementation process which will promote the usage and positive impact of the information system;
- the nature of schools as organizations, particularly the features of policy-making and information usage within them.

Sections I and II of this book present the body of knowledge accumulated in the field. The third and final section is oriented towards the future.

In chapter 8, Wild & Smith present views on the probable developments of ITEM in the foreseeable future. Leading software vendors from various countries were canvassed for their opinions of what their products would look like and what support for education management they would provide over the next decade. The users' perspective was drawn from interviews with a range of users. The views from (non-) governmental organizations were solicited in the United Kingdom, Australia, Finland, France, Hong Kong, New Zealand, The Netherlands, and The USA. Finally, members of the IFIP Working Group 3.7 (ITEM) were asked to put forward their views forecasting the future of ITEM. These sources of information have been integrated into the eighth chapter.

The final chapter draws conclusions on the major points and addresses the question of what should be done to 'get things right', i.e., to utilize the potential of professional school information systems as fully as possible as soon as possible.

The book is the result of the contribution of many people whose roles we gratefully acknowledge. Firstly, we would like to express our gratitude to Kluwer Academic Publishers for producing this edited book that will make the accumulated knowledge accessible to anyone around the world. Secondly, we appreciate the co-operation of all the contributors, their willingness to report on their research and to share with us their perspectives on the future of information technology in educational management. More than twenty people from seven different countries have contributed to the work and without their commitment and investment it would have been impossible to produce this book. In addition to their intellectual input, Arthur Tatnall and Ray Taylor made a significant contribution to the language editing of the contributions for which we are extremely grateful. Finally, we would like to thank Marja Mulckhuyse for her valuable and accurate secretarial support at various stages in the production of this book; she transformed the raw manuscripts into the chapter versions you find in this book.

Acronyms

There are many acronyms used in the text which we feel usefully abbreviates the reading but which may be new to some readers. Although these are described when they are first used, for the reader's convenience we reproduce them on the next page.

Enschede /Loughborough/Hong Kong,

Adrie J. Visscher, *University of Twente, The Netherlands*
Phil Wild, *Loughborough University, United Kingdom*
Alex C.W. Fung, *Hong Kong Baptist University, China*

LIST OF ACRONYMS

4GL	Fourth Generation Languages
AIP	Artificial Intelligence Paradigm
ASP	Application Services Provider
BBC	British Broadcasting Corporation
CAI	Computer-Assisted Instruction
CASE	Computer-Aided Software Engineering
CBAM	Concerns Based Adoption Model
CBDS	Common Basic Data Set
CCTA	Central Computer and Telecommunications Agency
CDS	Communication and Delivery System
CMI	Computer-Managed Instruction
DES	Department of Education and Science
DFD	Data Flow Diagrams
DfEE	Department for Education and Science
DSL	Digital Service Link
DSS	Decision Support Systems
ED	Education Department
EIS	Executive Information Systems
EMB	Education and Manpower Bureau
ER	Entity-Relationship
FMS	Financial Management System
GCSE	General Certificate of Secondary Education
HKBU	Hong Kong Baptist University
HKEA	Hong Kong Examinations Authority
ICT	Information and Communication Technology
IS	Information System
ISS	Information Systems Strategy
IT	Information Technology
ITEM	Information Technology in Educational Management
ITSD	Information Technology Services Department
JAD	Joint Application Design
JAD	Joint Application Development
LAN	Local Area Network
LEA	Local Educational Authority
MIDAS	Management Information Data Access System

MIS	Management Information System
MRS	Management Reporting System
MUSAC	Massey University School Administration by Computer Project
ODBC	Open DataBase Connectivity
OFSTED	Office for Standards in Education
OMR	Optical Mark Reader
PI	Performance Indicator
PMIS	Pedagogical Management Information System
POA	Primary One Allocation
PRINCE	Project In a Controlled Environment
RAD	Rapid Application Development
RDBM	Relational Data Base Management
RML	Research Machines Limited
RSF	Relevant System in Focus
SAMS	School Administration and Management System
SAR	Special Administrative Region
SCHOLIS	School Information System (for Dutch secondary schools)
SCRIPT	Schools Control and Recording of Information for Pupils and Teachers
SENCO	Special Needs Education Code of practice
SIMS	School Information Management System
SIS	School Information System
SFA	Secondary Four Allocation
SMI	School Management Initiative
SOA	Secondary One Allocation
SSA	Secondary Six Allocation
SSADM	Structured System Analysis and Design Methodology
STAR	Students Teaching and Academic Record
TPS	Transaction Processing Systems
VOR	Virtual Optical Rendering
WCBS	West Country Business Systems
XML	Extensible Markup Language (current replacement for HTML)

SECTION I

Introduction to the nature of computer-assisted school information systems

CHAPTER 1

COMPUTER-ASSISTED SCHOOL INFORMATION SYSTEMS: THE CONCEPTS, INTENDED BENEFITS, AND STAGES OF DEVELOPMENT

Adrie J. Visscher
University of Twente, The Netherlands

1. INTRODUCTION

This chapter first focuses on the question of what is meant by the 'school information systems' (SIS) concept followed in section 3 by an analysis of the intended benefits of using SISs. Section 4 provides a detailed analysis of possible modules of SISs and the types of support which can be provided for school staff. A brief description of the history and the growing importance of the field in support of education, with an overview of the growing research interest in SISs, conclude the chapter in sections 5 and 6.

2. CONCEPTUALISATION

The 'information system' concept has become generally very popular, including in the field of education. However, the meaning is not always clear or precise. One can use the concept in the very broad sense and include all formal, informal, manual, computer-assisted, and verbal activities to store, process, obtain, and distribute data. In that case we are referring to the information system of an organization such as a school. A more narrow definition of the term, however, is more usual: a system supporting the *computer-assisted* storage, manipulation and production of data. Various related terms, such as 'administrative information systems', 'decision-support systems' and 'management information systems' are also found in this context.

Central to this book is the concept of the 'school information system' (SIS) together with an analysis of what such computer-assisted system can mean for schools.

It is difficult to state precisely what a computer-assisted SIS is because the technology on which it is based is changing continuously. This implies that the types of support school information systems offer, and the computer applications they consist of, also change. It is, therefore, better to define school information systems in abstract terms:

3

A.J. Visscher et al. (eds.), Information Technology in Educational Management, 3–18.
© 2001 *Kluwer Academic Publishers. Printed in the Netherlands.*

an information system based on one or more computers, consisting of a data bank and
one or more computer applications which altogether enable the computer-supported
storage, manipulation, retrieval, and distribution of data to support school management.

This definition implies that the specific nature of a particular school information
system is dependent on the number and character of computer applications (e.g.,
student administration, personnel management, student timetabling, etc.) included in
the information system. The features of SIS-subsystems can vary considerably.
Sometimes they mainly support the routine registration of data and the production of
standard lists. In other cases the computer also provides policy-making information
to school organizational staff that supports them in their strategic management
activities.

The activities of teachers and clerical employees in schools result in a data bank
filled with, hopefully, up to date data on the school organization and its
environment. This data bank enables the production of valuable managerial
information (e.g., trends, patterns, forecasts) as detailed later.

School information systems are not only designed for assisting school managers,
but are also used by clerical staff in registering, processing and outputting student,
finance, personnel and other data for day to day, routine work. Actually, the research
shows (Visscher et al., 1999 and Visscher & Bloemen, 1999) that SISs in schools
are mainly used for clerical work, with managers so far failing to receive much
benefit from these systems. It is therefore important that we try to find ways in
which we can promote the use of SISs by school managers (cf. chapter 7).

As mentioned earlier, the term 'information system' is used in various contexts
and for different types of systems. The definition presented here implies that quite a
few of these systems fall outside the focus of this book. A relevant example is a
student monitoring system for evaluating long term student progress (Gillijns, 1991;
Vlug, 1997). Student progress data can be entered into these computer-assisted
systems which thereafter produce student progress reports that can be used at both
teacher and school management levels.

The external school systems designed for feeding back school performance data
(indicating schools' performance data compared with that of other schools) are
sometimes also called 'school information systems' (cf. Fitz-Gibbon, 1996; Visscher
& Coe, forthcoming). Integration of such systems into SISs is weak at present but
will grow in importance for school management with a move towards performance
related pay such as in the UK.

Integrated learning systems according to Underwood (1997) operate on the
behaviorist model of learning that uses drill and practice to deliver a core curriculum
of knowledge and skills, through individualized tutoring and practice. In other
words, these systems support teaching-learning processes instead of the clerical and
managerial activities that are central to this book.

There is, however, a trend towards more integration of the computer-assisted
registering of classroom data and administrative and managerial school data.
Hogenbirk (1997), for instance, reports on a Dutch tool for planning and monitoring
the teaching-learning process. The tool supports students in planning their learning
activities, and assists teachers monitoring the learners who study fairly
independently. It is designed to be linked to existing computer-assisted school

information systems as well as to educational courseware and student assessment tools. Also in other countries classroom activities are becoming more important in computerized school information systems. The authors of chapter 4 for example point to the importance of the so-called 'classroom manager' module in the New-Zealands MUSAC school information system.

The Internet offers various possibilities to assist in the running of schools. One can, for instance, think of the web-based exchange of data between schools, external bodies and parents.

Having pointed to various types of 'information systems' that fall outside the central focus of this book, we will now restrict ourselves to its narrow meaning. The rest of this chapter and in most of the book the focus is computer-based tools for assisting clerical and managerial school staff in their administrative and managerial activities.

3.   AN OVERVIEW OF SIS-MODULES AND TYPES OF ASSISTANCE

3.1   A SIS-framework

A detailed overview of the potential of school information systems, a so-called school information system framework (Visscher, 1992) is shown in Figure 1. The framework is the result of an in-depth analysis of the clerical, administrative, and managerial work, outside the classroom, in Dutch secondary schools (Essink & Visscher, 1989). The goal of the analysis was to identify all possible and valuable types of computer support where the computer could replace existing manual work as well as assisting in new activities that have become possible as a result of the introduction of the computer. Visscher (1992) also describes the possible forms of support the computer can give within the subsystems of the school information system framework, in terms of so-called elementary activities. These can not be presented in full here for reasons of space but Figure 1 shows that the SIS-framework includes two types of subsystems/modules relating to administrative and managerial functions.

The administrative subsystems support various types of data handling activities on student, financial, personnel and other school data. Logically, the student administration subsystem is the heart of the school office assisting in all data handling in the 'life of a student', like his/her enrollment, absenteeism, student counseling, assessment (report marks and central examination marks), and the deletion of students. In the same way that this has been done for the 'student administration' subsystem, each of the other six school administrative subsystems can be elaborated into sub-subsystems, such as those supporting all stages of the life of a school employee (subsystem II), school budget (subsystem III) and timetable. In section 3.2 we will elaborate on the types of support and benefits for school staff when using these administrative subsystems/modules.

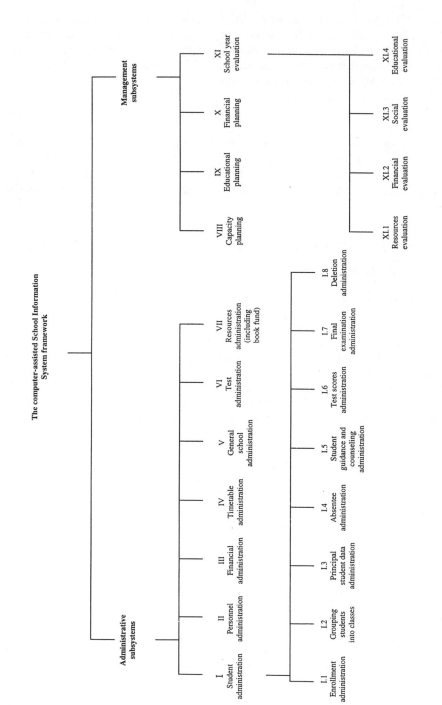

Figure 1: Administrative and managerial subsystems of a computer-assisted information system for secondary schools (source: Visscher, 1992)

Management subsystems in Figure 1 concern information system modules that have been developed to assist school managers to control activities carried out frequently and which are common to most schools (the latter makes the development of these modules cost-effective). The advantage of these modules is that school managers themselves do not have to define complex programming statements to obtain the management information they need. If the modules have been developed then selection of the option provides the required information directly via a system menu.

Three of the management subsystems in Figure 1 support school *planning* activities. The *'capacity planning'* module assists for example in the planning of:
- the number of lesson periods and task periods that will be allocated to teaching and non-teaching staff;
- the technical infrastructure, e.g., computers for students and for school staff, photocopiers and other machines;
- school buildings.

The *'educational planning'* subsystem is closely connected with the capacity planning subsystem as the results of the latter provide the starting point for the former. In educational planning the available lesson periods are allocated to individual teachers, and the student, classroom and teacher timetables are constructed.

In the last planning subsystem, *'financial-economical planning'*, a school budget estimate is drawn up on the basis of financial data for previous years, expected trends, available finances and financial planning parameters. The subsystem can also provide support in forecasting the liquid assets of a school over a defined period.

The last management subsystem *'school year evaluation'* provides an evaluation of what has taken place within a defined timeframe in the school. The evaluation subsystem helps, for example, in retrieving the following evaluative information:
- the budgets spent in a school year (e.g., where did we spend more than planned, where less);
- the personnel aspects (e.g., illness of staff) in a school year;
- the academic results (e.g., the percentage of students in the final grades passing this year's final examinations in comparison with other school years; the percentage of students promoted to higher grades);
- the utilization of other than financial resources (e.g., the classroom-student ratio);
- the percentage of students that has achieved the various school-type grades, or that has passed an examination of a certain type;
- the 'bottleneck grades' in terms of student flow-through;
- per subject, per teacher statistics on final examination scores in comparison with previous school years and with school internal examinations;
- the magnitude of student absenteeism after a school truancy reduction policy has been implemented;

- patterns in students' choices of subjects and school types;
- trends in cost types (the ones that increased, decreased, or remained the same).

Incorporated within these four explicit management subsystems is the potential for wide-ranging and contextualized managerial support.

The questions of interest to school managers in performing their management tasks vary strongly between school managers because they operate in different schools and contexts. All their varying information needs simply cannot be included in a standard information system menu. However, if the relevant school data have been collected in the clerical subsystems, and if the database is of the relational kind that can be approached by means of modern query languages, then an enormous variety of interrelationships between the data can be analyzed to support school managers in their work. It will, however, require particular skills to define the queries to satisfy the variety of information needs. This may be acquired in training courses where school managers can learn to exploit the wealth of information schools possess with modern, computerised school information systems. Further in these chapters we will show that there is currently a lack of such skills and training.

3.2 Five Types of Support

So far, an overview has been given of the nature and content of the information subsystems that a management information system for schools may include. The support computer-assisted school information systems can provide can also be analyzed from the perspective of the data processing functions SISs can provide for school staff:

1. *computer database update*: recording changes in the relevant school organizational environment and in the school itself. (E.g., student application data are entered into the database of the information system);
2. *information retrieval and document production*: reporting on the school organizational situation for operational activities requiring little or no problem diagnosis because the data lead directly to the action to be carried out. (E.g., a computer report on those students who have applied for admission but who still have to hand in some data relevant to the admittance decision);
3. *decision-making*: the computer 'itself' makes a decision on the basis of available information. (E.g., when admission criteria have been defined unambiguously automatic admissions by the SIS are possible);
4. *data communication*: mutually connected computers exchange messages and other data between school staff and other organizations. (E.g., data on admitted students);
5. a. *decision-making support*; some managerial problems are *structured*, i.e., they consist of a limited number of variables, the way in which they can be solved is known, and also the number of solutions. (E.g., the composition of lesson groups, or school timetables). The computer, as a result of its enormous computing capacity can compute all possible solutions for these structured problems, from which school managers can choose the solution they prefer.

5. b. Most problems school staff face are not structured but *ill structured*. These are characterized by uncertain causes, many variables that may have caused the problem and various possible remedies of unknown effect. This type of problem requires problem-diagnosis and the search for solutions is an important prerequisite for dealing with the problem. The computer, through flexible reporting, can provide decision-makers in schools with specific information relevant to the problem solving required. In our view SISs can be very valuable in these situations as they enable more informed decision-making in contexts where uncertainty can be enormous.

Unfortunately, school managers have not gained great benefit from the capacity of SISs to inform their decision-making on ill-structured problems (Visscher, 1996). This may be due to the fact that the usual circumstances of school administration and management do not permit informed dialogue, decision-making, action-taking and evaluation (Goodlad, 1975). This results in relatively low levels of information usage and uninformed decision-making continues to be common in this type of organization. Many school managers do not put much effort into evaluating how their school is performing. The advent of SISs does not seem to change this without enormous effort.

In most cases full rational decision-making on ill-structured problems will not be possible. 'Bounded rationality', finding 'satisfactory' instead of the best solutions, is often what can be achieved as a result of the complexity of organizational problems, the political factors involved and the limitations of the human information processing capacity (Simon, 1993). Information does not automatically lead to decisions, decisions are the product of many interacting variables, and many factors beyond information play a role (Weiss in Alkin, 1990).

Moreover, SISs contain only part of the information that 'drives the organization' (Mintzberg, 1989) and that is preferred by school staff. SIS information can also be too old, too general, and too inaccessible. In combination with the formal, quantitative and aggregate data SISs produce, informal, qualitative, and detailed information is essential for school decision-making. Neither informal data alone nor formal SIS-data alone form a sufficient basis for managing schools (Sproull & Zubrow, 1981).

Though SIS output will not directly lead to undisputed solutions for all ill-structured school problems it may well enable more informed decision-making by providing information on the organizational functioning of schools, possible causes of ill-structured problems, and the likely effects of actions that may be taken.

Visscher (1996) points to the following five types of SIS-output that can help in the diagnosing and solving of ill-structured school managerial problems:
1. Information on *relationships between variables*, e.g., between:
   • the school criteria for admitting students and the student pass rates on final examinations;
   • student absenteeism and student achievement;

- the magnitude of student absenteeism and school timetable features (e.g., when are students playing truant most?);
- lesson drop out (the number of lessons cancelled) and lesson group achievement;
- school examination scores and national examination scores per subject and per teacher.

2. *Information on patterns*, for example patterns in:
   - school costs/budgets;
   - teachers'/departments' results;
   - student flow-through;
   - student achievement over the years.

3. *Answers to what-if questions*, e.g.:
   - how many teachers will be needed if student intake grows by X %, or decreases by Y %;
   - how changes in student promotion criteria will impact on student promotion figures;
   - the results of alternative allocations of teaching lesson periods to teachers;
   - the effects of alternative strategies for allocating financial resources.

4. *Evaluative data* e.g., to what degree:
   - the percentage of class repeaters has increased after the grade promotion criteria have been changed?
   - student results have improved since the introduction of extra mathematics lessons.

4. INTENDED BENEFITS

The development and implementation of school information systems is usually motivated by expected efficiency and effectiveness benefits. The empirical research evidence for these claims, however, is still small. This does not mean that the opposite effects were found, just that it is very difficult to prove these benefits unambiguously (e.g., in pre-test post-test comparisons). The research that has been done in this area consists mainly of studies in which school information system users are asked for their perceptions on the extent to which SISs have improved their efficiency and/or effectiveness (e.g., Visscher & Spuck, 1991; Visscher & Bloemen, 1999; Visscher et al., 1999).

Despite the lack of empirical proof for these high hopes, there are plausible grounds for expecting efficiency and effectiveness benefits as a result of introducing SISs.

Efficiency is defined here as the ratio between input and output, for instance, the ratio between the manpower and time needed to produce a certain amount of information. It is expected that the computer enables the storage, manipulation, production and distribution of the same amount or more data with the same or less manpower and time. The efficiency of school activities may be improved in the following ways:

- in the pre-SIS situation the same data are registered separately and repeatedly at several locations (e.g., by the caretaker, school office staff, counselor, and deputy heads) which requires much school staff time. The single entry of data in a central database saves time, facilitates the multiple usage of the same data by all staff, and prevents errors which may have occurred as a consequence of the repeated registration of data by various staff;
- the computer-assisted manipulation of data (e.g., making computations, sorting data, etc.), and the production of internal and external lists, reports, etc. saves time because in the pre-SIS situation the information demands of external bodies and persons requires the repeated manual or typed registration of these data on specific forms which now simply can be 'spit out' by the computer;
- the computer-assisted exchange of school data can be done most efficiently if the recipient accepts the data in a form that can be retrieved from the school database by school staff.

Improved school effectiveness, defined as a better attainment of the school goals as a result of the usage of computer-assisted information systems, is even more difficult to prove in research. However, there is good reason for positive expectations:

- school managers often spend considerable time on clerical work. Because of the probable efficiency benefits described, they can spend more time on other activities that may improve the quality of school functioning like developing better educational material, school policies, and improving school quality assurance procedures. Hopefully, these activities will help schools to better achieve their goals.
- school staff can find better solutions for structured allocation problems (e.g., composing timetables, the allocation of students to lesson groups, or the allocation of teacher-lesson group combinations to the timetable) because the computer can compute alternative solutions for complex allocation problems from which the best one can be chosen and implemented (previously the first solution found was accepted). As allocation results often influence daily school life (e.g., via a timetable) the SIS has an impact on the life and well-being of students and school staff and therefore impacts on the effectiveness of schools;
- the SIS is not just an automated variant of the card-index box in which data can be registered in computer files. The information system can also help to signal that certain aspects of schooling require attention. If certain standards have been defined in advance, such as a student has played truant too often or the percentage of low marks within a class is too great, and transcribed into software, the computer can provide a warning to school managers if the standards are not being met. This may improve process control, lead to more timely corrective actions, and lead to a more effective school;
- if the school information system enables an investigation of the interrelationships between variables (e.g., between truancy and student achievement) more informed school policy-making becomes possible (and by that, the reduction of

uncertainty), as well as the evaluation of the effects of school policy measures, such as whether the number of truants has been reduced after a school policy measure to achieve this was introduced. It seems likely that improving the conditions of school decision-making will affect the quality of school policies, and as such, the results achieved by schools.

5. THE HISTORY OF SCHOOL INFORMATION SYSTEMS

In the 1990s the history of the development and implementation of computerized SISs was analyzed for seven countries by the authors of a special issue of the Journal of Research on Computing in Education (Visscher, 1991). The results of their analyses are summarized in Figure 2.

stages	goals	approach for analysis and design	standardization versus flexibility
teachers: initiation stage (1960-1985)	efficiency	- application- directed - expert - decentralized	tailor-made
software vendors: expansion stage (1970s-1985)	efficiency	- more integration - expert - central	standardization
special projects: integration stage (1980s-?)	efficiency & effectiveness	- fundamental - participative - central	compromise
stabilization stage (?)	-	-	-

Figure 2. Stages in the Development of Computer-assisted SISs

5.1 The Four Stages

Nolan (1977, 1979) has presented a well-known theory on the growth stages which organizations pass through when automating their data processing activities. Zisman (1978) has transferred this theory to the field of office automation, an area with many similarities with school administrative computerization. The stages that Zisman distinguishes can also be observed in the history of SISs in schools, so we have applied Nolan's stages (initiation, expansion, integration, stabilization) to the history of SISs.

Figure 2 represents the *subjective* appraisal of the contributors to the special issue (Visscher & Spuck, 1991). It is also important to point to the fact that the label given to a country is an overall evaluation. In other words, big differences may exist between schools within one country. For example, if some or most schools are in the expansion stage, other schools may still be in the initiation stage. Despite these limitations, some interesting general trends are emerging. Basically, the same 'initiation picture' can be observed in most countries that started their activities between the 1960s and 1985. Pioneer teachers, in most cases teachers in one or more of the science subjects, enthusiastically created the first amateurish school administrative applications tailor-made for their own. High hopes existed, especially as far as the computer-assisted construction of school timetables (e.g., Bird, 1984) was concerned. It was expected that it would now be possible to enter all relevant data on students, teachers, classrooms, subjects and constraints, and that the computer thereafter could 'spit out' the timetable. In most countries, however, the complexity of school timetabling proved to be so enormous that, although the computer fulfills an important role in this process, the last and most difficult parts of the timetabling process still have to be done by humans.

The United States was the pioneer country in this field, developing the first business applications for applications such as finance and payroll back in the 1960s. Many other countries needed 15-20 more years to reach the same level of school administrative computing. Some countries, especially developing countries, still await the entrance to the *initiation stage* due to a lack of capable professionals, technical infrastructure and finance. Countries active in this area (e.g., Hong-Kong, the United Kingdom, the USA, New Zealand, and the Netherlands) all had their first school administrative computer-applications by the end of the 1970s.

In the second stage, *the expansion stage* in the 1970s and 1980s there was growth in both the number of schools using SISs and the number of applications being developed. Software vendors entered the school market producing their own software, or adapting already existing software that had been developed by pioneer teachers, to more professional standards.

The *integration stage* was characterized by the move from the management of computers to the management of *information*. It is interesting to note that some countries that were lagging behind considerably (e.g., Hong Kong, Australia) have changed their position dramatically in a relatively short period. In fact, they became countries operating in the forefront of the use of computerized SISs in a few years. In other words, if a nation decides to direct serious attention to supporting school administration and management by means of modern, computer-supported SISs, and if it is able and willing to commit the required resources, it can change the state of the art in this area dramatically quickly. This is good news for all countries that plan to start their initiatives in this area. They can learn from the experience gained in other countries and avoid repeating the same mistakes and waste of resources .

A special project initiated by the national or the state government, or a project group, has provided the stimulus to enter the integration stage in a considerable number of countries (e.g., the SAMS-project in Hong Kong, the PMIS-project in Israel, and the SCHOLIS-project in The Netherlands). Without these projects progress proves to be much slower. The projects aim to produce better school information systems, that is, systems that enable more school efficiency and school effectiveness.

In the final stage, the *stabilization stage,* the maintenance and refinement of information systems, such as the adaptation of available systems in support of new developments within the school organization, or external to it, is central. Although some countries think they are in the stabilization stage, or expect that they will enter this stage in the near future, it is our view that this last stage of development is still unachievable since it presupposes the accomplishment of the full potential of computer-assisted school administration and management. Although administrative applications have been developed in a considerable number of countries, software for the full support of managerial work is still elusive. Moreover, new technological and scientific developments, such as the Internet and psychometry, promote new types of support for administrative and managerial school staff.

5.2 Design Strategies, and Tailor-made or Standard SISs?

In each of the first three stages presented in Figure 2 different automation goals, analysis and design approaches, and ways of addressing the so-called standardization-flexibility problem can be observed.

In the initiation and expansion stages teachers, individual schools and school districts developed school administrative applications to improve the efficiency of school office work. The strategy applied for the analysis and design was amateurish due to the fact that professional expertise of the autodidactic teachers was limited for this type of work. The strategy followed was of the 'first things first' kind in which a teacher noticed an area where the computer was expected to be of value, such as 'registration of pupil data'. He analyzed these activities in his school and developed software that assisted in some way. The approach was application-directed. Subsequently various computer-applications were developed by teachers who operated as 'experts', taking design decisions autonomously within their schools, but without a total picture of the information system to be developed. The software was developed in a decentralized way, for usage within one school, with little transportability between schools.

In the expansion stage the software vendors developing and adapting software maintained the narrow goal to increasing the efficiency of clerical operations in schools. The software was often based on the analysis of a few schools and thereafter adapted, based on the experiences of users. The design strategy was not purely a matter of developing one application at a time and by this time some consideration was given to the interrelationships between applications. Full integration, however, remained a distant goal only to be achieved much later. Several loose, non-integrated school administrative applications were developed in this stage and the lack of integration of modules had two disadvantages. Firstly, it required the repeated entry of the same data into different applications. Secondly, it limited the possibilities for school managerial support since managers are interested in relationships between data (see previous sections) whereas the storage of data in separate applications does not allow the analysis of their interrelationships. Just as in the previous stage of development, the developers played an expert role. User participation was limited and only indirect with representatives from schools presenting feedback on software prototypes that frequently were already in nearly final form.

An important difference between the pioneer teachers and the software vendors is that the latter did not develop information systems for one school but, logically, tried to sell the system to as many schools as possible. As a result of their centralized developmental approach standard systems were developed so that schools had to adapt themselves to the systems.

The third group of system designers initiated special projects aimed at accomplishing a new generation of school information systems to address school effectiveness alongside administrative efficiency. New benefits of system use were now considered important such as managerial assistance and computer-supported data communication. These attempted to provide wide-ranging and useful forms of computer-support. The integration of modules enabled growth to the level of *management* information systems. It was at this stage that the value of management information was well recognized. Management information was considered an important asset in making decisions about the operation of schools. In other words, computer-supported planning and control became important. The advent of relational database management systems (RDBMs) and local area networks (LANs) facilitated new management-oriented forms of assistance. By relating data elements within a database to each other, the production of valuable management information becomes possible. An important prerequisite for such an information system, however, is a thorough analysis of the school organization delineating the procedures and activities taking place within schools, and indicating how school activities, managerial decisions and data are interrelated ('the fundamental design approach'). The development of such systems does not only presuppose a professional approach but also considerable sums of money. By the mid-1980s only a few countries had progressed to this stage.

The fundamental approach for system design followed in this stage includes extensive user participation. The goal is to develop a standard system at central level for as many schools as possible. System standardization is required because of the high costs of system design, development, user support and maintenance.

Nevertheless, designers also know the importance of SIS-flexibility and therefore try to offer this to users wherever possible by trying to achieve a compromise between standardization and flexibility. This is done by offering schools the option to choose the SIS-modules they prefer, as well as options within SIS-modules. Relational database management systems and query languages also provide some flexibility since users can then decide for themselves what information they want to retrieve from the SIS-database.

Although the fundamental approach can be observed in a number of countries, it is still not widespread. Experience, however, has shown that although this approach is costly, the money invested will produce a better return because the developmental work is very likely to result in a system with a long life-cycle, with a greater contribution to improving the efficiency and effectiveness of schools.

In the stabilization stage no new design and development approach is being followed as the maintenance of available SISs is the central feature of this stage.

6. THE INCREASING IMPORTANCE OF THE FIELD

The field of computerized SISs as a support for education as well as a field of scientific research has grown in importance considerably during the 1990s. This is shown by the enormous sums of money invested, in order to let educational institutions benefit from the capability of computerized SISs to support clerical work and management activities, and ultimately improve the quality of learning and teaching. Hong Kong, for example, has invested 70 million US dollars to develop and implement an integrated computer network linking the Education Department and more than 1,500 primary and secondary schools.

Another indication of the increased interest and importance of the field of computerized SISs is suggested by the paper presentations at the World Conference on Computers in Education. In 1990 (Sydney) only one paper was presented on the use of computers for school management purposes (Visscher, 1990) but subsequently about 15 research papers on this topic were presented at the next World Conference held in 1995 (Birmingham). More importantly, a professional group of 20 experts from ten different countries worked together during the conference week in 1995. They produced a report addressing the development, research, and implementation topics central to the ongoing growth of IT and educational management (ITEM) and the research methods and strategies to generate the required knowledge and understanding (Nolan & Visscher, 1996). In addition to this activity, the first international conference on ITEM was held in Jerusalem in 1994. Since then, a conference has been organized every two years.

Although a considerable number of computer applications supporting school administrative work have been developed, in many countries there is still much to be done. This is especially true for applications assisting school management activities. Since the full utilization of available SISs has not been realized, investment in the exploration of aspects such as alternative design strategies and implementation approaches is needed which hopefully will lead to better SIS-implementation so that school staff benefit more fully from the potential of these systems.

Large-scale empirical research into the design and use of SISs has grown in the last five years (e.g., Visscher et al., 1999; Wild & Smith, 2000; Visscher &

Bloemen, 1999) and our knowledge about and understanding of strategies for the effective design and implementation of SISs have increased.

The next eight chapters show how this has come about through the synthesis and documentation of experience and research, which in turn points us to knowledge that still evades us and guides us to future research.

REFERENCES

Dale, D.M., & Habib, A.G. (1991). Administrative Computing in the Australian Educational System. *Journal of Research on Computing in Education, 24* (1), 120-145.

Alkin, M.C. (1990). *Debates on evaluation.* Beverly Hills: Sage Publications.

Bird, P. (1984). *Micro computers in school administration.* London: Hutchinson.

Essink, L.B.J. & A.J. Visscher (1989). *Een computerondersteund schoolinformatiesysteem voor het avo/vwo.* [A computer-assisted school information system for schools for general secondary education, and schools for pre-university education]. University of Twente: Faculty of Educational Science and Technology.

Fitz-Gibbon, C.T. (1996). *Monitoring Education: indicators, quality and effectiveness.* London, New York: Casell.

Gillijns, P. (1991). *Student monitoring system.* Tilburg: Zwijsen.

Goodlad, J.I. (1975). *The dynamics of educational change: Toward responsive schools.* New York: McGraw-Hill.

Hogenbirk, P. (1997). An educational tool for planning and monitoring the teaching-learning process in Dutch secondary education. In A. Fung, A.J. Visscher, B. Barta & D. Teather (Eds.). *Information Technology in Educational Management for the schools of the future.* London: Chapman & Hall.

Mintzberg, H. (1979). *The structuring of organizations.* Englewood Cleffs: Prentice Hall.

Mintzberg, H. (1989). *Mintzberg on management.* New York: Free Press.

Nolan, R.L. (1977). Restructing the data processing organisation for data resource management. In B. Gilchrist (Ed.), *Information Processing 77, Proceedings of IFIP Congress 77.* Amsterdam, the Netherlands: North Holland Publishing Company.

Nolan, R.L. (1979). Managing the crisis in data processing. *Harvard Business Review,* 57(2), 115-126.

Nolan, P. & Visscher, A.J. (1996). Research on Application of Information Technology in Educational Management. In J.D. Tinsley & T.J. van Weert (eds.), *IFIP World Conference on Computers in Education VI WCCE'95, Post-conference report,* 163-168. Birmingham: IFIP.

Simon, H.A. (1993). Decision making: Rational, non-rational, and irrational. *Educational Administration Quarterly, 29*(3), 392.411.

Sproull, L.S., & Zubrow, D. (1981). Performance information in schools systems: perspectives from organization theory. *Educational Administration Quarterly, 17*(3), 61-79.

Underwood, J.D.M. (1997). Integrated learning systems: where does the management take place? *Education and Information Technologies 2,* 275-286.

Visscher, A.J. (1990). The computer as management tool: promises and pitfalls. In A. McDougall & C. Dowling (Eds.), *Proceedings of the Fifth World Conference on Computers in Education,* pp. 609-614. Amsterdam: Elsevier Science Publisher B.V.

Visscher, A. (1991). School administrative computing: A framework for analysis. *Journal of Research on Computing in Education,* 24(1), 1-19.

Visscher, A., & Spuck, D.W. (1991). Computer-assisted school administration and management: The state of the art in seven nations. *Journal of Research on Computing in Education,* 24(1), 146-168.

Visscher, A.J. (1992). *Design and evaluation of a computer-assisted management information system for secondary schools* (Ph.D. dissertation). Enschede: University of Twente, Department of Educational Science and Technology.

Visscher, A.J. (1996). Information Technology in educational management as an emerging discipline. *International Journal of Educational Research, 25*(4), 291-296.

Visscher, A.J. & Bloemen, P.P.M. (1999). Evaluation and use of computer-assisted management information systems in Dutch schools. *Journal of Research on Computing in Education, 32(1), 172-188.*

Visscher, A.J., Fung, A. & Wild, P. (1999). The evaluation of the large scale implementation of a computer-assisted management information system in Hong Kong schools. *Studies in Educational Evaluation,* 25, 11-31.

Visscher, A.J. & Coe, R. (forthcoming). *School Improvement through Performance Feedback.* Lisse/Tokyo: Swets & Zeitlinger Publishers.

Vlug, K.F.M. (1997). Because every pupil counts: the success of the pupil monitoring system in The Netherlands. *Education and Information Technologies 2,* 287-306.

Wild, P. & Smith, D. (forthcoming). Has a Decade of Computerisation Made a Difference in School Management? In Nolan, C. & Fung, A. (Eds.), *Institutional Improvement through IT in Educational Management.* London: Kluwer.

Zisman, M. (1978). Office Automation or Evolution? *Sloan Management Review,* 19(3), 1-16.

CHAPTER 2

THE COMMERCIALLY DEVELOPED SIMS FROM A HUMBLE BEGINNING

Phil Wild & John Walker
Loughborough University, United Kingdom

1. INTRODUCTION

This chapter gives an outline of general developments in SIS in England, Wales and Northern Ireland over a period of the last twelve years and gives a more detailed description of the current market leader called School Information Management System (SIMS). There have been two quite distinct phases of development of SISs in these parts of the United Kingdom, the demarcation line being drawn at the time of Central Government funding through a variety of Education Support Grants available to Local Education Authorities (LEAs). After a general overview of the historical context of Information Technology in Educational Management (ITEM) in the UK, the detail of the development and current state of SIMS will be described. The authors have a wide experience of the development of SIS, being involved with early developments in their own schools, and then respectively as a university researcher of ITEM and Support Centre Manager for SIMS implementation within one LEA.

2. THE CONTEXT AND HISTORY OF SISs IN THE UK

By the late 1970s and early 1980s significant developments had taken place in the implementation of computers in the curriculum and by the mid-1980s most schools, especially in the secondary sector, had significant IT provision found largely in dedicated computer resource rooms and active learning facilities with some stand-alone machines in departments. Whole school networks were being implemented and the potential for links between schools and other agencies were being investigated. These were hindered by the two non-standard operating systems of Research Machines Limited and BBC computers which made up the bulk of school-based systems (the BBC computer was made by Acorn Ltd but, in association with the British Broadcasting Corporation, it was badged as the BBC computer). This had an unfortunate side effect for the UK educational software industry because little of the software that was developed was portable from one machine to another or to industry standard machines. Thus, totally different software

19

A.J. Visscher et al. (eds.), Information Technology in Educational Management, 19–38.
© 2001 *Kluwer Academic Publishers. Printed in the Netherlands.*

was available for each platform, some for both in entirely different versions and with a plethora of software houses emerging. At this time many LEAs also set up their own software production operations, some achieving national credibility.

Owing to these non-standard operating systems, the UK educational software industry was not able to capitalise in other countries on its early lead and many eventually ceased trading due to the restricted user base. To compound this problem, in the early days much software was offered to schools at no cost or at very subsidised rates with the end result that schools were not educated to the real cost of software. To this day they remain resistant to paying market prices. Whilst the RML machines were able to support some industry standard software, it was not until the advent of Windows that more generally available products, such as those from Microsoft and Lotus, became available for general school use.

This was not the environment in which to introduce software for school administration and management and most LEAs maintained a watching brief on developments without any formal intention to create an implementation programme. However, there were exceptions, with much in-house development by individual teachers with some foresight and a growing knowledge of computer programming.

It was in this environment that many schools started to implement computer-based student record keeping systems providing some analysis features and improved information provision on such things as examination results and finance. Individual establishments were therefore showing interest in the use of computers for administration purposes. Soon the need for some standardisation became apparent if data transfer between schools, LEAs and central government was to become a reality.

One of the first 'national' computerised administration initiatives that can be identified was developed by Public Examination Boards and offered purpose written computerised entry, forecast grade, amendments and results transfer by modem direct to the Board, together with email facilities. Reduced entry fees and free modems were offered to participating centres. Many schools, often prompted by LEA initiatives, took up the offer with clear benefits to both the schools and the Examination Board. Although these systems were later developed fully, at this time there was no integration with any other administration software in schools, the result being that pupil details had to be keyed into the software even if they were already available in electronic format.

The picture was thus one of only a small minority of LEAs supporting computerised administration. There was little national co-ordination or direction and the most promising development was the dozen or so LEAs that were in active discussion with each other and already saw the benefits of combining resources to promote system development. Of interest to many LEAs was a Bedfordshire LEA initiative that started life in a single school as a result of personal interest by two teachers. The acronym SIMS (School Information Management System) was used.

Schools in the United Kingdom experienced much organisational change over the 1990s with the devolution of financial and managerial responsibility to schools and out of central and local government.

Following the Education Reform Act in 1988 (DES,1988), the government of the day entered the picture through a variety of central funding support, designed to encourage the implementation of computers in school administration and management. Whether this was an altruistic approach or designed so that the DES (later the DfEE) could subsequently ease its own data input and expand its requirements for information collection from schools is a matter of debate. It was however seen by the government of the day as an essential precursor to schools operating there own budgets. In brief, the government made available £325million over three years to provide computer systems to accommodate the extra managerial load and use of these computerised systems has since become increasingly important in the management of educational institutions (see for example Visscher, 1996). Government funding was initially at 70% of the cost with Local Education Authorities (LEAs) providing the balance. This decreased after two years to 60%, so there was a strong incentive to take up funding early on in the process and the majority of LEAs took up funding in the first year (1989). As a result many LEAs started to implement new IT systems at a rapid pace. Previous studies have shown that these installations were assessed from an accountancy perspective at the expense of assessment of system usability and user acceptance. (Wild, Scivier & Richardson, 1992). Independent schools did not receive any funding at all from Government sources.

Naturally, the availability of funding created significant opportunities for commercial suppliers of software and for some LEAs to promote their own systems more widely. It was quickly evident that a small number of systems were achieving market prominence in England and Wales with SIMS and SCRIPT being the main contenders at the time with general market penetration. Other systems were restricted to single LEAs or very small user bases across the country. SIMS achieved a dominant position very early in the accelerating nationwide movement to implement systems in schools and by the year 2000 the then main competitor (RML Key Solutions) had only 20% of the market.

In parallel with the developments in the state schools, the private schools were tending to use commercial companies to develop computer based finance packages due to the business-oriented nature of such schools. The finance packages created were full accounting packages adapted mainly from commercial accountancy programmes. However, at about the same time that LEAs and a small number of schools were realising the potential of computers for general school administration, the commercial companies in the private sector started to develop similar ideas. In many cases they used teachers from the state sector with experience of such systems to begin their own wider developments. One such company, Dolphin Computer Services, already had a wide user base of their finance systems in private schools but failed to capture much more of the overall market with their more comprehensive school administration systems. The main reason for this lack of penetration was one of cost. The overall software package and support was more professional and comprehensive but at a cost beyond the reach of state schools. Capita, who already owned SIMS, has now bought out Dolphin. The overall number of 'players' in the SIS market has reduced due to such mergers and buy-outs.

3. THE DESIGN OF SIMS

It is evident from previous studies that the early SIMS modules were designed to mimic a manual school administration system. This is perhaps one reason why it was initially so readily accepted by LEAs and schools (Wild et al., 1992). The design process was therefore one of trying to match the known requirements of a school office at the time. After a period of time the teachers who had carried out the early development gained in their own knowledge of what could be done and started to be more proactive in designing modules to fit wider school management needs and employed computer programmers. Early developments were therefore best described as 'trial and error' probably due to a lack of knowledge of software design on the part of the teachers. As readers will find later in the book, such a 'design' process is unlikely to result in an effective system that is acceptable to teachers and efficiently implemented throughout an organisation.

Many computer professionals working within local Councils envisaged the implementation of school systems as very simple, requiring only general purpose packages such as generic spreadsheets or data bases. This attitude, caused by a lack of knowledge of the operation of schools, completely ignored the unique management demands of schools, the lack of any previous experience of operators and the degree of training required to achieve proficiency in these packages at the time. There were significant hurdles for many LEAs in discussions with their controlling council colleagues.

At this time the SIMS vendor was part of Bedfordshire LEA with no commercial ambitions, seeing the implementation of systems as a partnership between the LEA, other LEAs and schools. It was however a requirement of the SIMS licence that subscribing LEAs set up training and first line support to their schools. Initial training and on-going support was available to LEA teams directly from SIMS. The licence costs included an annual maintenance agreement based on the number of schools actually using the system. Initially the system consisted of three software elements, the core consisting of basic student information, curriculum and finance module groupings. Those LEAs that had commenced earlier programmes saw the initiative as principally student-based whereas many of those coming later perceived the implementation as predominantly finance systems based. This was often reflected in the nature of the implementation, the controlling department and in the background of personnel supporting the initiative.

4. CURRENT STATUS AND FUTURE DEVELOPMENT

Many of the SIMS modules were originally written for the DOS environment and the maintenance and extension of functionality of these modules consumed much programming and development time. SIMS development sought to ensure backwards hardware compatibility (laudable from an LEA and school point of view since it gave extended life to older machines) but there were serious delays in issuing Windows versions of the software. In the early to mid 1990s new users, both LEAs and individual schools, required a totally Windows based system. However, existing users tied to older machines were more reluctant to move to Windows, perceiving great difficulties in obtaining funding for the more up to date hardware required for this environment. The SIMS company, following consultation with users, eventually adopted a harder line than previously taken and published programmes of development which included the dates of withdrawal of support and development of DOS modules and the issue of Windows based alternatives. All of the new modules written since the early 90s have been in Windows versions only, with many of the 'older' modules continuing to exist in both DOS and Windows (although only the latter are being further developed).

National requirements for comparative monitoring of pupil and school performance, reporting to parents, Special Educational Needs Code of Practice (SENCO), data required by the UK Office for Standards in Education (OFSTED) have all produced new but reactive opportunities for further software development. Such requirements have pushed the development towards school management processes and information needs rather than simply administrative tools for the storage and reproduction of data. This is undergoing further development in the UK at present but there is little consensus on the most effective ways of monitoring and reporting on school and teacher performance. The conversion of data into useful management information remains an incomplete goal, with Government requirements on schools and teachers pre-empting software and data capability.

The original implementation envisaged the use of the software as principally for administration and computers were only to be found in school offices. For many years, however, most schools have been broadening the use and access to the system by teaching and management staff rather than those in the central offices. Typical examples now include:

- Senior staff having access to reports, comparative analysis and planning functions;
- Heads of Year accessing pupil assessment details and analysis of attendance;
- Examination secretaries (teachers) using the external examinations packages for comparative analysis between similar schools;
- General staff having access to read only pupil records such as personal information, home information, timetable, historical information, attendance and assessment records through a recently introduced analysis module;
- Department based access to assessment information and direct use of the Assessment and Reporting suite of modules.

In many schools the administration network has grown to include twenty or more workstations and the current solution to access problems is to merge the curriculum and administration networks allowing access at many more physical points in the school. Clearly, problems of data security have needed to be addressed and the restrictions of station use or staff access have required careful consideration.

The entire suite continues to be developed and was available in Windows from the end of 2000. The vision for the future of SIMS is continually hampered by the need for reactive developments in response to government legislation on schools that affects data and information requirements. However, as detailed further in chapter 8 of this book, there is development leading to web-based systems that will broaden both access and functionality and lead to more direct user support rather than relying on LEAs as 'middle managers'.

4.1 The Current SIMS Software Suite

SIMS is a modular but integrated system in that once entered, core data is available to other modules. The producers of SIMS have tried to address the need for schools to keep accurate records whilst handling student and staff information in many different contexts, from class lists to staff cover rotas. It now covers a range of functions including accounting, personnel, curricula applications, pupil records and library management software, all assembled in a modular format. In most institutions the system is networked and runs in either Novell or Microsoft NT environments. A degree of flexible but not co-operative working is allowed in the system in that certain modules such as Timetabling, SENCO (see 4.1.18) and Assessment Manager can be set up as satellite systems. This allows work to proceed away from the main system, locking affected areas to prevent data editing and leaving other areas of the system in a usable condition. Subsequent data import from the satellite system would then be needed to unlock the affected areas.

Use is made of alternative input devices, notably optical mark readers (OMR) for Examinations, Attendance, Options (see 4.1.14), Analyst, Assessment Suite modules and bar code readers for Library and Options. There are links built in for third party products which use swipe card or remote radio linked keyboards for attendance data. File export is possible from most modules and report generators to generic packages such as spreadsheets, databases and word processors.

Briefly, the details of the current range of major modules is:

4.1.1 Alert Manager

Monitors data in SIMS and reports when critical criteria have been met. This might be used to monitor attendance records for a year group or of individual pupils, or report when a department in school exceeds 80% of budget expenditure. Staff are able to set their own 'trigger points' and will be notified automatically when these are met.

4.1.2 Analyst

Collates, analyses and presents results across a range of user defined reviews and surveys such as opinion polls, curriculum audits and curriculum mapping. Presents results in tabular or graphical formats with choices of filters.

4.1.3 Assessment Suite

This suite consists of three modules which monitor and analyse pupil performance.

Assessment Manager provides support for recording pupil marks, grades and other scores to meet school requirements for internal and National Curriculum purposes. National curriculum criteria is included with the module and updated as necessary. Users can define their own 'aspects' to record data on pupils. The system offers aggregation, mean, difference and other such facilities to analyse individual or group performance. All assessments are time and date stamped allowing historical records to be built up and monitored against targets. Users can define group or individual reporting sheet layouts for, say, reporting to parents.

Assessment analysis carries out statistical calculations on data in Assessment Manager including progression lines with residuals, predictions and targets offering comparison with externally generated regression lines from national averaged data for comparative purposes.

Assessment reporter contains a number of templates which allow users to customise reports containing tables, graphics and text comments linked to grades, marks or scores stored in Assessment Manager. Multiple comment banks can be developed allowing comments to be adapted to suit the target audience.

4.1.4 Attendance

Designed to record attendance and allow monitoring of school, group and individual attendance achievements. It meets all the analysis and reporting requirements of the DfEE.

4.1.5 Curriculum Planner

Designed to assist with the planning of subject matter for courses taught throughout the school. Study units are built up as the basic building blocks each containing an outline, associated activities, programmes of study being addressed, assessment forms, necessary resources and time allocation. Once the course has been planned Curriculum Planner produces textual outlines of the course, planned outcomes in terms of attainment targets, assessment techniques and resources used.

4.1.6 Development Planner

This module provides a structure for creating a development plan which defines individual projects and associated tasks with details of targets and monitoring techniques.

4.1.7 Equipment Register

Assists with the maintenance of a complete inventory of equipment in the school, facilitating stock checks, health and safety checks and audit requirements for acquisition and disposal. The module has links with the Finance module for acquisition transfer and depreciation if required.

4.1.8 Financial Management System (FMS)

A comprehensive double entry accounts package addressing general ledger, order system, accounts payable and accounts receivable. Links are provided for integration with Central Finance systems such as LEA Treasurers and the module links with Personnel and STAR (see 4.1.19) for staff salaries and pupil billing.

4.1.9 Budget Planning

Allows users to model budgets based on previous years or entirely new plans. Percentage increases can be applied to previous budgets for both income and expenditure. A number of alternative plans can be developed which vary the income, expenditure and allocations to cost centres as well as exploring the effect of proposed or actual staffing changes. Once approved, the chosen plan can be exported to the Financial Management System module.

4.1.10 Key Stage Diagnostics

Produces tables and graphs enabling schools to compare their performance in Key Stage tests and teacher assessments against national benchmarks. It can be used to identify particular strengths and weaknesses within individual pupils or groups of pupils. It is possible to define sub-groups to investigate attainment against such issues as gender. Frequency graphs and item analysis allow evaluation of test performance too be carried out, including facility indices.

4.1.11 Management Information Data Access System (MIDAS)

MIDAS was designed to give easy access to information held across the SIMS system, including staff and student personal details, curriculum data, special needs, financial details, timetables, individual and school attendance statistics and statutory returns. It also includes event and conduct logs for students. The module was specifically designed for senior managers to access information easily without the need for detailed knowledge required to operate all the individual modules holding the data.

4.1.12 Examinations

Designed to assist with the administration of both internal and external examination seasons and sessions, the examinations module communicates online with the Examinations Boards. Entries, amendments, forecast grades and coursework marks can be sent online with results, syllabus details and component details received from the Boards in the same way. OMR sheets can be printed for the input of entries and forecast grades. The module supports the nationally agreed EDI format and has comprehensive reporting and analysis functions.

4.1.13 Timetabling

Starting with a list of teachers, pupils, rooms and simple details of the timetable cycle (all imported from STAR, see 4.1.19) Timetabling first assists with the production of the curriculum plan. Several different plans can be constructed and costed before the actual timetabling process begins. The module has both manual and automatic scheduling routines and once the timetable is constructed students are assigned to the classes. A wide range of printing and analysis routines are provided.

Integral within the package is the Staff Cover module which maintains details of teacher absence and assists with the business of assigning cover, notifying cover staff , maintaining a database of supply teachers and offering analysis functions for managing and planning staff cover.

4.1.14 Options

This module facilitates the process of student subject options allocation, whether in a free choice or directed choice situation. Options will advise on the numbers of classes required in each subject, the block structures and will try to optimise the class sizes in keeping with the subject and ability range. The module produces teaching and subject group lists and exports the data directly to the Timetabling module for incorporation in the timetable.

4.1.15 Personnel

The Personnel module stores personal, professional and contractual information about all teaching and non-teaching school staff. The module also links with the SIMS EMS system allowing the automatic exchange of staff information changes between a school and the Local Education Authority.

4.1.16 Photo Importer

Allows the import of bitmap format images from whatever source such as digital camera, scanner or video camera and then links with the STAR (see below) or Personnel modules to import student or staff photographs for use in the SIMS modules. Many school photographic services now offer individual bitmap images for the whole school on CD ROM as part of the annual school photograph activity.

4.1.17 RepGen Lite

RepGen Lite allows the design of individual reports from data held in the rest of the system and will report across several different modules. Pre-defined reports are included but users can add others, including filters and the order of printing fields which can be stored for future use. Files can also be produced for export to other applications such as word processors or spreadsheets.

4.1.18 *Special Educational Needs Code of Practice (SENCO)*

This module was produced to help schools comply with the Code of Practice for the Identification and Assessment of students with Special Educational Needs. The module can hold special educational needs information on any pupil, including past and future reviews, special provisions, links with adults (e.g., educational psychologists, doctors, teachers etc.) and Individual Education Plans. SENCO will produce lists of actions necessary in the next chosen period, automate letter production, and provide status reports on outstanding correspondence.

4.1.19 *Students Teaching and Academic Records (STAR)*

STAR is the main database of pupil records, holding personal, medical, historic, school and academic information on each pupil. Routines are provided for new intakes. End of year procedures and global editing features ease data entry. Photographs can be imported though Photo Importer and the system uses extracts of the national post code database to ensure data accuracy with the entry of contact addresses. Various modules produce outputs for statutory Government specified reports based on the data held in STAR.

4.1.20 *Value Added*

This is used in setting school and pupil improvement targets and investigating individual and school performance based on GCSE and GCSE A-level data. SIMS collects data from participating schools in August each year and creates benchmark statistics that can be used by schools for comparison purposes. Predicted outcomes in various subjects at GCSE Advance level examinations (at age 18) can be produced which are based on individual pupil performance at GCSE (at age 16).

4.1.21 *Visitor Log*

The Visitor Log module is designed for use in the reception area in order to maintain an accurate record of visitors. It will print personalised badges (with a photograph if linked to a digital video camera), record entry and departure times, maintain records of purpose of visits, recall previous visitor details, and provides analysis functions.

5. IMPLEMENTATION PROCESSES

A typical LEA responded to the implementation of SIMS by going through a series of planning stages:

- Initial discussions with teacher representatives, other LEA groups, Treasurers and Trades Unions regarding the nature, funding, likely aims and benefits of any proposed implementation programme.
- Working groups carried out an evaluation of the existing software and hardware platforms based on the functionality, links with industry standards, 'look and feel', discernible development paths, status of supplier, rapport with education

and costs. There is little evidence of any formal analysis of contextual or organisational needs at this time.

- LEA team visited existing users.
- Software systems trials in a number of (mainly secondary) school sites.
- Development of an implementation plan ranging over a six to seven year period for all the schools within a larger LEA, and detailed local plans for each school predetermined by government funding provisions in order from larger secondary schools first to smaller primary schools and special schools.
- Development of the local plans for the identification of staff, training requirements, premises (and the adaptations necessary such as blinds, power points, security, etc.), network provision and identification of staff needs and location of stations to satisfy those needs. A full development plan for each school might have spanned over three years.
- The provision of computer systems, software and training (often free of cost to the school). Many LEAs also provided additional hours of clerical time and cover for teachers on such courses.
- The establishment of centrally based support teams (as required by the SIMS licence) comprising staff drawn from a variety of backgrounds such as clerical, treasurers, teaching, IT and staff with school management experience.
- A full range of training opportunities offered to schools from initial discussions with headteachers through to detailed training in the management of the SIS and the use and implementation of modules.

Any discussion of the reasons for SIMS achieving market dominance would include the following readily identifiable features of the software and implementation processes at the time:

- Licence, support and training costs that were affordable for both LEAs and schools.
- An obvious rapport with educational issues, the administrative needs, national and local developments and an understanding of the problems facing both LEA and schools in developing programmes of implementation. The most significant feeling for LEAs was one of dealing with people who had actually done the job, either at LEA or school level. Furthermore, the company was not at this stage commercially aggressive.
- The look and feel of the software was readily acceptable to computer-inexperienced school staff, unlike much commercial software of the time that presented very formal and busy screens.
- School office staff were being trained to use a system which very closely paralleled what they already did manually.
- The early establishment of user groups to advise on development and strategies.
- The use of industry standard i.e., IBM compatible hardware and MS-DOS operating system, allowing links with other industry standard and most recent versions of generic software such as word processors.

The source of training and support for schools varies with the type of licence agreement with SIMS under which individual establishments are operated. Schools within LEAs that took out licences with SIMS would normally be offered full training programmes and support directly from the LEA local support unit whilst the LEA teams were offered initial training from SIMS. Single site licence holders, usually independent and other non-LEA schools, together with some schools residing in 'non SIMS' LEAs would normally take training and support direct from SIMS. However, these boundaries are now blurred, as some single site schools have purchased support contracts with their local LEA support unit.

Training typically covers the detailed use of SIMS modules for operators and such areas as awareness for managers on what is available, advice on implementation and preparation for using new areas of the system and potential use of systems. In addition, training for optimising module use for the provision of management information and general good practice are now included. Where relevant, training also includes joint courses with other advisors such as those involved in assessment policies, treasurers department staff, LEA audit staff and senior management. These provide a co-ordinated approach and encourages best practice, not only in the use of SIMS, but for school policies in general. For example, pupil assessment module training would includes an introductory day for senior management comprising discussion on the development of whole school assessment policies. This would be followed by examples showing how SIMS might support any locally developed implementation. Should the school subsequently decide to adopt the SIMS assessment suite, detailed training in the operation of modules would be offered to appropriate staff determined by the school.

It is difficult to be precise about the duration of each course, but most are 'hands on' one day courses, although in the case of more involved modules, such as 'Timetabling' or the 'Assessment Suite' there would be further days to develop more in-depth understanding. Most LEA teams would also follow up such courses with individual visits to schools to advise and assist in the implementation to meet specific local requirements.

It can be argued that the most successful support, training and implementation teams in the early days were those which included a significant number of teachers. This gave them credibility in the training due to a realistic understanding of the way schools operate, the constraints on innovation and the demands being made in terms of staff, finances, organisation, premises and developing external requirements such as performance monitoring. As found by Mitchell and Wild (1993), a counter argument is that the early SIMS modules and the training from 'insiders' imposed a straightjacket on the administrative systems which meant that clerical staff maintained paper records for ease of data access . Subsequently, the balance of need shifted towards more technical IT support as networks and operating systems grew in complexity and users become more educated and sophisticated in their requirements.

These initiatives were taking place at a time when the expansion of computers into every day life was only just beginning; there was little general appreciation of the ultimate role of computers and many people were sceptical of their worth. With the benefit of hindsight, much of what was done was rather basic but at the time it was totally innovative with no precedents. It is generally accepted by all those involved, many of whom are still working in the field, that with today's knowledge the design and implementation process was crude, with no vision of how computers could enhance the school administration. Early SIMS merely 'did the same' as was done manually but used the computer as a tool to try to do it faster. The original outcome was slow and cumbersome which is why many school staff actually used paper-based copies for speed of access! Fortunately, as is reported below in the results of the evaluative studies carried out by the authors, there have been great strides forward more recently in user acceptance.

In summary, this period saw the LEAs as the principal originators of development, prompted by government funding at the time. In turn this put pressures on LEAs to react, resulting in condensed evaluation periods, followed by somewhat hectic implementation activity. The period saw SIMS achieve market leader status.

Limited market penetration by other SIS producers and the cancellation of LEA 'in house' initiatives resulted in massive investment in SIMS. There was a period of rapid growth for the company, putting pressures on their own development plans, support arrangements and internal management of a rapidly expanding workforce. In fact, SIMS, now part of the Capita company and known as Capita Education offers a portfolio of services to the Education sector, including consultancy and training on general educational issues. This 'inclusion' of the SIS into wider educational issues will potentially enhance system integration into school management processes.

6. EVALUATIVE STUDY

In 1998 the authors sent out questionnaires to schools in England that used SIMS. A thousand sets of three questionnaires were sent to approximately 25% of all secondary schools in England with a return rate of approximately 45%. The sample of schools was taken from Local Education Authorities that were known to promote the use of SIMS, thus ensuring a high number of SIMS users responded. The basic questionnaire was that used by the book editors in the international studies (Appendix A) but with relevant adaptations in the context of English schools and the SIMS software.

Questionnaires were sent to staff that had various different roles within each school. These were the Headteacher, the SIMS-administrator and a member of the clerical staff. The Headteacher questionnaire included an additional section on management tasks and responsibilities relating to the use of SIMS, otherwise all questions were the same for each group of respondents.

Questions solicited information on various factors including the user's computing background and SIMS knowledge, training and support, system functionality employed, system usability and its effect on their jobs. In addition, Heads were questioned on how they used the system in support of managerial decisions. Respondents were asked in detail for their views on system usability.

6.1   Quality of the System

6.1.1   Basic System

Users were questioned on various aspects of system reliability (Table 1). This is of course a pre-requisite to users feeling comfortable with using it and, although only reported by a small percentage of users, there are still some problems reported even after over ten years of use.

Table 1. Basic System Quality

Hardware Performance	62% happy/very happy	8% unhappy/very unhappy
System Reliability	90% said it did or usually did always work	10% said systems did not always work

In addition 69% were unhappy with the working environment due to interruptions to work, which is not conducive to accurate data entry.

6.1.2   Data Quality compared to the Previous System used

There is some feeling amongst school staff that SIMS stores more information than is needed, with 49% having the view that most/all of information is relevant and 49% reporting that only some/a little of the material is relevant. However, since the survey was carried out, teachers have been required to show the impact of their teaching on pupil achievement gains for performance related pay. This means that they must now use previously unused data, possibly changing this view.

Table 2 shows some further measures of users' perceptions of the data within SIMS which are more positive and show that, although there are still problems, the percentage of users that think the system is poor is small (neutral % not shown)

Table 2. Perceptions of Data Quality

Data Currency	73% better or much better*	4% worse*
Data Completeness	60% better or much better*	9% worse*
Data Accuracy	77% good or very good	3% poor or very poor
Ease of Access to Data	55% happy or very happy	9% unhappy/very unhappy

* = than previous system

6.2   Use of SIMS

6.2.1   Frequence of Module Use

As would be expected, the modules most commonly used varied according to the different roles of users within the organisation. The scale used to measure frequency of use was everyday 1, once a week 2, once a month 3, a few times a year 4, never 5. Modules such as EXAMS, Form 7, Photoimporter, Curriculum Planner and Curriculum Modeller, Development Planner, Analyst and Value Added would be expected to be used at the 3-5 range because of the *modus operandi* of schools and staff functions.

Table 3. Module Use by User Role

Module	Clerical n = 160-180	Deputy Headteacher n = 38-48	Headteacher n = 77-94	IT-co-ordinator (Teacher) n = 2-4	IT Manager n = 20-26	Office Manager n = 13-18	SIMS Manager n = 21-28	Teacher n = 21-26	Unspecified n = 7-11	Average of means
	Mean	Mean	Mean	Mean	Mean	Mean	Mean	Mean	Mean	
Star	1.9	2.3	3.1	2.3	2.3	1.3	1.4	2.3	2.4	2.1
Midas	2.6	2.2	2.8	2.5	2.3	2.7	2.2	2.1	2.6	2.4
Timetable Module	2.9	2.5	3.3	3.3	2.8	3.2	2.0	2.5	3.6	2.9
Repgen Module	2.8	3.3	4.4	3.3	3.0	2.1	2.6	3.0	3.4	3.1
Financial Management	3.1	3.4	3.6	4.8	3.4	4.4	3.7	3.8	2.5	3.6
Attendance Module	3.4	3.3	3.7	4.0	3.5	2.9	2.9	3.3	3.9	3.4
Personnel Module	3.5	3.7	3.8	4.8	3.4	3.2	3.4	3.8	3.0	3.6
Exams	4.2	3.5	4.3	4.0	3.9	4.4	3.0	3.3	4.3	3.9
Assessment Manager	4.4	3.7	4.3	5.0	3.5	4.3	3.3	3.7	4.7	4.1
Cover	4.5	3.3	4.2	4.8	4.0	4.8	3.8	3.9	4.3	4.2
Options	4.4	4.3	4.4	4.0	4.5	4.6	4.1	4.4	4.4	4.3
Form 7 Module	4.4	4.3	4.4	4.7	4.4	4.6	4.3	4.2	4.3	4.4
Key Stage Modules	4.6	4.4	4.8	4.5	4.3	4.8	4.4	4.1	4.9	4.5
SENCO Module	4.6	4.3	4.8	5.0	4.5	4.8	4.5	4.5	4.7	4.6
Profiles Module	4.7	4.5	4.6	4.8	4.4	4.8	4.3	4.5	4.9	4.6
Photo	4.7	4.6	4.7	5.0	4.5	4.9	4.4	4.7	4.2	4.6
Equipment Register Module	4.6	4.7	4.8	5.0	4.7	5.0	4.7	4.6	4.9	4.8
Performance Indicator Mod	4.8	4.5	4.7	5.0	4.6	4.9	4.3	4.5	4.4	4.6
Curiculum Module	4.8	4.6	4.6	5.0	5.0	5.0	4.9	4.9	4.7	4.8
Library Module	4.8	4.8	4.8	5.0	4.7	4.9	4.8	4.7	5.0	4.8
Curric. Planner Module	4.8	4.7	4.8	5.0	5.0	5.0	4.9	4.8	4.9	4.9
Scheduler Module	4.9	4.9	4.8	5.0	4.9	5.0	4.9	4.8	4.8	4.9
VA Module	4.9	4.9	4.8	5.0	4.7	5.0	4.9	5.0	5.0	4.9
Curric. Modelling Module	4.9	4.8	4.8	5.0	5.0	5.0	5.0	5.0	5.0	4.9
Alert Module	4.8	4.9	4.9	5.0	5.0	5.0	5.0	5.0	4.8	4.9
EMS Transfer Module	4.8	5.0	4.9	4.7	4.9	5.0	5.0	5.0	4.8	4.9
Analyst Module	4.9	4.9	4.9	5.0	5.0	5.0	4.8	5.0	5.0	4.9
Dev. Planner Module	4.9	4.9	4.9	5.0	5.0	5.0	5.0	5.0	5.0	5.0

The results showed that most staff, particularly by Clerical staff, used STAR quite regularly, which was to be expected since it is the core student information database of the SIMS system (see Table 3). MIDAS was the next most widely used module, indicating that this module, introduced quite late in the SIMS development, is playing the role of information provider for which it was designed. Alert and Development Planner were the least used modules overall.

The respondents with a clerical role in the organisation reported that after STAR, the Report Generator, MIDAS, Timetable, Attendance and Options were the modules they used most commonly. Deputy Heads used STAR, MIDAS and Timetable (probably for planning teacher cover) most frequently as did SIMS Managers who used STAR, MIDAS, Timetable and in addition, FMS. Office Managers used STAR, FMS and Personnel, Head Teachers used STAR, MIDAS, Timetable and Attendance.

The degree of some module use was unexpected. For example, according to two Local Education Authority's, 'Attendance' is run on a daily basis in every High School therefore an overall result of 1 representing close to 100% use could therefore be expected. The average across all users was however only 3.4 indicating a much lower use. This could be indicating that the people responding to the questionnaire do not have high individual use of this module but that overall its use is serving a purpose for all users when needed.

The data in Table 4 indicate that the work patterns of staff involved with data processing in schools are quite widely dispersed with a high degree of managerial involvement in hands-on work with the system. It is probable that this reflects the wider use of networked systems which now create greater staff access. Also likely is the wider range of modules supporting managerial functions, with teacher and pupil quality measures resulting in broader use from school management and individual teachers, with headteachers now using the system for particular monitoring needs.

Table 4. Number of Hours spent per Week using SIMS

Staff	Hours per week direct use	Hours per week indirect use
Clerical	11-20	1-4
Teacher	5-10	1
Deputy Head	1-4	1-4
Head	1	1-4
SIMS Manager	5-10	1-4
Average	5-10	1-4

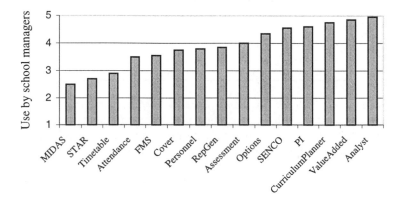

Figure 1. Module Use by Head Teachers and Deputy Head Teachers

Figure 1 clearly shows that the modules most commonly used by Headteachers and Deputy Headteachers can be used as a source of management information. Although the questionnaire returns do not provide detail on how this information is being used, it is unlikely that such school staff would spend time retrieving it if they did not have a specific purpose in mind. The Assessment and Cover Modules were also quite frequently used in this context. An anomaly occurs in the results for the Performance Indicator Module that provides compulsory external returns for exams and attendance. When investigated further, it was found that several schools used spreadsheets such as MS-Excel which were used in preference to the SIMS software module to make their returns. It is expected that, with new Government directives on performance management and target setting, the Performance Indicator module will grow in use.

6.3 Training in System Use

It is clear from the overall implementation procedures for SIMS outlined above that this aspect of implementation was taken seriously. The external training was carried out mainly by the LEA-teams with some further training carried out directly from SIMS. In addition, many respondents reported that they had been trained internally. Table 5 shows the time which users spent on training.

Table 5. Hours spent by Users on Training

Training Time	% of users receiving internal training	% of users receiving external training
< 1 hr	53%	11%
1-4 hrs	28%	23%
5-10 hrs	11%	19%
11-30 hrs	6%	14%
<30 hrs	2%	24%

However, even with the emphasis place by SIMS on training, only 44% were happy or very happy with the quantity of external training and perhaps more importantly 20% were (very) unhappy with it. However, in terms of quality, 63% were happy or very happy, and only 8% were (very) unhappy.

Alongside training, the access to help in case of problems is important in any implementation and this was available both within schools and outside schools. However, the help systems perhaps needed more careful thought as only 48% reported that they found it easy or very easy to get help within the school and only 37% found it easy or very easy to get help outside the school. This leaves a lot of SIMS users feeling that they have been left to struggle when problems arose.

6.4 Effects of System Use

Figure 2 shows the effects of the system on reported workload and stress of users. Workload was reported as lower despite the fact that more data must now be processed in schools than has ever previously been required. However, the workload was spread among many staff, including those whose job was specifically designated as being responsible for the automated administration of the school. Stress levels have reduced since earlier studies (Wild et al., 1992), probably because people are more comfortable with the computer systems and there is more general exposure to IT. There is a 'don't know' category in the study because some respondents had not used any other system than SIMS so could not compare workload or stress with previous systems.

SIMS has made it possible for schools to take over many of the management roles previously carried out by external agents, such as LEAs. At the same time schools have been made more responsible for their own well-being in terms of academic and financial management. The main outcome of using SIMS has therefore been to provide access to information previously unavailable.

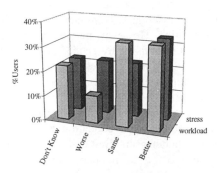

Figure 2. Workload and Stress Levels for Users; 1999 Survey

6.5 User's Comments and Conclusions

A few of the salient points that appeared in user's comments were that SIMS had made an invaluable contribution to administration efficiency although there were some qualifications including that the cost of updating and maintaining SIMS was a problem within limited school budgets. Some SIMS modules were not well quality controlled before shipping and SIMS needed to keep pace with developments in education. It needed more flexibility in all modules particularly in user-assigned fields and more presentation options needed, even at a basic level of font styles, for example. The general feeling was that SIMS was a good system, and users had not found a better one. However, most people felt that the system needed fine tuning, that it had bugs and that they were always waiting for upgrades to sort out problems. They also said that the quality of SIMS varied greatly between modules.

These comments summarise concisely SIMS, current position as a near monopolist supplier to the education market in England, Wales and Northern Ireland. Development is continuing and the present Executive Managers responsible for the direction of SIMS are clear that the future will see many changes in the way school staff access and interact with SIMS (see chapter 8). As teachers and school managers become more used to using data and information from SIMS, they are starting to demand more from it. The data is now being turned into useful information which is accessible to teachers.

7. LESSONS LEARNED

It has taken over ten years for SIMS to reach a stage where the great majority of users are happy that the many real and perceived problems which were prevalent in the early days of operation have been overcome. SIMS was started when the writing of computer applications on a large scale was in its infancy and it was first put together by teachers with little knowledge of computer programming. No one would now have to start from that position. However, part of the problem was a lack of research and observation of what schools really needed and what the computers and users were capable of doing. No one really asked the fundamental question "what does the school really need to support management and administrative structures". It has taken over ten years to start to answer the question.

There is little doubt that even greater emphasis on training, with more training provided on using the SIS to support the education process, would have given teachers and school managers a better grounding and motivation for the integration of the systems. This is just starting to happen, not only because SIMS has developed, but because demands are now being made on teachers that ensure that they will have to use the SIMS based information systems. Teachers now need the information. Before they could leave it to someone else. The key lesson is therefore to ensure that school staff are more aware of the need at the start of the development and implementation process.

REFERENCES

DES (1988), *Education Reform Act*, London, DfEE

DFEE (1998). *Education Green Paper*. London: DfEE.

Mitchell, S. & Wild, P. (1993). A Task Analysis of a Computerised System to Support Administration in Schools, *Educational Management and Administration*, 21(1) 53-60.

Visscher, A.J. (Ed.) (1996). Information Technology in Educational Management. *International Journal of Educational Research,* 25(4), 289-390.

Wild P., Scivier J.E. & Richardson S.J. (1992). 'Evaluating Information Technology-supported Local Management for Schools: The User Acceptability Audit.' *Educational Management and Administration* 20(1) 40-48.

CHAPTER 3

SAMS IN HONG KONG: A CENTRALLY DEVELOPED SIS FOR PRIMARY AND SECONDARY SCHOOLS

Alex C.W. Fung & Jenilyn Ledesma
Hong Kong Baptist University, China

1. INTRODUCTION

This chapter describes how SAMS[1] has been developed and implemented in Hong Kong schools, and the degree of usage at the end of the five-year project. Through the presentation of quantitative and qualitative findings, the problems that were faced in implementing a large-scale School Information System (SIS) in 1,200 Hong Kong schools are discussed. Strategies used in the system design and implementation are reviewed and factors affecting the implementation and usage of the system are reported. Evidence provided indicates the need of a client-centred approach in SIS development and implementation for success. After the future of SAMS has been discussed the chapter ends with a number of conclusions on what can be learned from the SAMS experience. The authors have long-standing experience of the SAMS system and implementation process. Fung's work in this field began as a headteacher of a Hong Kong secondary school before he engaged in more focused research into SAMS on his move to his present post. Jenilyn Ledesma joined him as a research assistant to support the work of the SAMS Training and Research Unit set up at Hong Kong Baptist University under Fung's guidance.

2. EDUCATIONAL CONTEXT IN HONG KONG

Hong Kong is one of the most densely populated cities in the world, with nearly seven million people living on less than 400 square miles. Its return of sovereignty to China in 1997 marked the end of the British colonial administration and the beginning of a Special Administrative Region (SAR) and a 'one-country-two-systems' concept. The thirteen year period of transition, after the signing of the Joint Declaration between the People's Republic of China and the British governments in 1984, was marked with uncertainty for many people. As witnessed by the world, the transition in July 1997 was smooth overall. The SAR has remained politically stable,

---

[1] SAMS stands for 'School Administration and Management System', a SIS developed centrally by the Education Department of Hong Kong for all schools in the public sector.

A.J. Visscher et al. (eds.), Information Technology in Educational Management, 39–53.
© 2001 *Kluwer Academic Publishers. Printed in the Netherlands.*

and business has been kept as usual although the region was caught in the economic crisis of 1997 as in neighbouring countries.

Understandably the education system in Hong Kong in the past one and a half centuries has followed the British system, with nine years of free and compulsory schooling put in place in 1979. Opportunities for obtaining a higher education were limited to less than 5% of the age group before the 90's. The system was selective and competitive with success in society 'normally' pegged to success in examinations and proficiency in the English language. The scenario began to change, interestingly and perhaps incidentally, in the early 90s during the transition period when university education was dramatically expanded. Today 18% of the collegiate age group can have access to 14,500 first year university degree places offered by seven universities and one institute of education, on top of other non-degree opportunities.

In the school sector, which consists of government, aided, and private primary and secondary schools, the curriculum is quite generally controlled by the Education Department. Students follow much the same path during their six years of primary, three years of junior secondary, and two years of senior secondary schooling. Thirty percent of students finishing the five years of secondary are selected for secondary 6-7 matriculation/pre-university studies. The past practice of providing pre-vocational and technical education over and beyond the mainstream grammar school experience is fading out. The new reform proposals for the education system in Hong Kong recently announced by the Education Commission will bring about significant changes to the system in the coming years (Hong Kong Education Commission, 2000).

3. THE HISTORY OF COMPUTER-AIDED SCHOOL ADMINISTRATION IN HONG KONG

Hong Kong was one of the early adopters of computer education in schools. Computer Studies was introduced in secondary schools as a new subject in the curriculum in the early 1980s. Unfortunately, it was not until 1997 that the government recognized the need for Information Technology (IT) in the primary schools. At present, almost all secondary schools offer Computer Literacy to junior form students (ages 12 to 14) and Computer Studies to senior form students (ages 15 to 16). The use of IT in education (with an emphasis on using IT in support of teaching and learning) is now a high priority on the SAR government's agenda, and schools are busy getting equipped, installing infrastructure, getting on-line, and getting teachers trained. The SAR Government's 5-year IT in education strategy, announced in 1998, has committed a very large investment on information technology in schools, covering the provision of hardware, software, communications networks and professional development of teachers (EMB (Education and Manpower Bureau), 1998). The government policy aims at providing students with a broad range of IT skills that will be of undoubted benefit to these students. Further, if the investment is wisely used with proper implementation of the policy, there is the potential of offering enduring benefits to students, employers and the Hong Kong society.

Secondary schools in Hong Kong also have had a long history of using computer-aided school administration. With the availability of computers for teaching Computer Studies in the early 1980s, some schools developed their own systems for record keeping and preparation of report cards. The use of computers in school administration was quite common among Hong Kong secondary schools by the beginning of the 1990s. This was not true in the primary schools. However, the systems that were in use were 'home-grown' to meet individual functional demands. As such, they were limited in scope, defied standardisation, and, accordingly, were not compatible with each other.

Computer-Aided school administration and management in Hong Kong advanced from an ad hoc developmental stage to a popularization stage in 1993 when the Hong Kong government launched a five-year Information Systems Strategy (ISS) aimed at improving the efficiency and effectiveness of Hong Kong education. With an investment of 70 million US dollars, an integrated computer network was developed centrally, linking the Education Department (ED) and all government and aided sector primary and secondary schools. The ISS included the implementation of a standardized School Administration and Management System, SAMS, in all public-sector schools. This SAMS project marked the beginning of the government taking a leading role to implement in Hong Kong a centralized, integrated system of supporting school administration and management processes, and for electronically transmitting information between schools and the Education Department.

In the following sections, the structure and functions in SAMS are first described, followed by the design and implementation strategies. The degree of SAMS usage among schools at the end of the five-year period, together with difficulties and problems encountered, are then reviewed.

4. AN OVERVIEW OF THE STRUCTURE AND CONTENT OF SAMS

The SAMS consists of 12 core applications and four supporting applications. Each school in the public sector (totally about 780 primary and 420 secondary) was given a local area network with four or five PC workstations to operate SAMS on the Chinese Windows platform. The system is bilingual, accepting both Chinese and English input and output. It was written in Chinese FoxPro for the Windows 3.1 environment. The system is a standard package for both primary and secondary schools. Typically a primary school would have 24 classes from P1 to P6 and an enrolment of around 900 pupils and 40 teachers. At secondary schools, there are 30 classes from S1 to S7 with about 1,100 students and 50 teachers.

4.1 The 12 Core Applications

1. *School Management* – for storing school information such as the class structure, subjects offered, and other basic information of the school. It should have been named as the 'School Basic Information' module rather than the misleading 'School Management' module.
2. *Student* – for maintaining student personal data, keeping information similar to a traditional student record card.
3. *Student Attendance* – for recording students' absence or leave from school.
4. *Student Assessment* – for recording student achievements in tests and examinations, in order to produce report cards to parents. Progression of students from one level to the next is also handled in this module. This module basically provides teachers and school executives with recording and printing functions for students' academic and non-academic (i.e., extra-curricular activities) performance, as well as supporting the year-end operation of allocating students to different classes.
5. *Staff* – for managing data about teachers and other support staff members of the school. It includes personal information, qualifications and duties.
6. *Staff Deployment* – for maintaining records of staff on leave or absence from duty, draws up substitute teaching schedule and automates the process of deploying substitute teachers. It can also process information of external substitute teachers and transmits applications for vacation leave to ED.
7. *Allocation* – for handling affairs related to school place allocation, which is centrally managed by the ED, and serves as a communication link between schools and the ED for this specific placement process. There are 2 allocation modules for primary schools, Primary One Allocation (POA) and Secondary One Allocation (SOA). For the secondary schools, there are 3 modules, namely Secondary One Allocation (SOA), Secondary Four Allocation (SFA) and Secondary Six Allocation (SSA).
8. *Timetabling* – is for preparing the school timetable and is used normally only once in a year. It processes and records the lesson arrangement for classes, teachers and venues.
9. *HK Exam Authority* – for secondary schools to prepare data for registering S5 and S7 candidates for public examinations managed by the Hong Kong Examinations Authority (HKEA). Students in Hong Kong graduating at S5 and S7 sit respectively for the Hong Kong Certificate of Education Examination and the Hong Kong Advanced Level Examination. The module also caters for recording examination results returned to schools by the HKEA after the public examinations.
10. *Programme Schedule* – this application is provided only to SMI schools (i.e., schools that have joined the 'School Management Initiative' which advocates school-based management). The module is to assist these schools in scheduling their educational programmes for students. It also serves as a database for part of the functions within the Financial Monitoring and Planning module.
11. *Financial Monitoring and Planning* – this application is also provided only to SMI schools for accounting matters, financial monitoring and planning.

12. *Special School* – for certain needs required only by special schools.

All of these twelve applications are mainly for clerical/administrative support. Each application consists basically of a Maintenance function (for capturing and recording of data), an Enquiry function (for searching what has been stored), a Report function (for printouts), and a Data Management function (for extracting data records). Except for a few statistical reports, the system cannot provide managerial information that impacts on school decision-making or policy. No scenario building, for example, is available and no query functions are available to answer 'what-if' questions.

4.2 The Four Supporting Modules

1. The *housekeeping* module sets up a number of codified tables used by other modules in SAMS, and is the starting point in using SAMS. Some tables are pre-defined by ED as standards across the territory, such as codes for subjects and staff grades. Other codified tables are user-defined, to give flexibility for different schools, such as extra-curricular activities of students.
2. The *security* module defines access levels of different staff members to different modules and data in the system. This module also protects the integrity and confidentiality of the data.
3. *Inter-year Processing* carries forward data from one academic year to the next, filing at the same time the past year data as history records.
4. The *communication and delivery system (CDS)* module is, in reality, outside SAMS. It is an electronic delivery system that relates to SAMS and which provides data-transfer between a school and ED, using a dial-up modem over data lines. Within each of the 12 Application Modules is a 'Data Management' function that can be used to extract data for electronic transmission to ED or HKEA using this CDS. Each school is provided with an electronic mailbox for up-loading information, and ED also downloads to these mailboxes school information (such as ED Circulars and Student Allocation data). Schools, however, cannot communicate with one another via this CDS. The Data Management function also provides individual schools the facility to extract from SAMS the data that they wish to use for add-on programme development, or for certain administrative or managerial tasks not provided in SAMS.

5. THE DESIGN STRATEGY OF SAMS

The SAMS project of the Education Department was technically supported by the Hong Kong government's Information Technology Services Department (ITSD). The design of SAMS was intended to provide flexibility for the basic needs of various types of schools. In brief, it was tailor-made to suit both primary and secondary schools.

Fung (1996) has written an evaluation of the SAMS design and development strategy. The development of the SAMS package and implementation in schools were both carried out in phases. The first version of SAMS, version 1.0 containing a few basic modules, was piloted in ten schools in the summer of 1994. Mass distribution to schools then followed in batches ('rolled-out') beginning September 1994. By the end of 1996 SAMS version 2.01, after several upgrades since version 1.0, had been rolled-out to more than 600 primary and secondary schools, covering about half the schools in Hong Kong. The ED described this as an evolutionary process, both in the design and the implementation.

The ITSD adopted the Project In a Controlled Environment (PRINCE) methodology (CCTA (Central Computer and Telecommunications Agency), 1990) as the framework in specifying, designing, and implementing the SAMS project. Specifically, for the design and development, Structured System Analysis and Design Methodology (SSADM) was employed. SSADM basically includes the following structure:

1. Feasibility Study (Stage 0: Feasibility)
2. Requirements Analysis (Stage 1: Investigation of current environment; Stage 2: Business system options)
3. Requirements specification (Stage 3: Definition of requirements)
4. Logical system specification (Stage 4: Technical system options)
5. Physical design (Stage 5: Physical design)

Following the PRINCE methodology, the SAMS project had a three-tier organization structure with a Project Board, a Project Management Team, and a Project Assurance Team. Members of these committees were senior staff members from ED and ITSD, who were advised by a User Representative Group consisting of school heads and teachers. In theory at least, therefore, the SAMS project had involvement from the school users. In practice, however, the ITSD considered the ED rather than the schools as their client department and user, and no school representative sat on the decision-making Project Board.

6. THE LARGE-SCALE IMPLEMENTATION OF SAMS

As hinted in the earlier section, ED took an evolutionary and phased approach in implementing SAMS in Hong Kong schools. This was necessary as the scale of implementation was quite large for 1,200 schools, and had to be completed within five years as set by the policy.

At the macroscopic level, ED had to provide central promotion, training, and support for SAMS. It was also responsible, at the institutional level, for a number of things that had to be dealt with for each 'roll-out' of SAMS to a school, including:

1. Site preparation. A school had to prepare a site plan for the LAN, which had to be approved by the Architectural Office/Housing Department, before a contractor could do the wiring.
2. Data conversion. A school had the option of having their paper records converted by ED's sub-contractor; or by itself with some funding from ED.

3. Hardware procurement and installation. ED took care of procurement centrally and the successful contractor provided the hardware and installation.
4. Software installation. ED assigned sub-contractors to install the SAMS package.

To provide information to schools about the SAMS project, ED held a number of seminars for school heads explaining about SAMS and took the opportunity also to collect feedback. Schools could volunteer to join the implementation scheme at different scheduled times. Circulars and SAMS newsletters were also used to provide information to schools. Saturday 'clinic' sessions were held for school SAMS users to come together for problem solving and experience sharing. A SAMS electronic bulletin board system was also set up together with a hot-line telephone support.

Training was recognized as a major task in the implementation, which was costly in terms of money as well as time on the part of trainees. ED's policy on SAMS training was a provision for two teachers per school, including one who would be taking up the role of the 'SAMS Administrator' at school. To provide the training needed, a central SAMS training laboratory was set up in ED, together with a number of training laboratories established in pre-vocational schools located at different districts in the territory. Each laboratory had a simulated SAMS environment with about 20 workstations for training. Another unique effort by ED was to collaborate with a local university to set up a SAMS Training and Research Unit with 40 workstations, which shouldered part of the SAMS training on a contract basis.

In general, the SAMS training provided by ED was scheduled on a modular basis for the 16 applications. Training for a module varied from three to 15 hours depending on the complexity of the module, and were offered in morning or afternoon sessions. The training schedules were circulated to schools for nomination of trainees, who were often teachers (sometimes secretarial or clerical staff) who had to take time off from their normal teaching duties to attend. Most probably because of the limitation on funding, no substitute teacher could be given to schools when their teachers went off duty to attend the SAMS training. For this reason, schools usually sent different teachers to be trained for different modules. The consequence of this was that teachers who were fully conversant with the whole operation of SAMS were rarely found in a school. To fill this loophole, the SAMS Training and Research Unit at the Hong Kong Baptist University offered evening courses to individual school heads and teachers on top of the centralized SAMS training scheme.

Within the ED, a new division called the Information Systems (IS) Division was formed as a result of the ISS. Headed by an assistant director, this division oversaw the ISS project including SAMS. Under this IS division, a SAMS hotline service was created to support school users, and a new section called the 'Add-on Programming' was also established. As its name suggests, the latter attended to ongoing development of SAMS functions that schools would like to have, building on the core SAMS that ITSD developed.

7. EVALUATIONS OF THE SAMS PROJECT

Over the period of five years ED and ITSD had twice evaluated the SAMS project for internal purposes, once when halfway through and the other at the conclusion of the process. These evaluation reports are unfortunately not available in the public domain. However, independent studies have been done on the SAMS project in Hong Kong, mainly conducted by the SAMS T&R Unit of HKBU in collaboration with the staff of the University of Twente, the University of Loughborough, and the University of Birmingham. These included a preliminary study in early 1995 (Wild & Fung, 1997), a study between 1995 and 1997 when the project was half way through (Visscher, Fung & Wild, 1999), and a study in 1998 at the end of the five-year implementation.

These studies collected both quantitative data using surveys, as well as qualitative data from interviews. The first survey was conducted, using the "SAMS Questionnaire" (see Appendix), in January 1997 when SAMS had been rolled-out to 641 primary and secondary schools. After this survey, a series of semi-structured interviews were then carried out to collect qualitative data from 15 primary and 15 secondary schools. The second survey was done at the end of the five-year project, in November 1998, when SAMS had already been rolled-out to almost all primary and secondary schools. An adapted and shortened version of the SAMS questionnaire was sent to 1,265 schools for data collection, with 961 valid returns (response rate of 76%). In the following sections, some findings from the first survey are first presented; then more quantitative details are provided based on the 1998 study to give an evaluation of the SAMS utilization and its impact in Hong Kong schools.

7.1 System Utilization and Related Factors

Results of the 1997 survey indicated that the degree of use of SAMS at the time was on the low side (Visscher, Fung & Wild, 1999). Only a minority of schools had actually attained the level of data input that allows SAMS' full usage as an administration and management system. Many of the modules were not used, or only to a limited extent. Of the respondents, 57% were direct SAMS users (and 50% of these direct SAMS users were SAMS administrators responsible for the operation of SAMS). Principals tended to be indirect users, mainly using reports from the system for routine administrative task.

Results from that study strongly indicated that the limited use of SAMS was strongly affected by the factors depicted in the Visscher model (Figure 2, chapter 5). There were considerable user-criticisms on the quality of SAMS; users were mostly dissatisfied with the quality, particularly with the strategy used in the design and development of SAMS. The process of implementation was also problematic. The extent of user training was insufficient. The quality and quantity of both internal and external training were perceived to be unsatisfactory. As far as the effects of the implementation of SAMS were concerned, an interesting finding is that user motivation after using SAMS, in comparison with that before SAMS was installed, decreased considerably. Previous computer knowledge, perceived quality of information about SAMS, and the perceived clarity of the goals of the innovation process also partially explained the relatively low degree of usage. Although all these can simply be taken as user perceptions, they are critical success factors in SIS-implementation and should receive more attention in the design and implementation strategies.

Findings from the 1998 study indicated a mixed response from school staff towards the use of SAMS. On the one hand, users viewed the system to be having design limitations and performance problems such as being "too slow.... mechanistic and prescriptive" etc. On the other hand, there was a significantly positive response that saw SAMS' potential benefiting school management, particularly in relation to workplace requirements.

7.1.1 Degree of Use: The Extent of SAMS Usage in Hong Kong Schools

Results from the 1998 survey showed that schools did not necessarily start full operation with all modules in SAMS after the roll-out process, even though all the software modules had been installed. The amount of data input into different modules also varied from one school to another and only a small number of schools were found to be using all the SAMS modules. In general, the degree of SAMS usage (Table 1) was shown to be on the low side. Many SAMS modules were not used or only to a limited degree and usage of SAMS by school staff was not widespread at the end of the 5-year project.

Table 1. Use of SAMS Modules by Schools in 1998/1999

SAMS Module in use	Primary n=513	Secondary n=286
School Management	87%	89%
Student	91%	92%
Student Assessment	60%	73%
Student Attendance	28%	41%
Staff	87%	80%
Staff Deployment	16%	27%
Timetabling (Scheduling)	22%	50%
Allocation	24%	56%
HKEA	nil	64%
FMP	3%	14%
Programme Scheduling	5%	11%
Special Education	0%	0%
Communication & Delivery System (CDS)	89%	95%

It can be seen from Table 1 that the two record-keeping applications of Student and Staff were the most widely used SAMS applications in the schools, with Student

Assessment next. The CDS, with the largest number of schools in use, was actually a necessity as ED had made it the channel of delivery of circulars to schools in place of circulars by mail.

7.1.2 Users' Difficulties in Implementing SAMS

Schools were asked to indicate the five most difficult aspects in their SAMS implementation from a list of about twenty items. Table 2 is a summary of the difficulties encountered by schools in implementing SAMS.

Table 2. Five Most Difficult Items in SAMS Implementation as perceived by the School Staff

Primary schools	Secondary Schools
Not enough technical manpower in school (67%)	Low hardware performance (83%)
Insufficient external support for troubleshooting (60%)	Systems not flexible enough (66%)
Low hardware performance (57%)	Insufficient number of workstations (50%)
System not flexible enough (43%)	SAMS functions not meeting school needs 46%)
Inadequate training by ED (41%)	Not enough technical manpower in school (45%)

7.1.3 Users' Satisfaction with SAMS

An essential question in the survey was to ask schools about their overall level of satisfaction with the system. As shown in Table 3, the study revealed that 38% of the primary school staff felt satisfactory/very satisfactory, in contrast to 23% indicating unsatisfactory/very unsatisfactory (with a rather high 38% missing data). Among the secondary schools, 57% reported satisfactory/very satisfactory, and 21% otherwise (with 21% missing data). The reason for the rather high missing percentage of response to this question is not known.

Table 3. Overall Level of Satisfaction with SAMS

Level of Satisfaction	Primary (n=513)	Secondary (n=286)
Very satisfactory	2%	4%
Satsfactory	36%	54%
Unsatisfactory	21%	20%
Very Unsatisfactory	2%	2%
Missing	38%	21%
Total	100%	100%

7.1.4 System Support

According to the findings in the 1998 survey, most schools found the efficiency and quality of the support provided for SAMS to be unsatisfactory. These user perceptions are shown in Table 4. Support for SAMS included hotline support, hardware support, as well as user manual support. Apparently the primary schools had more difficulty in this aspect than the secondary schools.

Table 4. Level of Satisfaction with the Support provided

Level of satisfaction	Primary Schools Mean ± SD*	Secondary Schools Mean ± SD
EFFICIENCY		
SAMS support by ED	2.7 ± 0.7	2.4 ± 0.8
Hardware/network support by Vendor	2.6 ± 0.7	2.5 ± 0.7
QUALITY		
SAMS support by ED	2.6 ± 0.7	2.4 ± 0.7
Hardware/network support by Vendor	2.5 ± 0.7	2.4 ± 0.7

*1 = very satisfactory, 4 = very unsatisfactory

7.1.5 SAMS Training provided

Training is undoubtedly a crucial factor affecting the implementation and usage of SAMS. When asked in the questionnaire survey about the level of satisfaction with the training provided, the following feedback from the users, as shown in Table 5, was noted.

Table 5. School Satisfaction with the Training provided

Level of satisfaction	Primary Schools Mean ± SD*	Secondary Schools Mean ± SD
Quantity of training	2.6 ± 0.6	2.2 ± 0.7
Quality of training	2.5 ± 0.6	2.3 ± 0.6
Timing of training	2.7 ± 0.7	2.3 ± 0.8
Mode of training	2.6 ± 0.7	2.2 ± 0.7

*1 = very satisfactory, 4 = very unsatisfactory

7.1.6 Users' Suggestions for Improvement

At the end of the five-year project, when schools were asked to identify the five most needed improvement areas in SAMS, the items of concern were identified and are indicated in Table 6.

Table 6. The 5 Most needed Areas for Improvement in SAMS

Primary Schools (n=513)	Secondary Schools (n=286)
Improve hardware performance (56%)	Improve hardware performance (79%)
Effective hotline support (52%)	Increase system flexibility (64%)
Increase system flexibility (45%)	More workstations (55%)
More training/support for add-on	Match with user requirements (50%)
program development (44%)	
More internal training (38%)	Effective hotline support (37%)

8. THE IMPACT AND THE FUTURE OF SAMS

At the macroscopic level, the five-year SAMS project has at least raised the awareness of the potential of ICT in educational management, both for the central office and the schools. By and large the level of IT literacy among teachers has been upgraded through the training provided. The experience gained by schools in managing and operating SAMS is perhaps one of the most valuable side benefits for their managing IT in support of teaching and learning, under the recent Hong Kong SAR Government's five-year IT in education strategy, announced in 1998. Whether communications between schools and ED have improved or not is difficult to say, but the use of the CDS for electronic distribution of circulars, for handling school place allocation, for registration with HKEA, and for reporting statistical data to ED have all become a matter of routine.

At the school level, the impact of SAMS does vary from one school to another. Although there are continuous complaints of various kinds, there are also schools that have reaped benefits from SAMS, particularly the primary schools which did not have computer-aided administration systems before. Workload on the part of teachers does not appear to have lessened because of SAMS, but to the contrary have increased together with stress especially on the SAMS Administrator. The creation of this latter post in a school has impact not only for staff promotion considerations, but also affects the power structure within the school as the SAMS Administrator assumes an important role with his/her technical expertise.

There is no argument about the good intention of ED with the SAMS project in improving school management effectiveness and efficiency. Irrespective of the difficulties encountered, the experience of schools with SAMS is a building block to more successful institutional improvement through IT in educational management. Under the current government policy of integrating IT in support of teaching and learning at school, there is a need to not only manage IT better, but also a need for schools to be managed better through the use of IT.

Although the five-year project has already come to an end, it is envisaged that SAMS will not be discarded as the innovation cannot be reversed, nor can it be left stagnant as it is. On-going development is a necessity, and such development (or re-development) should be done with the educational needs of the school and the technological advances of IT in mind. As schools in Hong Kong are moving down the road of self-management according to the Education Commission's recommendations, the next generation of SAMS would be expected to provide not only improved administrative functions, but also support for school policy and decision making. While school improvement is being advocated under the school-based management policy, it would be reasonable to expect, as a concrete example, that the SAMS would support school-based self-evaluation. The system designers must be prepared to adopt such a client-centred approach in order that the next generation of SAMS truly reflects its name as an administrative and management system that schools can fully embrace.

The thrust of the evidence provided in this chapter strongly suggests that SAMS needs to be redesigned and rebuilt to support properly the current and future needs of schools in Hong Kong. However, there are technical difficulties that will need to be confronted. These difficulties stem from the use of Microsoft's FoxPro database management system for the construction of SAMS. The decision to use FoxPro would have seemed sound at the time it was taken because it offered superior performance to other desktop database management system software. Additionally, FoxPro is scalable (that is, it functions equally efficiently and effectively with databases of widely ranging size), and it operates across Windows, Macintosh and Unix hardware platforms, and, most importantly both Chinese and English language versions were available. However, to accommodate larger and more complex databases, SAMS would need to be redeveloped to run on more powerful file servers operating with Windows NT, Oracle, or, less likely, UNIX systems.

The development of new SAMS software must also take into account the advantage of having school-based LANs installed in schools. Again, it should not be assumed that a similar LAN topology will be installed in all schools, and that systems of online data entry of assessment data by teachers in classrooms will be acceptable. One should learn from the UK experience where teachers were equipped with laptop computers that they took with them as they moved from classroom to classroom. They could plug those computers into LAN ports in each classroom for online entry and recall of assessment data. Overwhelmingly, the teachers rejected that approach, principally because they saw it as being disruptive of their teaching practice. Many argued that it was an instance of educational practice being shaped by technology rather than technology being effectively exploited in education practice. No doubt there were many contributing causes to this outcome but it is clear that teachers will not use, or will be reluctant to use, technology that they see as merely adding to their clerical workload and which offers no real educational advantage.

Over the past five years, technological advances have much surpassed the hardware (some schools still use 486 machines) and system platform (Windows 3.1) of SAMS. In the age of the Internet, communication and connectivity is the key to success and the future-SAMS will very likely have to be developed with web-based technology. This is further discussed in the chapter on the future developments regarding SISs (chapter 8). Functionally it will also have to be developed with an integration of teaching and learning supported with ICT.

In terms of sustainability, the concept of SAMS being centrally funded, developed, and supported has to be re-visited. This centralised bureaucratic model is simply not flexible enough to meet the different and fast changing needs of schools. Apparently some senior officials in the Information Systems Division of the ED have already recognised this and there is a likelihood that the future development of SAMS will be opened up to market competition. This is in line with the decentralisation of funding to schools in the school-based management initiative. Hopefully in the not too distant future, schools will find in the market suites of SIS-programs available which they can choose to meet their needs.

9. CONCLUSION

This chapter has described and raised many issues about the design and implementation of SAMS in Hong Kong schools. At the end of 1998, when the five-year project was completed, research data suggested that system use was still very limited and tended to be of an administrative rather than managerial nature in the schools. The studies described also revealed various constraints existing in most schools that adversely affected SAMS usage. A crucial element cutting across all these limiting factors appeared to be the lack of a client-centred approach in both the design and implementation process.

It is important to draw lessons from the Hong Kong SAMS experience for future efforts of similar SIS projects throughout the phases of design, development, implementation and maintenance (including training and support). Most of the teachers interviewed in the study presented in this chapter believed that the introduction of IT in the classroom / school level has the potential to change substantially their day-to-day working life. Some opined that front-line teachers should be involved in aspects of systems development in order to produce a system that would far more likely benefit the schools, teachers and students. They also stressed that such systems must reflect and support the operating rhythms of the school, allowing more flexibility in daily operations. Unfortunately, SAMS failed to cater for such needs as characterized by its rigid, standardized operating procedures. The large-scale implementation of SAMS has been an ambitious computerization project. However, whether schools are willing to replace their individual systems depends much on the design of SAMS and how well it is being implemented (Fung, 1996).

If SAMS is to be redesigned to accommodate such demands, a different systems design and implementation strategy from that used in the past must be employed. In particular, systems designers and teachers must work closely together as equal partners to develop systems of data capture that do not place unreasonable additional burdens on teachers. They must also develop processing systems that can provide feedback on student progress that is truly useful for teachers and students, as well as managerial information to support school decision and policy-making. If teachers genuinely feel that they and their students derive real educational benefit from the system, they are obviously far more likely to be enthusiastic about it and to integrate its use into their teaching. Additionally, because organisational arrangements and management systems differ among schools it may be necessary to develop flexible modes of data entry so that schools can adopt the form that best meets their particular characteristics. This suggests that various prototype systems should be developed and extensively pilot-tested in different kinds of schools.

It is also relevant to consider the history of the development and implementation of SAMS. There is little doubt that there are many contributing reasons to the limited success of SAMS. Some of these contributing causes have their origins in organisational arrangements and project management procedures that did not confer sufficient influence in decision making on the ultimate end users. Development and implementation of more innovative information technology across the education system is a vastly more complex technical and organisational undertaking than simply the re-programming of SAMS. If it is to be successful it must occur in a carefully planned and incremental fashion and in an appropriate organisational context. The evolutionary approach in designing different versions of SAMS is also worth pondering. This has caused a number of schools to adopt a 'wait and see' attitude toward the innovation.

In summary, there are opportunities opening up for the Hong Kong education system in general to make more extensive and more effective use of information technology in school administration and management. Realizing those opportunities, it makes good management sense to design and develop a common, computer-based system that provides core functionality in a manner that will allow for flexibility in implementation while maintaining integrity of data and database structure. It will also require close collaboration between all institutional elements of the Hong Kong education system and a staged, carefully monitored, implementation of new approaches. Policy and planning must not merely reflect an unfettered embrace of technology. Such policy and planning, should rest on an understanding of the potential use of information in educational management.

REFERENCES

CCTA (1990). *PRINCE overview: the PRINCE project management method*. London: Her Majesty's Stationery Office

Education Commission (2000). *Reform proposals for the education system in Hong Kong*. Hong Kong: Government Printer.

EMB (1998). *Information technology for learning in a new era: five-year strategy 1998/99 to 2002/03*. Hong Kong: Hong Kong Education and Manpower Bureau.

Fung, A.C.W. (1996). An evaluation of the Hong Kong design and development strategy. *International Journal of Educational Research*, 25(40), 297-305.

Visscher, A.J., Fung, A.C.W. & Wild, P. (1999). The evaluation of the large-scale implementation of a computer-assisted management information system in Hong Kong schools. *Studies in Educational Evaluation*, 25 (4), 11 - 31.

Wild, P. & Fung, A.C.W. (1997). Evaluation of ITEM for proactive development. In: A.C.W. Fung, A.J. Visscher, B.Z. Barta & D.C.B. Teather (Eds.), *Information technology in educational management for the schools of the future*. London: Chapman & Hall, pp. 105 – 116.

CHAPTER 4

MUSAC IN NEW ZEALAND:FROM GRASS ROOTS TO SYSTEM-WIDE IN A DECADE

C.J. Patrick Nolan, Margaret A. Brown & Bruce Graves
Massey University, New Zealand

1. INTRODUCTION

With a stroke of the legislative pen late in 1988, the whole New Zealand school system was restructured away from central Government control that had been in place for over a century to school self-governance and management by local school boards of trustees. Overnight, New Zealand schools became referred to as 'Tomorrow's self managing schools', mandated by Government to achieve levels of organisational efficiency and effectiveness greater than was ever possible or realised in the past. For some years prior to restructuring, a small but steadily increasing number of schools had been experimenting with and using computer-assisted school administration and information systems (see Visscher, 1991, for discussion of developments internationally). Restructuring was perhaps the single event that pressed schools to take computerised school administration more seriously than in the past as a means to assist them to pursue the organisational efficiency and effectiveness goals they were mandated to achieve. Researchers and developers who had either developed computerised systems or understood their potential began, much more actively, to promote computer-assisted school administration as a direction for the future. This chapter summarises the development of computer assisted school administration in New Zealand but its principal purpose is to tell the story of one particular system developed and marketed to schools by the Massey University School Administration by Computer Project (MUSAC). The two first authors of this chapter are respectively a senior academic of the university College of Education and a university researcher. Their work and positions in the university are independent of MUSAC, maintaining only an arms length relationship with MUSAC. The MUSAC operation, though in the University as a system development and dissemination centre, is not part of the university in the conventional sense of contributing directly to university research and teaching. It is, however, frequently the subject ofresearch and MUSAC staff members make contributions to teaching programmes by invitation, as do other New Zealand system developers who are in competition with MUSAC. The third author is acknowledged because of the key role that he played in providing data and information useful to the senior authors when analysing system uptake and utilisation.

A.J. Visscher et al. (eds.), Information Technology in Educational Management, 55–76.
© 2001 *Kluwer Academic Publishers. Printed in the Netherlands.*

By the year 2000, nearly 2000 of New Zealand's 2795 schools had acquired and routinely use the MUSAC system. Its development, adoption and utilisation over nearly twelve years, by and large, is the story of computer-assisted school administration in New Zealand. While schools across the country use approximately ten systems in all, little dispute exists that the MUSAC system more than any other currently in use has transformed the operating administrative and management environment of New Zealand schools. It is a moot point as to whether it has changed the technical core of the schools (Fulmer, 1995), i.e., their curricula, pedagogy and systems of assessment and evaluation. A complex of factors brings about such change.

Two factors in New Zealand in the future may have a determining influence on the development of systems applicable for school administration and management in the technical core. The first is increasing teacher participation in school management and governance and teachers' consequent need for tools to manage curriculum, pedagogical and assessment data and information across a range of school levels. The second is increasing acceptance by practitioners and school administrators alike that the development of schools as learning communities is a preferred school development path for the future, though this is not to deny that learning communities still need to be efficiently and effectively organised. This is the case for both primary and secondary schools, though it is primary more than secondary schools that are noticeably moving in the learning community direction. As school development and change occurs in the directions indicated then computerised school information systems must evolve in ways that support the development.

The development of the MUSAC system, like most others, is predicated on the concept and operational needs of schools viewed as organisations. As the operational conditions of the schools have changed over the past decade, however, at times quite dramatically, the MUSAC system has grown and new programs have been developed in ways that permit the schools effectively to address and deal with their changing organisational conditions. Additionally, in the 1990s MUSAC began redeveloping its programs to operate in the emerging new Windows environment. That is to say, MUSAC is progressively replacing its somewhat loosely integrated set of twenty-six DOS programs with four generic Windows programs. The development appears to be timely. Market analyses are revealing how schools increasingly want more compact and tightly integrated generic programs capable of performing a wide range of functions. These functions are intuitively and immediately useable by a wide range of educational practitioners, from the principal to classroom teachers. Discussion later in the chapter assesses the extent to which the re-designed and evolving MUSAC system actually accommodates the views and needs of end-users. Nowadays, end-users seemingly have a more sophisticated and educationally broader perspective of what might count as a school information system suitable for leading and managing the schools of today. Moreover, the definition of a 'good system' also appears to be changing, perhaps as a by-product of an increasingly discerning and sophisticated end user.

2. PURPOSE

This chapter documents and examines the development, adoption and implementation of the MUSAC system in New Zealand. The period of development covered is from 1984 to the present. Planned development beyond 2000 is also discussed in recognition that while circumstances may change dramatically over ten years, planning for the future is vital even though the goals and objectives of the plan may have to be modified, even replaced. To achieve its purpose the chapter is organised in sections covering:

1. the development of computerised school information systems in New Zealand including key influencing factors;
2. the development circumstances of MUSAC including its design and design philosophy;
3. a description of the evolving structure and contents of MUSAC in three broad stages (establishment, expansion and consolidation) along with examination of its qualities as a system suitable for utilisation by schools;
4. analysis and discussion of utilisation patterns and implementation strategies; and
5. conclusions which discuss the overall impact of MUSAC on New Zealand schools.

The conclusions identify ways that system developments of the future, both MUSAC and other systems, might support school development in a broad sense and wider than the conventional automating and informating functions (Fulmer, 1995) characteristic of system utilisation to date.

3. SCHOOL INFORMATION SYSTEM DEVELOPMENT IN NEW ZEALAND

As in other countries (Visscher & Spuck, 1991) during the later 1970s, teacher enthusiasts, with skills in computer programming, pioneered the development of SISs in New Zealand. Generally, the pioneering developers defined their mission as that of developing programs to help school administrators economise on the use of their time, i.e., be more efficient. Thus, programs were developed to deal with such recurring, but key, administrative tasks as scheduling, pupil registration, school accounting and marks analysis. In some instances the developers formed school-based businesses and generated revenue for their schools. The MUSAC software was itself initially developed in this way. Others left teaching and formed small school software businesses and marketed their products to schools in the local region.

Computer-assisted school administration, thus initiated and largely uncoordinated was ad hoc, resulting in a diversity of functional, integrated and single purpose software solutions and strategies. Designed by teachers and school administrators, who understood schools and how they worked, the solutions tended to be well received because they met administrative and management needs as defined by the schools themselves. As the principal developer of the MUSAC software once commented: 'Our first priority was to develop computerised methods and procedures that would help schools become masters of their own destinies and managers of their own affairs' (Butler, 1999).

From around the early to mid-1980s, commercial organisations such as banks, accountancy firms and business software houses entered the field. Not infrequently, they sold business software to schools straight off the shelf. Following the 1988 restructuring, computer-assisted school administration in New Zealand went through a transition from initiation to a stage of expansion (Visscher, 1991). Both the business community and the schools themselves began to recognise more clearly, though from somewhat different perspectives, the potential of computers to support school administration and management. On the whole, the school software businesses seem to have been more successful than the commercial organisations for two reasons. Firstly, they understood better than the commercial organisations the distinctive data and information processing requirements of schools. Secondly, they designed special purpose applications capable of doing what the schools wanted. The more advanced packages incorporated an integration feature with the capability to transport data between applications.

During the expansion stage, individual schools grappled with the different but related challenges of: (i) managing the computer environment in a technical sense; and (ii) understanding how the benefits for school administration, much vaunted by vendors, might be realised. The acceleration of school administrative hardware and software purchases during the late 1980s and through to about 1996 indicates that New Zealand schools were by now integrating computer technology into their day-to-day management and administrative practice. (See MUSAC figures in Figures 1 and 2, which depict the rate of acquisition, though not the rate of use.) It is a reasonable speculation, however, that by the mid-1990s many schools had achieved the automation of activities goal (viz. the improvement of the efficiency of clerical activities) characteristic of initiation and expansion. Moreover, a significant minority appears to have shifted attention from the management of computerisation to the management of information. However, findings from case studies around this time (Nolan & Ayres, 1996) also showed that the way schools were actually managing information (i.e., their use patterns) varied markedly.

4. MUSAC ORIGINS

MUSAC was established in 1989 as a Massey University-based initiative with a formal mandate to create and market to New Zealand schools a comprehensive computerised school information system that would enable school administrators and teachers to:
1. meet the challenge set for them by Government to govern and manage themselves;
2. direct their own development rather than be directed from without as in the past; and
3. make their own decisions and become wholly responsible for their own affairs.

Given the limited budgets within which most New Zealand schools operate and the relative paucity of their computer knowledge at that time, three further requirements were built into the MUSAC development brief, which remain in place today. The MUSAC system, and its component programs, must also be affordable, user friendly and robust.

The University did not develop the MUSAC system from scratch. Its initial core programs had already been developed under another name and marketed as a system to approximately 100 schools (see Figure 1) by the person who later became the general-manager and chief developer of MUSAC (R. Butler). The original system was selected as the MUSAC platform for three reasons:

1. it had built into its design most, if not all, the functionality already observed in competing local and overseas systems (e.g., the OASIS package from New South Wales, Australia - see Dale & Habib, 1991);
2. it was already known by schools to be a robust and useful system; and
3. the software design philosophy, involving such attributes as responsiveness, flexibility and inventiveness, fitted with the values of the University Education Faculty who understood the role that a computerised system might play.

Consistent with research on information system design elsewhere (Nolan, 1977; Spuck & Atkinson, 1983; Honeyman & Honeyman, 1988; and Essink & Visscher, 1989), the MUSAC system was conceptualised holistically from the outset as a fully integrated system. The design philosophy provided for a modular architecture into which new programs could be incorporated as they were developed in response to expressed or anticipated needs. As Visscher (1991) points out, this capability, alone, establishes the superiority of an integrated modular system over others. It permits single entry of data for access by multiple users, thereby eliminating in one stroke, so to speak, duplication of clerical activities that long had been the bane of the school office.

5. MUSAC DEVELOPMENT STRATEGY

The MUSAC development plan, formulated during its establishment in 1989, was based on the assumption that acceptance, uptake and implementation of the MUSAC software would require that the schools participate in the design and development process, i.e., have a stake in the enterprise. To this end the design approach of the plan contained three key elements:

1. the welcoming of flexibility and divergent thinking in the design of software which involves listening to, and valuing, the ideas of others in and outside of MUSAC, especially end-users, converging towards best/preferred design solutions;
2. the adoption of a concept of 'user friendliness' somewhat broader in scope than conventional definitions involving a user group, help desk and rewards to users for good ideas and error detection; and

3. the software developers and customer support staff subscribing to a problem-solving approach, with solutions provided by end-users being regularly incorporated into software updates.

All three of the elements, working together, helped to create a culture within MUSAC that encourages MUSAC staff, to this day, to be responsive and anticipatory in their approach to software design and adaptation for advancing technology. On the one hand, existing software is constantly revised to match existing school needs. On the other, new software is constantly under development, anticipating changes and new needs. For example, the new *Classroom Manager for Windows (2000)* contains an array of integrated learning assessment tools for use at many school levels and by a wide range of school staff. This particular program thereby accommodates the contemporary redefinition of teachers as classroom managers and as participants in the making of school-wide decisions.

During the establishment of MUSAC, program modifications were often made based on MUSAC staff perceptions of school needs. However, during expansion and consolidation, the development of new programs and the modification of existing programs were informed much more by feedback based on data, often provided by consultants and directly from the schools. While MUSAC software was designed primarily to support school-based administration and management, in time it had to incorporate suggestions from the Ministry of Education that increasingly came to recognise the value of receiving information processed and transmitted by computer. A number of MUSAC programs were thus developed or modified to meet the requirements of Government regulations. Equally, MUSAC abandoned some programs for two reasons. Firstly, they were tangential to the core business of MUSAC of supporting school administration and management, such as *Payroll*. Secondly, programs were withdrawn because government regulations changed. In the case of *Exam Entries*, the government wrote its own program and said that all schools must use it. Thus, school use of *Exam Entries* rapidly diminished.

MUSAC planners now estimate that the half-life of any given program is about eighteen months. Thus, to stay in business, MUSAC program revision and development is constantly in progress. In 1996, MUSAC explicitly adopted what might best be called 'vision led planning'. This incorporated the responsive strategy of the past but overtly sought to anticipate the future and plan new program development that in the future will address emerging technological advances such as new and emerging operating environments. The new motto derived from the strategy is 'both to lead and to follow'. In this respect, the key lesson to be learned from the MUSAC experience is not so much 'adapt or perish' but plan and develop creatively and produce software programs that schools need and can use. The lesson is salutary in light of the fact that some MUSAC programs have been too advanced for the current level of knowledge and expertise available in schools.

6. STRUCTURE AND CONTENTS OF THE MUSAC SYSTEM

Figure 1 presents the structure and contents (the programs) of the MUSAC system as it evolved and developed in the three stages of establishment (1984-89), expansion (rapid and steady from 1989-97) and consolidation (1997-2002). Over the full development period, the underlying transition has been from DOS-based to Windows-based software. The DOS environment, and associated lack of the relational capability later provided by Access databases, necessitated the development of single purpose programs that proliferated up to 1997. While the MUSAC System during this time was relatively well integrated as a system and permitted networking, its functionality remained limited by proliferation. The advent of Windows and Access database programming provided developers with the capacity they needed to redevelop the whole system yet retain, refine and expand the processing capabilities that had been identified as useful over twelve years of development.

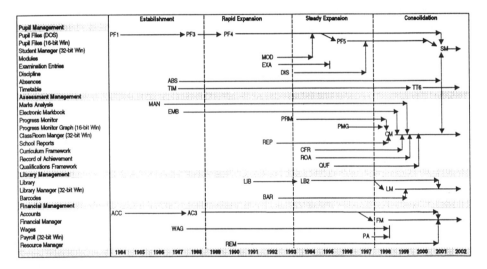

*Figure 1. MUSAC Programs by Year of Development**

As Figure 1 shows, the pattern of program development from 1997 onwards is one of convergent evolution as new multi-purpose generic programs were developed and field-tested in, and with, schools. The new programs group together and amalgamate the previously single purpose programs, related by their connection with a common information processing function. For example, *Classroom Manager (1998),* referred to above, links together all programs previously connected with the

---

* Appreciation is expressed to Bruce Graves, Manager of the MUSAC Helpdesk for the assistance he gave in producing the figures.

management and administration of information related to the assessment of learning and to the reporting and recording of student achievement and progress. Three other generic programs are currently under development and due for release during 2001. *Student Manager* (2001) covers all aspects of the management of students, from placement into classes to the recording of absences and the issue of receipts. *Library Manager* (1998) addresses all aspects of the operation of school libraries, including learning and teaching resources and other materials linked to the professional work of teachers and their classrooms. *Financial Manager* (1998) deals with routine financial accounting to school budgeting processes and resource allocation. To ensure continuity during development and testing, the schools are continuing with single purpose programs rewritten for Windows.

Each of the programs permits a full range of both automating and informating functions. Thus it is possible for, say, teachers and office staff alike to use the list producing functions of Student Manager to routinely generate a range of lists from class lists of students, sports teams, cultural clubs and the like. The same program can be used also, however, for various investigative and analysis purposes, e.g., to examine the relationship between patterns of school attendance/absenteeism and such factors as achievement levels and student attributes such as gender, ethnicity and socio-economic status. Equally important, data in one generic program can be correlated with data in another. This could be for the purposes of showing connections, identifying trends and analysing patterns. For example, in any given school it may be important in setting school policy on library acquisitions to base decisions on students, preferences and borrowing patterns. To this end, data from Library Manager can be cross-tabulated with data from Student Manager. The MUSAC website (http://musac.massey.ac.nz) contains a full description of the MUSAC programs identified above and encompassing all aspects of the administration and management of schools as outlined in the School Information System Framework developed by Visscher (1996).

6.1 Establishment

The precursor MUSAC programs, *Pupil Files* and *Accounts* laid the foundation for the MUSAC System from 1984. When MUSAC was formally established in 1989 they, along with five other programs developed in the interim, constituted the initial MUSAC System. *Pupil Files* linked with *Marks Analysis, Electronic Markbook, Absences* and *Timetable* to address a relatively wide, though still not comprehensive, range of pupil management and assessment functions. *School Wages* was linked with *Accounts* to address a comparable range of financial management functions. Early on, *Pupil Files* was also core in the sense that it was the central program from which all other programs could be used to access pupil data for more specific processing tasks. For example, *Timetable* linked with it in the preparation of the school timetable and *Accounts* for the issue of invoices and receipts. At this time the System was not, and could not have been, fully relational in the sense that it is today in the Windows operating environment and with the use of Access databases for program development.

6.2 Expansion

By 1994, the MUSAC System had been developed as a comprehensive, fully field-tested and integrated suite of 15 school data and information processing programs. Figure 1 shows how they fit with the four school management strands and the four new generic programs discussed above. The system, in its turn was now able to perform a full range of automating and informating functions (Fulmer, 1995) and encompassed the administrative and management sub-systems of schools and their associated activities as outlined in the Visscher (1996) school administration and management framework mentioned above.

During expansion, both the MUSAC System developers and users explored and began to see more clearly the scope of school management and administration amenable to support by computer. Together, they progressed in their understanding of the difference between automating and informating functions and the role of a computerised school information system in the management of information:

1. Automating as the routine processing of school data associated with such administrative functions as the entry of student data into teacher maintained records, the processing of school accounts and the compilation of information for external agencies, e.g., the Ministry of Education; and

2. Informating as generating information by computer to support school management and leadership functions at various levels, namely the principal and senior management level, the department level and the classroom level.

Survey research (Nolan & Ayres, 1996) on acquisition and use patterns in the mid-1990s, showed that understanding of the distinction remained confined, by and large, to senior school managers and administrators. Interestingly though, around this time educational practitioners and some researchers (Fulmer, 1995) were suggesting that the power of computerised school information systems might be more fully realised when the full range of educational professionals were permitted and encouraged to use them. Teachers came increasingly to want administrative and management tools they could use, especially as they sought to meet demands for evidence of their efficiency and effectiveness. Such wants necessitated not further expansion of the MUSAC system but consolidation and refinement of it in the form of greater versatility of use and scope for using the same tools by a wider range of users.

Two foundations for refinement existed in the form of the MUSAC networking capability and program integration. Together they permitted decentralised practitioner access and interaction through remote terminals. The inclusion of these features with MUSAC still operating in DOS, was a thoughtful and deliberate commitment by the developers to the development of professional collegiality and collaboration through information sharing.

6.3 Refinement and Consolidation

Reciprocity seems to be integral to the development of computerised school information systems. The changing circumstances and needs of end users suggest directions for software and system development. Reciprocally, technological advances (e.g., Windows itself and Access databases) suggest new ways to design systems and process information. The net effect in the MUSAC development environment was two-fold. First there was a need to convert existing key programs (*Pupil Files* and *Accounts*) from DOS to Windows. Second, it was necessary to reduce the twenty six programs, that by 1997 had made MUSAC unwieldy and vulnerable to loss of market share, into the four generic programs identified above. The graph of Figure 2 indicates that the shift from DOS to Windows was timely and that the decline of the DOS programs in schools has been matched by the uptake of the new Windows single purpose and generic programs.

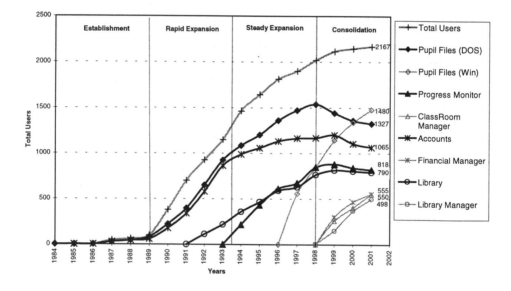

Figure 2. Key MUSAC Programs by School Acquisition

Figures 1 and 2 together illustrate the transition from DOS to Windows quantitatively in terms of the peak in 1998 and then the drop-off of the number of key DOS programs in schools and the rapid replacement of them with the two types of new Windows programs, viz. the single purpose programs for Windows (e.g., Pupil Files 5, 1997) and the multi-purpose generic programs for Windows (e.g., Classroom Manager, 1998). MUSAC Timetable remains stand-alone and is currently being redeveloped for Windows. By 2002, current redevelopment of the MUSAC system will be complete and the completion will mark the single most significant and substantive development phase since the completion of establishment in 1989. In this period, it is probably fair to say that the MUSAC System has increased its system capacity, power and functionality by close to an order of magnitude. Yet, such is the speed of advances with information and communication technology today, that the half-life of current new MUSAC programs remains less than two years. The MUSAC development team is even now planning the further refinement and perhaps renewal of the MUSAC System to render it accessible and usable via the Internet.

7. THE SYSTEM QUALITY OF MUSAC

The MUSAC system encompasses all aspects of school administration and management as outlined in the School Information System Framework developed by Visscher (1996) and elaborated in chapter 1. Additionally, it now includes specific programs that teachers can use in their classrooms and other work places to support curriculum planning and delivery and learning and teaching. In this respect, it conforms to the concept of a classroom focused information system (Frank & Fulmer, 1998).

A systematic analysis (Nolan & Ayres, 1996) of the MUSAC software during its expansionary stage revealed that, at that time, the MUSAC system also satisfied technical criteria of a capable system. In general terms it could be employed to 'collect data, automate processes and informate the work of multiple decision makers from different organisational levels' (Fulmer, 1995, p. 6). Its bottom-up design and incorporation of a help desk and a user group facility meant that the system was, and still is today, responsive to user needs.

More specifically, the design of the MUSAC system met, and still meets today, the five criteria of system quality identified by Fulmer (1995) in the following ways:
1. networking and remote terminals create multiple input ports enabling both administrator and teacher access to, and use of, the full range of data stored in the system;
2. user defined fields in most programs, but especially in Classroom Manager, provide for a wide range of units of analysis (including categories such as gender, ethnicity and socio-economic status) for the aggregation of data and the investigation of patterns and trends;
3. a broad spectrum approach to data permits the collection of diverse kinds of data (e.g., nominal, ordinal, interval ratio, biographic, self evaluation, etc.) within and across programs, with the system as a whole able to store most types of data and present them in formats appropriate for each type, from box and whisker diagrams to qualitative comments;
4. a wide range of analysis tools, including conventional spreadsheet, data-base and statistical techniques, permit the use of a corresponding wide range of inquiry and analysis methods, e.g., comparative analysis of student achievement data as a factor in deciding the composition of classes or 'what if' analyses of financial data for developing alternative school budgets; and
5. an open entry windows environment permits variable levels of access for data retrieval and processing of system data at any organisational level, e.g., attendance and absentee trends for specific classes or spending patterns across subject departments.

The incorporation of these features into the MUSAC system reflects the commitment by MUSAC developers to the development of professional collegiality and collaboration through the information sharing referred to above. The extent to which schools actually practice information sharing depends on how many and which MUSAC programs they possess and the manner in which they use them.

Ongoing research is required to clarify how much and how schools use MUSAC, especially since the introduction of the newer Windows single purpose and generic programs. On the face of it, the design of the newer programs further illustrates ongoing conformity of the MUSAC system to Fulmer's (1995) criteria of a good system. Discussion later on in the chapter addresses the notion of 'good system' itself, and the extent to which reformulation of the criteria of a good system may now be required or additional new criteria added.

8. MUSAC SOFTWARE USE PATTERNS

Over the past two decades, the MUSAC system and its precursor software have gradually replaced the manual systems used by New Zealand schools throughout the course of the twentieth century. Their utilisation is the result of grass-roots initiatives which stand in contrast with government mandated initiatives that appear to have been commonplace elsewhere (Visscher & Spuck, 1991). In New Zealand, responsibility for system uptake and implementation has rested with the schools, not the Government. The schools constantly challenge the developers to provide them with the systems they need. The question of how schools (managers, administrators, practitioners) actually use their MUSAC software, or are assisted to use it and to what effect, remains largely unresearched, although this is not to gainsay the earlier comment that widespread utilisation of MUSAC software has transformed the administrative and management environment of schools.

An analysis (Nolan & Ayres, 1996) of use patterns conducted across 1994-96 showed that, overall, all types of schools[1] in New Zealand (primary, intermediate, secondary and area) are using their computerised information systems to support a full range of school management and administrative functions. A recent re-analysis of the acquisition patterns in 1998 (unpublished), showed that schools nation wide still had the full range of programs currently available. The combinations of programs fell into discernible patterns of acquisition and, by inference and anecdotal reports from twelve support agencies and the MUSAC Help Desk, associated use

---

[1] School types in New Zealand: Primary schools (2221) consist of contributing (970) and full (1251) primaries, which cater respectively for 5-10 year olds (K to 5) and 5-12 year olds (K to 7). They range from single teacher schools in geographically remote areas to large, urban schools with 20 or more teachers. Intermediate schools (149) and a form of two-year Middle School, common in the USA cater for the education of 11-13 year olds in grades 6 and 7 with students fed to them from surrounding, contributing primary schools. Secondary schools (338) may include 11-17 year olds (grades 6-12), though typically they encompass the lesser age range from 13-17 (grades 8-12). Area schools (87), typically in remote areas where only one school is justified to serve a community, encompass the full age range and grade span for 5-17 years (K to 12).

patterns similar to 1996. The re-analysis of 1998 revealed a broadly similar pattern of acquisition and use:

1. a relatively limited use of software by a fairly large minority of schools using between 1-2 MUSAC programs, but only one program from any given strand in Figure 1 (primary = 40%, intermediate = 30%, secondary = 28% and area = 36%);

2. a moderate use of software by a solid core of schools across all school types, but in up to three strands in Figure 1 (primary = 45% with 3-6 programs/school; intermediate = 35% with 3-6 programs/school; secondary = 26% with 3-13 programs/school; and area = 37% with 3-8 programs/school);

3. a wider range of software use across all four Strands of Figure 1 but with wide variations in the number of programs used by each school type (Primary = 15% but no more than 8 programs/school, intermediate = 35% and up to 10 programs/school, secondary = 46% and up to 15 programs/school and Area = 27% and up to 10 programs/school).

Overall, the relatively large percentages of schools from all four school types contained in lines (ii) and (iii) above (primary = 60%; intermediate = 70%; secondary = 72% and area = 64%), indicates that computer-assisted school administration was well established in the New Zealand school system by 1996. It has very likely become better established in the last two years with the introduction of new software for teacher use. This is despite the fact that a significant minority was then, and appears still to be, at an early stage of computerised information system mastery and use. Even among the mature users, anecdotal evidence gathered recently through the MUSAC User Group and Help Desk suggests that use of individual programs to perform specific tasks for particular administrative purposes remains the dominant use pattern. The integration capability of the system is brought into play only when it serves a practical purpose, e.g., interfacing output from Timetable with Pupil Files to create class lists.

It could be the case that, below the surface of the use patterns identified here, lies a more in-depth and extensive use pattern. This is unlikely, however, because it seems that in most schools the people who actually deal with computerised data and information on a day-to-day basis are not the same people who make strategic decisions and plan school development, e.g., school boards of trustees. Typically, school leaders and administrators receive, from office staff, routine summaries of data and information. Their consequent unfamiliarity with the 'raw data' denies them the opportunity to consider alternative processing strategies.

A simple but potentially successful solution might be to make school staff who routinely process school data and information party to key school decision processes (Stewart & Prebble, 1993), for example, the school executive officer and the staff responsible for time tabling. They could act as experts to help teachers and administrators better understand the functionality of the MUSAC system and ways of using the system to explore the data. In this way, the participation of such staff in the making of decisions would broaden the possibilities for informed decision and action.

At a more general level, ongoing research is required to disclose the complete picture of use patterns. On the assumption that Visscher's (1991) stabilisation of system use has been reached by many schools, research is needed urgently to: (i) identify existing exemplary practice that might be emulated by others; and (ii) establish the base-line of existing information system use from which to conduct school-based training and development. That is to say, the difficulty appears to be that the functions of the systems and how to use them are insufficiently clear to the users. Thus, school administrators and teachers need training and development in order to master a computerised system, and explore ways of applying the system in the directions and at levels beyond automation and informating functions. To a degree, schools already avail themselves of this training but a well developed culture in schools of ongoing professional development to support fully fledged and widespread computerised school information system use has yet to emerge.

Many MUSAC programs have been explicitly designed to assist with teacher classroom administration and management and help them teach better, e.g., *Classroom Manager*. In fact, it could be said that 'impacting on the technical core of the school' (Fulmer, 1995, p. 5) with a view to enhancing learning and teaching has now become a primary goal of the MUSAC system. If schools have not realised that goal as fully as they might, then perhaps responsibility rests with the providers of professional development, as much as it does with the schools, to suggest ways of more effectively utilising the MUSAC System widely in the technical core of schools (viz. classrooms, syndicates and departments). This is because teachers are more likely to make use of computerised systems if it can be shown to them that use of the systems will reduce their workload, provide immediate, useable feedback, help them meet external review requirements and promote collaboration.

It is a moot point as to whether any one school-type, primary, intermediate, secondary or area, is further ahead than another in using MUSAC programs for policy analysis, strategic planning and programme development purposes, i.e., to perform higher order management functions. Secondary schools commonly have more teachers with the capability and experience to use a wide range of MUSAC programs, but it seems they use them to perform quite specific one-off tasks, perhaps reflecting the compartmentalised structures in which they work. In the secondary schools that do use MUSAC programs to carry out higher order functions, this activity tends to be confined within the schools' management team.

In contrast, a small but significant number of primary and intermediate schools use their somewhat fewer computer resources to make key data about the school, such as details of the school budget, available to the whole staff (including school trustees) as the basis for collaborative problem solving and shared decision making. Recent experience of working closely with secondary schools indicates that this approach is not well understood by them and it appears, as yet, to be seldom used.

For some time now, the New Zealand Government has been pressing schools to put in place assessment and evaluation procedures that document their effectiveness in educational terms. If nothing else, this external pressure for change may push schools to use their MUSAC systems to monitor and evaluate their educational programmes and, where necessary, plan and deliver more effective ones. That is, external pressures, perhaps more than spontaneous teacher and school administrator initiative, will push schools to interface their MUSAC information systems with the school curriculum and with the learning and teaching which lies at its core. As Fulmer points out (1995), if schools are to meet this challenge, then teachers and school administrators need to become better acquainted with, and better able to employ, their existing computerised information systems.

9. MUSAC IMPLEMENTATION

While only one element of the Visscher (1996) model of the relations between design, use and effects of information systems, implementation is strategic in the sense that it lies at the interface between the intentions of developers and the ways that information systems are actually used. If this is the case, then effective implementation strategies appear to be a key factor influencing the extent to which such systems may enhance school administration and management and impact positively upon the content and delivery of school education.

Anecdotal evidence suggests that during the early years of computerised school information system use in New Zealand, and even now, the importance and nature of implementation was little understood and little, if any, real attention was given to managing implementation processes. Individual system developers, like the chief developer of the MUSAC software, when he was head of a secondary mathematics department, canvassed local schools to purchase his software and he developed and modified the software hand in glove with the school administrators who were using it. He, like others, used word of mouth, school networks and local principals associations to generate interest, something akin to the orientation and awareness activities that typically are associated with formally orchestrated implementation strategies (McKinnon & Nolan, 1989 and Nolan et al., 1996).

In one sense, implementation enacted in this way is a strength in that the schools that came to implement the MUSAC system did so because they chose to. The weakness is that implementation may extend no further than specific individuals who use the system for particular purposes. This implementation pattern is commonly evident in secondary schools that typically exhibit highly segmented utilisation patterns linked to specific software programs used for particular purposes. In fact, until fairly recently the 'MUSAC Computer Admin System' was contained, by and large, in the administrative office of the school. Smaller primary schools are an exception. Here, size and propinquity promote information sharing and more widespread use.

Until recently, teachers as a whole have seen little value in seeking access to and using computerised schools information systems. School administrators, for their part, have tended not to encourage teacher use of the systems either, for at least three reasons, namely that such use might erode administrator power and control, administrators have lacked understanding of how teachers might generate information by computer and productively employ it for classroom use and the logistics of giving teachers access and use has been too difficult to manage (Frank & Fulmer, 1998). Teachers, for their part, have seen greater value in and adopted more readily computer tools to support learning and teaching. This has taken place in parallel with the development of computerised administrative systems over more than two decades. Arguably, a more formal joint implementation process may have been widely perceived as unnecessary by both teachers and administrators since it was not originally intended that the administrative system access and use would be widespread.

Developments over the past five years in institutional understanding of the wider uses to which computerised systems might be put, by a much wider range of school personnel, now means that schools as a whole better understand the complex and sometimes problematic nature of implementation. Moreover, the changing and more complex nature of the systems themselves requires that implementation be taken seriously, especially if schools wish to achieve more effective system utilisation.

Case study research on the implementation of MUSAC software (Nolan et al., 1996) yielded a research and theory based strategy derived from the Concerns Based Adoption Model (CBAM) (Hall, Wallace & Dosset, 1973; McKinnon & Nolan, 1989). The research showed specifically that when schools using MUSAC applied the strategy, which involved systematically working through key implementation processes of orientation, awareness, preparation and mechanical use, then wider staff acceptance and system utilisation was achieved:

- *Awareness* involves key personnel recognising that a computerised information system may actually be needed. The reasons may range from systemic pressures from a higher authority (e.g., the Ministry of Education in New Zealand) through community pressures to internal school reasons.
- *Orientation* involves key personnel seeking knowledge and ideas that will inform their decisions. For instance, it is likely that they will wish to know about such matters as tasks the computerised system will perform, the kinds of outcomes that might be expected, the levels of funding and support that might be required to both acquire and implement the system, and the relative merits and shortcomings of competing systems.
- *Preparation* engages personnel in the activities of setting up the system for practical use. Typically, this level of use includes acquisition and installation of the system, the determination of locations (e.g., where to place the file server and remote networked terminals), the assignment of staff roles and responsibilities, and the initiation of staff training.
- *Mechanical use*, the final step of implementation, involves staff members learning to use the system. Implementation ends when everyone who the school identifies as needing to use the system (or a part of it), has mastered the program(s) and is using it to carry out day-to-day tasks.

Use of the strategy works best as part of an adaptive yet systematic approach. This involves three key factors: (i) guaranteed funding and Board support; (ii) the assignment of key persons with a common view to drive the innovation and keep up the momentum of implementation; and (iii) regular, well-structured staff training and support provided on an as-needs basis so that staff can learn and master MUSAC programs by using them to carry out real management and administration tasks. In New Zealand, support agencies franchised to MUSAC provide schools with the guidance, training and support that they need. Interestingly, their philosophy is to help the schools become self-managing and not dependent on the agencies. They seem to understand that their aims must include: (i) helping schools to increasingly take responsibility for their own learning needs; and (ii) empowering schools to use their computerised information systems relatively unaided.

10. MUSAC SUPPORT AGENCIES

It could be said that the agencies that support MUSAC implementation and use, nationally, are vital to the MUSAC enterprise, for no matter how technically capable the MUSAC software, its effective and ongoing utilisation requires accessible, competent and frequent training and support. To this end, the MUSAC developers worked as hard, from the outset, developing support agencies nationally as they did actually developing and testing the software. In reality, the franchised support agencies, along with key schools from all parts of the country became co-developers in the sense of constantly making suggestions and producing ideas to improve existing programs and develop new ones.

MUSAC, based at Massey University, is located close to the geographic centre of New Zealand. Its own support agency and help desk is thus able to provide user support and training throughout the central region of the country. Two other principal agencies and their help-desks, supported by travelling consultants, cover the North and South of New Zealand. These two agencies are contracted to provide helpdesk support for all MUSAC-using schools and encompassing all four generic MUSAC programs covering pupil management, classroom management, library management and financial management.

The helpdesks are funded from income generated by membership of the MUSAC User Group. When schools purchase MUSAC software they invariably choose to become members of the User Group. User Group income pays for future development and maintenance of programs, the costs of sending out disks and documentation and access to the Helpdesk for help, but not training. The helpdesks of each support agency are funded by User Group income proportionate to each of the MUSAC programs supported by each support agency. User Group fees, in their turn, are charged on a sliding scale relative to size of school.

The Support agencies, not the MUSAC staff, deliver training and support in a variety of ways including telephone training, off-site seminars and workshops, one-to-one training sessions on-site and consultation. Training is in addition to the cost of purchasing MUSAC programs.

When a school purchases software from MUSAC they purchase a site license. This means that they may install the software on any machine in the school as well as on the at-home machines of school staff. Obviously price is critical to schools and the low cost of MUSAC could well have contributed to the wide take-up, in a similar way to the success of SIMS in the UK (chapter 2).

Research findings to date on implementation patterns are the result of exploratory rather than system wide surveys. However, this exploratory research indicates that implementation, when well executed, leads to system utilisation in the stages of routine use, integration, refinement and evaluation. To the extent that evaluations are favourable, a school may decide to expand the existing system by introducing a new component, i.e., initiate a new implementation stage. In this way, implementation of the MUSAC system studied in the research (Nolan et al., 1996) was seen typically to be on-going and incremental as schools progressively adopted new components. Interestingly, only in a very few instances (less than 5%) has any one school of nearly 2000 now using the MUSAC system attempted to implement in excess of three MUSAC programs at any one time. These have been large secondary schools whose staff possess a high level of technical computer competency and for whom implementation has been relatively straightforward and well supported by technical staff.

11. CONCLUSIONS

Use patterns are the bottom line against which to evaluate the impact of computerised school information systems. It was speculated earlier in the chapter that the majority of MUSAC-using schools could be classified as 'adult to mature system users', although a significant minority across school types is still at a neophyte stage. Within MUSAC-using schools as a whole, differences in use patterns may reflect different administrative requirements and administrative and management styles as much as they do levels of sophistication in the use of specific programs. In the absence of large-scale research that might reveal system wide use patterns, anecdotal feedback from the MUSAC Help Desk, MUSAC training seminars and school administrators doing post-graduate work, provides two useful insights. Considerable variation exists in kinds and levels of use and schools are not very adept at or willing to share good ideas and best practice. This is especially true of secondary schools.

In the past, school inspectors and the school advisory service played a role disseminating good ideas and effective educational and administrative practices. In New Zealand's school system today, this role is now performed by periodic Ministry of Education school development contracts, delivered by various professional agencies and organisations in the community. Such contracts, if let in the general area of computer-assisted school administration, could fund programmes within which knowledgeable and experienced educational practitioners might help their less experienced counterparts avoid pitfalls and pursue beneficial development paths. This could be an effective means of demonstrating how information sharing and collaboration between schools (as distinct from insularity and isolation) empowers schools to get the best value from their computerised school information systems.

The location of MUSAC in a university provides the software developers with three specific freedoms apparently important to the success of the enterprise:
1. freedom to exercise control over, and accept responsibility for, the manner and direction in which computerised school information systems are designed;

2. freedom to promote the interests of schools by adopting a 'school-centred' approach which places control over school management and development in the hands of school personnel; and
3. freedom to exercise discretion in deciding from whom advice and support might be sought (e.g., schools, government, business) and ultimately accepted or rejected.

The exercise of these freedoms implies that the developers pursue their objectives in a way that is consistent with knowledge creation and research values that define the mission of a university and set it apart from the institutions and organisations of government and business. On the one hand the developer's role is to produce software that is technically sound. MUSAC developers are well placed to do this in the university through ready access to the latest technical knowledge. On the other hand, their role, arguably, is to encourage innovative school administration and management by designing school information systems that incorporate the latest ideas from educational theory and research. In respect to this, MUSAC staff members are able to interact and exchange ideas within an Education Faculty actively working in the field of educational management, administration and school development theory and research. To date, however, the extent to which MUSAC software and other systems actually add value to the administration and management of New Zealand schools is not known in the sense of research findings which demonstrate the nature and extent of this value. System wide research is needed but as yet remains to be done.

In terms of its distinctive character as a 'grass roots' enterprise, MUSAC offers an alternative to the way in which computer-assisted school administration has been developed elsewhere. No claim is being made here that one approach is better than another. However, it is possible that the combination of being both university-based and 'grass roots' predisposes MUSAC to be flexible, proactive and responsive. These attributes may be more difficult to achieve in school systems which have adopted a top-down, centralised or Government mandated approach e.g., Australia, Hong Kong and the USA (Visscher & Spuck, 1991). Some of them have experienced or are experiencing serious difficulties with implementation (e.g., the OASIS system in New South Wales, Australia, and SAMS in Hong Kong).

Perhaps the New Zealand bottom-up, 'grass-roots' approach might suggest alternative ways of introducing computerised systems to schools and of effectively using them. This is not to say that the introduction and use of computerised systems in New Zealand itself is without difficulty. For instance, because the New Zealand Government gives schools little advice regarding, or funding for, the adoption and use of information technology, the schools are left to devise implementation strategies of their own. The various MUSAC support agencies around the country play a crucial role in assisting schools to implement their computerised systems. Utilisation of these agencies is, however, still left up to the discretion of individual schools and their capacity to pay. Many of them are unaware of the need to approach implementation systematically and of the necessity for well-informed support that expert advisers can provide. To the extent that schools actually get the support and training they need, the 'grass-roots' approach seems to work well helping schools to implement and competently use their computerised school information systems.

Software design strategy is no less important than implementation. The MUSAC 'fundamental strategy' (Visscher, 1991) is reflected in its modular architecture devised initially for a DOS environment and now re-developed and extended for Windows. The strategy has permitted MUSAC to respond constantly to challenges for the development of new programs (viz. the new Generic Windows programs) and address the common needs of most schools while accommodating special needs.

Findings from very recent case studies of MUSAC-using schools (Nolan & Lambert, 2000) suggests that, just at the point when MUSAC is consolidating its new generic Windows programs, quite different though not incompatible software may increasingly be required. The new software will be attuned to schools that operate more as learning communities than as organisations. In schools that operate as communities the principals and other school personnel commonly saw high use value in conventional spreadsheet generated results and information, e.g., reports on the academic progress of students. They also commonly required other kinds of results and information which their existing systems could not readily produce, e.g., digitised assessment and performance portfolios. Findings from the case studies showed that two factors were key in enabling school personnel to use their existing systems effectively:

1. the strength of commitment by school leaders and teachers to learning community principles; and
2. the technical understanding and know-how of the principal particularly and, to a lesser extent, the staff rather than system characteristics or design features (Visscher, 1996).

An implication of the studies is that senior school personnel and teachers must be acknowledged now, and in the future, to be the key factor in the ability of schools to effectively and fully utilise their (expensive) computerised systems to support the operation and development of schools.

This is the case for two reasons. Firstly, these personnel either possess or can learn the technical skills required. This aspect of the situation must not be under-rated. Even though designers strive to make their systems user friendly and intuitively useable, their effective use will require technical competency and confidence much more than can be acquired just by reading a manual or picking up the necessary knowledge by word of mouth. An implication, therefore, is that schools must be prepared to invest in the professional development of staff much more than in the past. Secondly, school personnel (trustees, teachers, senior administrators and managers and office staff especially) need to understand the nature of the data and information upon which to make informed judgements and decisions about directions for development at classroom, programme and school levels. These data and information encompass much more than is typically possible from school administration and management software designed around conventional alpha/numeric data base and spread sheet formats. However, the designs of the future will be much broader in scope and more accommodating than they are now of the inherent complexity, sophistication and subtlety of professional life and work in educational institutions.

By and large, the effect of school restructuring in New Zealand has been to focus the attention of school leaders and managers on meeting accountability expectations, operating the school smoothly as an organisation merely to produce increasing academic standards. Teachers have been expected to assess students against a myriad of pre-set achievement targets. 'Grass roots' attempts to provide computerised systems to aid teachers, administrators and managers has been replaced by systems to measure compliance to government as a motive for action. The computerised school information systems now being designed and developed in this climate have, by and large, embodied principles and precepts consistent with the concept of the school as a technical organisation rather than a learning environment, generating mandated returns, processing normative data and calculating and reporting performance statistics.

Computerised systems for schools of the future may still provide these functions of compliance. Increasingly, however, their purpose will be to support development in ways that take account of, and deal with, the complexity, sophistication and subtlety of the learning organisation as a whole. As this development unfolds, educational professionals at all levels will review and reflect upon their practice and strive to improve it. It is likely that narrative and stories, rather than just data, will increasingly become the objects of analysis and communication using computerised systems somewhat more sophisticated and multi-media capable than they are now.

REFERENCES

Butler, R. (1999). *Private Communication*, Rory Butler, MUSAC Central Massey University, Palmerston North, New Zealand.

Dale, D.M., & Habib, A.G. (1991). Administrative Computing in the Australian Educational System. *Journal of Research on Computing in Education, 24* (1), 120-145.

Essink, L.J.B., & Visscher, A.J. (1989). The Design and Impact of Management Education Systems in Educational Organisations. In H. Oosthoek, and T. Vroeyenstyn (Eds.), *Higher Education and New Technologies* (p.367-388). Oxford: Pergamon Press.

Frank, F.P., & Fulmer, C.L. (1998). Classroom-Focused Information Systems: Support for Teaching/Learning Entrepreneurs. In Fulmer, C.L., Nolan, C.J.P. & Barta, B.Z. (Eds.), *The Integration of Information for Educational Management.* Whitefield, Maine: Felicity Press.

Fulmer, C.L. (1995) Maximising the Potential of Information Technology for Management Strategies for Interfacing the Technical Core of Education. In Barta, B-Z., Telem, M. and Gev, Y. (Eds.), *Information Technology in Educational Management.* London: Chapman Hall.

Hall, G.E., Wallace, R.C., & Dosset, W.A. (1973). *A Developmental Conceptualisation of the Adoption Process with Educational Institutions.* Austin: The University of Texas.

Honeyman, J.C., & Honeyman, D.S. (1988). School Automation: A Paradigm for Analysis. *The Fifth International Conference on Technology and Education, Vol.1.* Edinburgh: CEP Consultants.

McKinnon, D.H., & Nolan, C.J.P. (1989). Using Computers in Education: A Concerns-based Approach to Professional Development for Teachers. *The Australian Journal of Educational Technology, 5* (2) 113-131.

Nolan, R.L. (1977). Restructuring the Data Processing Organisation for Data Resource Management. In B. Gilchrist (Ed.), *Information Processing '77, Proceedings of IFIP Congress 77.* Amsterdam: North-Holland Publishing Company.

Nolan, C.J.P., & Ayres, D.A. (1996). Developing a Good Information System for Schools: The New Zealand Experience. *International Journal of Educational Research, 25* (4), 307-321.

Conference on Information Technology and Educational Management, Auckland, New Zealand.

Nolan, C.J.P., Ayres, D.A. Dunn, S., & McKinnon, D.H. (1996). Implementing Computerised School Information Systems: Case Studies from New Zealand. *International Journal of Educational Research, 25* (4), 335-349.

Nolan, C.J.P., & Lambert, M. (2000). *Information Systems for Leading and Managing Schools: Changing the Paradigm.* Paper presented at the International Working

Spuck, D.W., & Atkinson, G. (1983). Administrative Use of the Computer. *AEDS Journal, 17* (1), 83-90.

Stewart, D., & Prebble, T. (1993). *The Reflective Principal: School Development Within a Learning Community.* Palmerston North, New Zealand: ERDC Press.

Visscher, A. (1991). School Administrative Computing: A Framework for Analysis. *Journal of Research on Computing in Education, 24* (1), 1-19.

Visscher, A.J. (1996). Information Technology in Educational Management as an Emerging Discipline. *International Journal of Educational Research, 25* (4), 291-296.

Visscher, A., & Spuck, D.W. (1991). Computer Assisted School Administration and Management: The State of the Art in Seven Nations. *Journal of Research on Computing in Education, 24* (1), 146-168.

SECTION II

Design and implementation of school information systems –
Learning from experience

CHAPTER 5

A HOLISTIC VIEW OF SISs AS AN INNOVATION AND THE FACTORS DETERMINING SUCCESS

Alex C.W. Fung[1] & Adrie J. Visscher[2]
[1]Hong Kong Baptist University, China
[2]University of Twente, The Netherlands

1. INTRODUCTION

In this chapter we first explain how we look holistically at the development and implementation of an SIS, using a multi-dimensional systemic perspective. Then we present a more detailed analysis of the variable groups that determine the usage and effects of computer-assisted school information systems. The chapter serves as a basis for further in-depth discussion of SIS-design in chapter 6, and implementation strategies in chapter 7.

2. A HOLISTIC VIEW OF SIS DEVELOPMENT & IMPLEMENTATION

Developing and implementing an SIS is a multi-dimensional systemic socio-technical innovation process (Fung & Visscher, 1996). This process is systemic in that it consists of a number of interrelated processes that are people-oriented as well as technology-oriented. Two aspects of integration are of concern in this innovation process. First, the technical design should aim at producing an integrated SIS for maximum organisational benefit; second, the change process has to be managed in a holistic manner such that sub-processes are integrated.

Figure 1 is an illustration of this holistic perspective where the SIS-innovation process is viewed as a 'working page' that contains five major 'sub-pages' and one 'linking page'. These interrelated sub-pages, as shown in Figure 1, are labelled respectively as Goals & Objectives, Design Strategies, Technical Design & Development, Implementation and Monitoring & Evaluation. Coupled with these is the crucial 'linking page' of User-Developer Collaboration throughout the entire process. We will discuss these in turn in the following paragraphs.

A.J. Visscher et al. (eds.), Information Technology in Educational Management, 79–95.
© 2001 *Kluwer Academic Publishers. Printed in the Netherlands.*

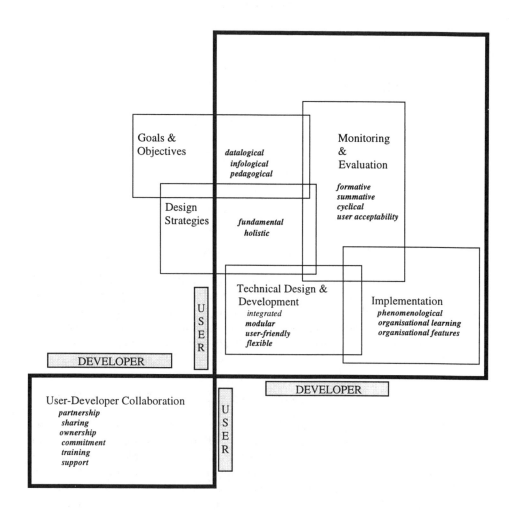

Figure 1. SIS Development & Implementation: A Multi-dimensional Systematic Socio-technical Innovation Process

2.1   The 'Working Page'

2.1.1   Goal & Objectives

Three levels of SIS-design objectives are discerned here with the first 'datalogical' level describing a system aimed at the automation of school administration. Such a SIS, in the end, can support mainly administrative functions. The next level of 'infological' SIS-design is one aiming to provide not only administrative but also managerial information support. Such a system, if properly used, should have impact on school decision- and policy-making. The third level is termed 'pedagogical' if the SIS can additionally provide support to teaching and learning, which after all is the primary function of the school. Shifting from the first level to the other two is in fact a move from efficiency alone towards effectiveness as well. Unfortunately, current SISs in use are by and large only at the first level. However, we are hopeful that SIS-development and usage will escalate from the first to the third level in the years ahead.

2.1.2   Design Strategies

International experience with school information system development shows that the design of SISs has been initiated by varying actors. In the early days (see chapter 1), amateurs developed the first school administrative computer applications in a 'home-grown' way in their schools. At a later stage, commercial vendors transformed these applications (as well as other applications that initially had been developed for the business sector) to the requirements of the school setting. Much later, special SIS projects were initiated. In Hong Kong, for example, the government decided to develop the information system SAMS (see chapter 3) to be used in all Hong Kong schools. In the Netherlands a group of academics with a computer science background, and academics from the field of educational technology joined forces to establish a system called SCHOLIS. In New Zealand a university worked in co-operation with a teacher pioneer who developed the first clerical applications for the school office, to set up a commercial enterprise to further the design and distribution of the MUSAC school information system.

More important than 'who did it' is the question 'how it was done'. The answers to both questions are interrelated because the system development expertise varies among those who carried out the design activities. What we advocate in this chapter is that the core of a good SIS has to focus on the information needs of the school as an organisation. The strategy is to have a profound study and analysis of the information requirements for managing the school efficiently and effectively, before designing and building an integrated system. Different design strategies are discussed in detail later in this chapter.

2.1.3 Technical Design & Development

Good SISs should be technically designed and developed with the four attributes of being integrated in architecture, modular in structure, user-friendly in interfacing, and flexible in meeting different user needs and in anticipating change.

SISs developed for regional or country use, in particular, have always to meet the challenge of standardization versus flexibility. A good system has to allow individual schools, with different characteristics and background, to enter the SIS use at different points compatible with the socio-technical environment of the school. At the same time, it should provide the schools with a developmental path for upgrading. Furthermore, user-definable data-fields and report-generators catering to individual needs will help to preserve school identities without which user-acceptance of the system will be jeopardised. Technical design is discussed more extensively in chapter 6.

2.1.4 Implementation

It is now quite well accepted that implementing an innovation is not simply a top-down event but a gradual process. Innovations implemented using a phenomenological approach that emphasises the meaning of the innovation to the participants are more likely to succeed (Fullan, 1982; Fung, 1995). In the case of SISs, this means addressing the issues from the perspective of the school users. Questions such as "Why do we want this SIS in our school?"; "How can it help me?"; "Will it increase my workload?"; "Is it intended to replace me?"; "Is it difficult to use?" and so on are all real and valid, and they have to be understood in the context of a particular school and inherent organisational features.

Successful implementation of a SIS, according to Fung's (1995) interpretation, is in effect the facilitation of the assimilation process of the SIS by the school. Essentially, it is an organisational learning process when the school goes through the phases of initiation, assimilation, and institutionalisation during the innovation. Classical terms like 'change agent' and 'implement', which carry a strong sense of an external expert descending upon an organisation to implant something new, are fading out. While the term 'facilitator' has become familiar in place of 'change agent', we suppose it will take some time before 'assimilation' takes over 'implementation'.

2.1.5 Monitoring & Evaluation

This activity penetrates through all the other processes discussed above, as depicted in Figure 1.

When we describe the development and implementation of a SIS as a systemic process, we are using the thinking behind systems theory. This means that we understand the innovation process to consist of sub-processes (as illustrated by the five 'sub-pages' in Figure 1) that are interacting with one another. In managing a SIS project, it is logical as well as necessary in practice to have a sequence of activities going through the phases of Goals & Objectives, Strategies, Technical Design & Development, and Implementation. However, we must bear in mind that decisions and actions in any phase could have impact or feedback on the others. The process is therefore non-linear and multi-dimensional. It is not simply the technological development of a computer system, but involves users, developers, and perhaps researchers and is thus socio-technical. Proper monitoring and evaluation is a key process throughout such a complex venture.

Monitoring is to understand 'where we are now' and 'where we are going'. To do this we need information, based on data collected as a result of evaluation. Monitoring is more than counter-checking whether planned tasks are completed on schedule or not. It covers also, perhaps more importantly, the functions of steering the project in the right direction, of attending to problems that are revealed through evaluation and of making decisions for adjustments where necessary through the sub-processes. All these are to be done without losing sight of the goals, while allowing room for revising, re-prioritising, or even dropping some objectives as circumstances warrant. This way of monitoring and evaluation is thus formative (in contrast to summative evaluation at the end of the project) and is cyclical, with the feedback collected at different stages used for informed decision-making. Feedback that is timely, valid and genuine is therefore a critical factor for SIS-development and implementation.

The success or failure of a SIS-innovation, after all, is reflected by how much and how far the school information system becomes institutionalised in the school(s). The degree of system usage, and the intended and unintended effects, are all indicators of whether the investment (money, time, and effort) is cost-beneficial. All these elements in one way or another are related to 'user acceptance' of the SIS. In this regard, Wild (1996) has advocated the use of a 'User Acceptance Audit' (UAA) for formative evaluation of SIS-development and implementation. One important contribution of user participation, besides generating 'ownership' of the innovation, is to provide constructive feedback as they and the SIS-developer(s) go through collaboratively the 'sub-pages' illustrated in Figure 1.

2.2 The 'Linking Page': User-Developer Collaboration

Mumford (1980) has shown that many automation projects are characterised by the fact that the computer expert determines the nature and content of the designed SIS autonomously. The possibilities of the technology ('technology push') are too often the starting point instead of the needs and characteristics of the users ('needs pull'). Ignorance of the needs and desires of users leads to the construction of information systems with a low degree of acceptance. Taking care of practitioners' needs and involving them in the design, development, and implementation of a SIS is important to make them 'owners' of the developed system. The influence of 'ownership' on the acceptance and use of an innovation is much stressed in the educational innovation literature (Fullan, 1982). The significance of this user-involvement applies to the entire innovation process, and is the concept we try to illustrate in Figure 1 using the 'linking page' labelled User-Developer Collaboration.

We have stressed throughout this chapter the importance of user participation for successful development and implementation of SISs. In this regard, Fung (1996) has written:

> "User-participation in information systems development is quite well accepted nowadays as one of the most critical factors for success (Mumford & Weir, 1979; Ives & Olson, 1984; Jarvenpaa and Ives, 1991). For instance, ETHICS is a method that specially advocates user participation throughout the systems design stage to produce a socio-technical system (Mumford & Weir, 1979; Mumford, 1983). JAD (Joint Application Design) similarly stresses user-involvement in the systems development process (Wood & Silver, 1989; Kettelhut, 1993). Furthermore, as King & Cleland (1987) have suggested, there is considerable evidence that the lack of involvement of users in different phases of systems development has been a significant factor contributing to the failure of many management information systems to perform as expected." (p. 302)

However, what exactly do we mean by user-participation? Different people might interpret this term very differently, especially regarding the level of participation. For example, a user representative group could be formed to advise on system development and project implementation, as in the case of SAMS in Hong Kong (see chapter 3), but without shared decision-making. Pondering over the issue further, we can ask when, where, what, who, and how to participate; or even ask the question of whether the participation is genuine. Without labouring ourselves to try to provide 'correct' answers to these questions, which probably do not exist, we would rather propose to promote 'user-developer collaboration' instead of 'user-participation'. In doing so, we clearly highlight the spirit of collaboration needed from all the concerned parties in a successful SIS-innovation. This is also the essence of the phenomenological approach that we recommend SIS-implementers (or better, SIS-facilitators) to adopt in managing the socio-technical innovation process.

In the next part of this chapter we will discuss the different factors (or variables) that affect the successful development and implementation of SISs. Success refers to the degree of system usage and the resulting positive impact, both intended and unintended. The framework explained above should be borne in mind and act as a kind of 'road map' for the SIS-innovation process, as we go through the variables.

3. THE VARIABLES THAT MATTER

Since a generally accepted framework including the factors influencing the impact of SISs was missing in the past, the relevant variable groups have been identified via studying the relevant literature in the field of educational innovation, business administration, and computer science. The following variable clusters are mentioned frequently in the literature (Björn-Andersen, Eason & Robey, 1986; Fullan, 1982; Mayntz, 1984; Rogers, 1983; Stasz, Bikson & Shapiro, 1986) as factors influencing the outcomes of innovation processes, including educational ones:

1. features of the innovation contents;
2. features of the innovating unit; and
3. features of the innovation strategy used.

As the design and introduction of computerized school information systems is an innovation in schools, these three groups of variables are relevant for studying the implementation and effects of SISs.

In our case of SISs, variable cluster (1) concerns the quality of the innovation, and hence the quality of the SIS concerned. Variable clusters (2) and (3) indicate that the results of the implementation of SISs are also dependent on the characteristics of the innovating units, casu quo schools, and of the strategy used for implementing SISs into schools. Besides these three variable clusters, we add a fourth one since we expect the nature and quality of a SIS to be influenced by the strategy followed for its design (see also Björn-Andersen et al., 1986, Maslowski & Visscher, 1999, Mayntz, 1984, and Rogers, 1983).

Visscher (1996) presents a model portraying the assumed interrelationships among these four variable clusters, and how they affect the usage and impact of SISs (see Figure 2). The validity of the model has been proven in several instances (Visscher & Spuck, 1991; Visscher et al., 1999; Visscher & Bloemen, 1999). Since the blocks in Figure 2 are interacting with one another, a choice in one block has consequences for what happens in one or more of the other blocks. In Figure 2, SIS-usage (block E) is supposed to be influenced by the SIS-quality (block B) which results from the design strategy used (block A). The nature of the implementation process (block C), and the characteristics of schools as organizations (block D), also influence SIS-usage (block E). Finally, the degree of SIS-usage, and the way in which the SIS is used, are expected to lead to both intended and unintended effects (block F).

The fact that within each of the variable blocks alternative decisions are possible means that we do not have to worry about what is called 'technologic determinism'. This term refers to the idea that the computer is regarded as "...an autonomous force having some predetermined impact..." (Björn-Andersen et al., 1986). In the view of Björn-Andersen et al. (1986), and Bennet and Lancaster (1986), this deterministic perspective should be rejected. On the basis of their international study Björn-Andersen et al. conclude that most computer usage impacts are accidental impacts, deficiency impacts, contingent impacts or planned impacts.

Each of the blocks in Figure 2 is discussed in depth below.

3.1 Block A: the Design Strategy

School information system design strategies can vary with respect to:
- The goal(s) of system design (variable A1 in Figure 2);
- The way decisions are being made about which school activities will be supported by the information system, and what the nature of this support will be (variable A2);
- The extent of user participation in the design of a SIS (variable A3);
- The way in which the standardisation-flexibility problem is addressed (variable A4).

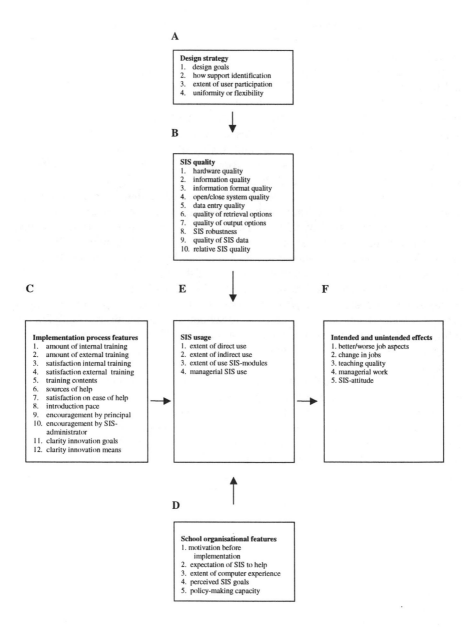

Figure 2. The contents of the clusters and the interrelationships between them

3.1.1 The Goal(s) of Information System Design

As stated in chapter 1, one simple goal of designing a SIS may be the reduction of paperwork, or, more generally, improving the efficiency of the work of school staff. At a higher level, a SIS can be considered as a tool for raising school effectiveness, the latter being defined as the degree to which the school goals are achieved.

Some of the goals in system design can be threatening for some of the people involved. For instance, a goal to evaluate teachers more intensively may be viewed as a threat by teachers. Keen (1981) states that IS-development is not only a technical, rational problem but also a political one since relations, power and authority may change as a result of the design and introduction of an IS. The political character implies that the degree to which each of the involved parties can influence the automation activities is of great importance.

3.1.2 What will be supported and How?

When the Nolan (1977) developmental stages were discussed in chapter 1 an analysis was presented of how computer-assisted school administration and management started with the partial automation of school administrative work, with the computer used to tackle a specific problem like student timetabling, or student attendance registration. Fung (1988) called this the 'application/task-oriented approach' which he illustrated with the metaphor of building a house, one room at a time, without regard to an over-all plan, or to the relationships between the rooms of the house. The consequence of such a strategy might result in a garage built on the second floor.

Another strategy, the 'functional' approach, represents a higher order alternative where, at different spots within the school, departments computerise activities according to their own functions in the school. The result is an information system with little (and only in the most important areas) or no integration of applications, no or little sharing of information across boundaries, and repeated data entry and overlap of data at several locations within the school.

Fung (1988) proposes a holistic approach as a way to design a school information system that will serve the whole organisation (and if desired also the district, state, government etc.). Elsewhere, Essink and Visscher (1989a,b) have also made a plea for such a strategy which they label the 'fundamental' approach. The approach includes a careful analysis of the information needs at various levels (within and external to the school) which is meant to result in the following output:

- a description of the activities (especially the managerial and clerical ones) carried out in schools, including an indication of the information essential for their execution;
- an analysis of the interrelations between various school organizational activities, especially from the viewpoint of data use (e.g., which pupil data are used for the construction of the timetable?);
- a definition of where and how the computer can assist those who carry out these activities. In other words, which existing school activities can be executed by the

computer, and which new activities become possible now as a consequence of the availability of the computer?

An advantage of the fundamental strategy, in comparison with a more incremental, evolving design approach is that it enables the design of a modular SIS-architecture, and thereafter the gradual design of the contents of each module or application. Integration of applications is then achieved with the same data being used in various subsystems providing single entry and multiple use of data.

A SIS built in line with the fundamental approach will probably have an upgradable path and a long life cycle. The probability that its structure has to be completely changed as a consequence of the identification of new applications, perhaps not identified in the early analysis of need, is small. Moreover, if new developments such as changes in governmental regulations require new forms of computer support, the modular and integrated SIS characteristics make SIS adaptations relatively easy.

The down side of this strategy is that it requires considerable expertise, tools, manpower and money. Amateur developers generally do not possess these, and for commercial software houses the small school market may prevent them from taking the risk of large investments.

3.1.3 User Participation

Another important aspect of decisions taken on the nature of information systems concerns the extent to which target users can influence these decisions through user participation (variable A3). This has already been discussed in the earlier part of this chapter and is not repeated here. We need only reiterate that ignorance of the needs and desires of users will lead to the construction of information systems with a low degree of acceptance. It is now common sense to take care of practitioners' needs and involve them in the design of systems to make them 'owners' of the developed system.

3.1.4 Uniformity versus Flexibility

The core of this topic can be formulated as follows: "How to develop a system that can be used in as many schools as possible?" There is often friction between the goal of developing the same standard SIS for as many schools as possible, and at the same time allowing for the unique characteristics of each school. The first goal should result in the development of a uniform SIS for a large number of schools. The second goal is meant to produce a system that takes account of the differences between schools as well as of the varying information needs of school managers. A SIS ideally is so flexible that it satisfies varying and specific information needs and also supports activities that are carried out only in a limited number of schools. The problem of providing for differences, however, is that the resulting systems are hard to maintain.

3.2 Block B: School Information System Quality

The design activities in block A of Figure 2 result in a SIS of a certain quality. Its characteristics will indirectly influence the degree of SIS-usage. Since SISs can differ so much with regard to various quality aspects one cannot speak of 'the impact of SISs'. Each information system, because of its features, will be appreciated and used by school staff to a certain extent, and have specific intended and unintended effects on users and on the institution in which it is used. Careful analysis should be conducted to find out which types of SISs produce the most of the intended effects, and least of the unintended ones.

Critical aspects of the quality of SISs are, for instance:
- the robustness of the hardware (variable B1) and software (B8);
- the quality of the data from the SIS (e.g., the number of errors, its completeness, and management support; B9);
- the convenience of opening and closing the information system (B4);
- the ease of entering (B5), retrieving (B6), and outputing (B7) data;
- the degree to which the information (B2) and the information format (B3) the SIS can produce are valued by its users;
- the quality of the SIS compared with the quality of alternative computerised and manual information systems (B10).

3.3 Block C: Implementation Process Features

Within block C the central question is what should be done to successfully implement a SIS with certain features and functions into a school. The literature on educational innovation and SIS implementation points to a number of factors that are of great relevance here. Many of these factors concern aspects of the modelling of the implementation process.

The roles of the principal and SIS-administrator, in encouraging school staff to use the SIS, is crucial. The principal in his/her leadership role can influence the attitude and behaviour of his subordinates in important respects regarding the innovation (variable C9). If s/he does not promote SIS-usage in the organisation, the probability that school staff will use the information system is considerably smaller. System administrators, because of their know-how regarding the potential of the system, and the way in which users can benefit from it most, can also promote system usage among colleagues (variable C10). A related variable concerns the sources of support for users, trying to work with the SIS, in the event that they experience problems.

It is often frustrating, when one tries to incorporate a new tool or method in his/her work, if the innovation causes problems because of the lack of user expertise, hardware/software problems, etc. To avoid frustration and low levels of SIS-usage, and to maintain motivation, users need quick and effective assistance (C6 and C7).

Visscher (1996) on the basis of an analysis of the literature also points to other implementation process variables. Clear innovation goals and means (variables C11 and C12) should lead the innovation process, and the planning of activities of the implementation process should be realistic (C8). As far as the latter is concerned Tomasso (1985) states that one computer application should be introduced at a time as schools require time to assimilate an application into their school administrative system. However, the pace of SIS introduction should not be frustratingly slow.

Bennet and Lancaster (1986) and Visscher (1988) stress the need of sufficient and adequate training and support for users. Users should be equipped to 'do the job' by providing them with the required training regarding the use of the SIS. User training for mastering the skills to enter, manipulate and output data is needed for clerical use. Simply providing a SIS and then waiting for something to happen will not lead to the desired results. Moreover, using information from the system for managerial activities not only presupposes these technical skills, but also requires the ability to determine what kind of information one would like to obtain, to interpret, and use in school decision-making. These are quite complex higher-order skills much more than learning to 'press the right button'. In chapter 7 this topic will be discussed in-depth.

Variables C1 and C2 refer to the amount of training users receive internally, such as from the system administrator, and from external trainers. The satisfaction of users with these two types of training is expressed by the variables C3 and C4. The fifth C-variable concerns the nature and the contents of the training activities. In many cases user training is too technical, focussing mainly on how the hardware works, and pays too little attention to how clerical and managerial staff can use the SIS in their jobs (Visscher et al., 1999; Visscher & Bloemen, 1999).

3.4 Block D: School Organisational Features

Another group of important variables includes the characteristics of the school organisations into which the information system is introduced (block D). Wyne and Otway (1983) and Keen (1981) stress the importance of this group of variables. These authors point to the organisational constraints for change and the pluralistic characteristics of organisations. The latter implies that members of organisations will view the innovation in various ways, because of the varying implications the SIS has for each of them.

First and foremost, it is of crucial importance that target SIS-users feel motivated for the innovation proposed (variable D1). If the innovator does not get their commitment and trust, 'dysfunctional behaviour' (Bennet & Lancaster, 1986) is likely to occur. In other words, not only technical and economic problems, but also 'people problems' (see Olson & Lucas, 1982) have to be solved, the latter ones probably being the most difficult ones. Crabb (in Bennet & Lancaster, 1986) speaks of 'to get people's understanding and co-operation'. Staff motivation is amongst other things dependent on the degree to which staff can benefit from a SIS through the quality features of SISs as discussed under block B. Ideally, the target user group has to feel a need that can be satisfied by the introduction of a SIS (variable D2).

Keen (1981) has pointed out the political aspects of SISs. A SIS may be threatening for some staff, because the system can be used to evaluate their performance intensively. As an example one may think of a SIS used for evaluating the teachers and/or schools performance. If school staff feel such a threat, 'counter-implementation' (Keen, 1981) and resistance are likely (variable D4).

The degree of computer experience may vary considerably among school staff (e.g., between older and younger staff) and so probably influences the degree of school information system usage. This variable is included in the D-variables (D3).

The literature on school policy-making questions the potential impact of computers within schools. Decision-making within schools is often characterized by means of the metaphor of 'garbage cans' into which every participant in the decision-making process drops his/her individual goals and problems, instead of organizational problems. In combination with the difficulty of determining causes of school problems (e.g., low student achievement) decision-making becomes diffuse, and taking decisions to solve school problems becomes increasingly difficult. The effect is often that taking decisions is postponed and/or that decisions are taken that neither harm anybody, nor solve a problem.

In addition to laborious and slow decision-making processes, the poor execution of decisions taken is often mentioned in the school administrative literature. The general picture of school policy-making is not one of a very decisive process. Although the effect of the introduction of SISs is always uncertain, some caution is needed regarding their use and their influence in the light of these school organizational characteristics.

Within the general school organizational features so far discussed, schools differ in some ways. One very important difference for the impact of SISs is the policy-making capacity of schools. Some schools only develop school-policy in the area of school resources, such as finance, buildings and the timetable, while others also formulate policies with regard to issues that touch the domain of the professional autonomous teacher through the content and method of the teaching process.

The policy-making potential of schools in each of these areas constitutes the possibilities and barriers of introducing computerised SISs. If one introduces a SIS into a school to improve its policy-making capacity, and if the school does not have in place a policy in that area, then one can be rather sure that the desired effect will not be achieved. The SIS will probably aggravate the problem if the limited policy-making capacity has not been first improved via some way of organisational development. Therefore, if one plans to introduce a SIS into schools, one must pay attention to these pertinent organisational differences among schools (variable D5).

3.5   Block E: Usage of the School Information Systems

This block concerns a number of indicators reflecting the degree of information system usage in schools.

Schools differ with respect to the extent to which they utilise the various types of support that SISs can offer (Visscher et al., 1999; Visscher & Bloemen, 1999). Suppose a SIS is available that enables all possible assistance like the support of routine clerical work, simple and complex school decision-making and strategic planning. Some users might use the system only for non-controversial, clerical, and structured allocation activities, a relevant example being student timetabling, while others might also make use of the possibilities to analyse data on pupils, teachers and finance as a basis for developing school policy.

In Figure 2 a distinction is made between 'direct' (E1; someone using the information system himself/herself) and 'indirect' system usage (E2; system usage through the use of printouts received from colleagues using the SIS). Apart from the number of hours school staff use the SIS in these two distinct ways, usage probably also varies in terms of the frequency with which they use each of the SIS-modules, and in the extent of managerial support (variables E3 and E4).

3.6 Block F: the Effects of School Information System Usage

Block F concerns the last and most important block in Figure 2 reflecting the impact of introducing information systems into schools in terms of its intended and unintended effects.

In chapter 1 we discussed the goals of school information system design and implementation and mentioned a number of ways in which schools may become more efficient and effective as a result of the usage of computer-assisted SISs. High hopes regarding the consequences of SIS-support in clerical and managerial work are contrasted by warnings for too much optimism (Ackoff, 1967; Beneviste, 1985; Honeyman & Honeyman, 1988).

Olson and Lucas (1982) present a model for analysing the impact of automation and indicate that SISs can influence:

- the nature of work: e.g., to be able to produce better reports, higher efficiency, specialisation and computer-mediated communication;
- the individual: more/less stress and work satisfaction;
- communication processes: the communication efficiency, the extent of direct contact and communication;
- management processes: the perception of managers regarding the rationality, flexibility and autonomy of their work; their methods and span of control;
- the interpersonal relations: the quantity and quality of social interactions and 'social reinforcement';
- interdepartmental relations: the number of conflicts between departments, the definition of departmental barriers;
- organisational structures and processes: changes in the definitions of organisational barriers and in the possibilities to react to structural changes.

Potential negative effects of computerisation like the fragmentation of work processes, de-skilling and re-skilling are also often mentioned (for example, Lancaster, 1985). Sirotnik (1987) moreover warns of an overload of information as a consequence of implementing SISs.

Visscher (1988) has translated these expectations and predictions to the world of school organisations. Although improving processes in schools may be valuable in itself, in accordance with Scheerens (1999) these improvements are considered prerequisites for the ultimate goal of more effective schools in terms of better student achievement. Since it will be extremely difficult to prove this effect by empirical research, it is nevertheless important to determine to what extent SIS-impacts occur in:

- the quality of clerical work (F2; e.g., ease of duties, reduction of monotonous work);
- the quality of managerial activities (F4; e.g., more informed management, more timely corrections);
- the quality of teaching (F3; since some SISs also support specific teacher activities, e.g., registering marks and better data on students; this variable is also included in the framework);
- a reduction of, or increase in workload and stress (F1);
- better information on how the school functions (F1).

The last criterion variable F5 concerns users' attitude towards and motivation for the SIS after having experienced the qualities of an information system for a certain period. The attitude is probably influenced most by the quality of the information system as perceived by users. However, it is also influenced by how the user experienced the implementation of the system. A high quality system might not be appreciated at all, for example, because the user was not trained well and therefore is not aware of the types of benefit that the school information system can offer.

3.7 Measuring the Variables

In this chapter we have set the scene for managing the development and implementation of a SIS as a multidimensional socio-technical systemic innovation process using Fung's road-map. Visscher's model for detailed analysis of the factors affecting a SIS-innovation has also been thoroughly discussed. We provide in the Appendix an example of how the variables in Figure 2 can be measured. It includes the questionnaire-items used for the evaluation of the SAMS introduced into Hong Kong schools (an adapted version of the research instrument was also used in the United Kingdom and in The Netherlands). The questionnaire items in Appendix A, which refer to one of the variables in Figure 2, are listed with a bold letter and number combination corresponding to the relevant variable being measured. Those items without a bold letter and number combination are variables not included in Figure 2. The instrument does not include items of A-variables since the Hong Kong study did not focus on this aspect.

REFERENCES

Ackoff, R.L. (1967). Management MIS Information Systems. *Management Science*, 14 (4).
Bennet, J., & Lancaster, D. (1986). Management Information Systems in Further Education: some observations on design and implementation. *Journal of Further and Higher Education*, 10(3), 35-49.

Benveniste, G. (1985). The Design of School Accountability Systems. *Educational Evaluation and Policy Analysis*, 7(3), 261-279.

Bjørn-Andersen, N., Eason, K., & Robey, D. (1986). *Managing computer impact*. New Jersey: Ablex Publishing Corporation.

Essink, L.J.B., & Visscher, A.J. (1989a). *Een computerondersteund schoolinformatiesysteem voor het avo/vwo; deel I: Analyse en informatiesysteemraamwerk [A computer assisted school information system for general secondary and pre-university education; part I: Analysis and information system framework]*. Enschede: University of Twente, Faculty of Educational Sience and Technology.

Essink, L.J.B., & Visscher, A.J. (1989b). The design and impact of management information systems in educational organizations (Leading Article). In *Higher Education and New Technologies*. Oxford: Pergamon Press, p. 367-388.

Fullan, M. (1982). *The meaning of educational change*. New York: Teachers College Press.

Fung, A.C.W. (1988). Trends and development in computer-aided school administration. *Proceedings of Microcomputers in Education Conference*. Hong Kong, A-20 - A-28.

Fung, A.C.W. (1995). Managing change in ITEM. In Barta, B., Telem, M., & Gev, Y. (Eds.) *Information Technology in Educational Management,* London: Chapman & Hall, London, pp. 37-45.

Fung, A.C.W. (1996). An evaluation of the Hong Kong design & development strategy. *International Journal of Educational Research*, 25 (4), 297-306.

Fung, A.C.W., & Visscher, A.J. (1996). Conclusion and agenda for ITEM research. *International Journal of Educational Research*, 25 (4), 373-380.

Honeyman, J.C., & Honeyman, D.S. (1988). School automation: a paradigm for analysis. *The Fifth International Conference on Technology and Education, volume I*. Edinburgh: CEP Consultants.

Ives, B., & Olson, M.H. (1984). User involvement and MIS success: A review of research. *Management Science, 30*, 586-608.

Jarvenpaa, S.L., & Ives, B. (1991). Executive involvement and participation in the management of information technology. *MIS Quarterly*, 12(2), 229-242.

Keen, P.G.W. (1981). Information systems and organizational change. *Communications of the ACM*, 24(1), 24-33.

Kettelhut, M.C. (1993). JAD methodology and group dynamics. *Information Systems Management*, 10(1), 46-53.

King, W.R., & Cleland, D.I. (1987). The design of management information systems: An information system analysis approach. In R. Galliers (Ed.), *Information analysis: Selected readings*. Sydney: Addison-Wesley Publishers.

Lancaster, D. (1985). The response to and impact of Information Technology in Schools and Colleges: the key individuals. *Educational Management and Administration*, 13, 140-145.

Mayntz, R. (1984). Information Systems and Organizational Effectiveness: The Social Perspective. In Bemelmans, Th., *Beyond Productivity Information Systems; Development for Organizational Effectivenss*. Amsterdam: Elsevier Science Publishers.

Maslowski, R. & Visscher, A.J. (1999). Formative evaluation in educational computing research & development. *Journal of Research on Computing in Education*, 32 (2), 239-255.

Mumford, E., & Weir, M. (1979). *Computer systems in work design – the ETHICS method*. New York: Wiley.

Mumford, E. (1980). The participative design of clerical information systems - two case studies. In N. Bjørn-Andersen (Ed.), *The Human Side of Information Processing*. Amsterdam: North Holland Publishing Company.

Mumford, E. (1983). *Designing human systems*. Manchester: Manchester Business School.

Nolan, R.L. (1977). Restructing the data processing organisation for data resource management. In B. Gilchrist (Ed.), *Information Processing 77, Proceedings of IFIP Congress 77*. Amsterdam, the Netherlands: North Holland Publishing Company.

Olson, M.H., & Lucas, H.C. (1982). The impact of office automation on the organization: some implications for research and practice. *Communications of the ACM*, 25(11), 838-847.

Rogers, E.M. (1983). *Diffusion of innovations*. New York: The Free Press, MacMillan Publishing.

Scheerens, J. (1999). Concepts and theories of school effectiveness. In Visscher, A.J., *Managing Schools towards High Performance* . Lisse/Exton/Tokyo: Swets & Zeitlinger Publishers.

Sirotnik, K.A. (1987). The information side of evaluation for local school improvement. *International Journal of Educational Research*, 11(1), 77-90.

Stasz, C., Bikson, T.K., & Shapiro, N.Z. (1986). *Assessing the forest service's implementation of an agencywide information system: An exploratory study*. Santa Monica, CA.: Rand Corporation.

Tomasso, C. (1985). What's in a name - SCAMP. In K. Duncan and D. Harris (Eds.), *Computers in Education, proceedings of the IFIP TC3 4th world conference on computers in education*. Amsterdam: North-Holland Publishing Company.

Visscher, A.J. (1988). The computer as an administrative tool: Problems and impact. *Journal of Research on Computing in Education*, 21, 28-35.

Visscher, A.J. (1996). The implications of how school staff handle information for the usage of school information systems. *International Journal of Educational Research,* 25(4), 323-334.

Visscher, A.J. & Bloemen, P.P.M. (1999). Evaluation and use of computer-assisted management information systems in Dutch schools. *Journal of Research on Computing in Education, 32(1), 172-188.*

Visscher, A.J., Fung, A., & Wild, P. (1999). The evaluation of the large scale implementation of a computer-assisted management information system in Hong Kong schools. *Studies in Educational Evaluation*, 25, 11-31.

Visscher, A.J. & Spuck, D.W. (1991). Computer-Assisted School Administration and Management: the State of the Art in Seven Nations. *Journal of Research on Computing in Education*, 24 (1), 146-168.

Wild, P. (1996). An assessment of strategies for information system evaluation: Lessons for education. *International Journal of Educational Research,* 25(4), 361-371.

Wood, J., & Silver, D. (1989). *Joint application design*. New York: Wiley Press.

Wyne, B., & Otway, H.J. (1983). Information Technology, Power and Managers. *Office: Technology and People*, 2, 43-56.

CHAPTER 6

DESIGN STRATEGIES

Arthur Tatnall
Victoria University of Technology, Australia

1. INTRODUCTION: THE DEVELOPMENT OF ORGANIZATIONAL INFORMATION SYSTEMS

Although some teachers believe that schools are unique organisations and that school administration is completely different to other types of organisational administration, this belief has little to support it. While schools do not operate with a profit motive, neither do many other organisations such as libraries and Government instrumentalities. All organisations, whether or not they aim to make a profit, must keep records, and all must manipulate data to produce reports. In particular, designing and building an information system for use in educational administration and management is not fundamentally different to building any other organisational information system.

Mistakes have sometimes been made in the past when developers assume that a school operates *exactly* like a business, but while there are many similarities there are also some important differences. Often, developers mistakenly assume that they know how a school operates, perhaps based on their own experience many years ago as a student. These mistakes can be avoided if the process of establishing user requirements and analysing system needs is undertaken properly.

The discipline of Information Systems is still relatively young, but the techniques for designing and building information systems have been continually refined over the years. It is clear today that business is the main user of information systems around the world, and that most of the information systems in use today have been built for business purposes. A large body of experience has been built up in creating these business information systems, but it is experience that is readily transferable to the building of other types of information systems.

2. EARLY ATTEMPTS AT DEVELOPING SYSTEMS FOR USE IN EDUCATIONAL MANAGEMENT

In the 1970s, after computers began to become available in schools, the first attempts at using them for educational administration tended to be by enthusiastic classroom teachers (Visscher, 1994; Tatnall, 1995) typically with a specific administrative application in mind. These teachers often developed their own

A.J. Visscher et al. (eds.), Information Technology in Educational Management, 97–113.
© 2001 *Kluwer Academic Publishers. Printed in the Netherlands.*

administrative systems by writing computer programs in BASIC to run on the school's mini or micro computer. The problem with this approach, however, was that these teachers often had only a very limited understanding of programming and of systems development, and the tailor-made systems that they built, while sometime quite effective at performing the tasks they were designed for, were function-specific and could not easily be adapted or extended to perform other management functions.

Soon, small software vendors entered the market and began to work on building information systems for individual schools (Visscher, 1994). These companies often employed ex-teachers with some knowledge of what schools required, but most had only a limited understanding of the range of administrative uses schools could make of information systems. Most of the systems developed during this period, while typically more robust than the earlier teacher-built systems, were usually also function-specific and performed only one or two particular administrative applications.

From about the mid-1980s, Government and private organisations in a number of countries around the world started working at the systematic implementation of computer-assisted school management for entire school systems (Visscher, 1994). In some countries this was Government sponsored, with the initiative taken by centralised education authorities attempting to develop educational management systems suitable for use in all schools. In other countries the task was taken on by private companies or non-government organisations, usually working in conjunction with the local educational authorities. The better systems they produced were designed using a process of top-down decomposition in which the administrative needs of schools were thoroughly analysed and then broken down into a number of sub-systems (Visscher, 1994) for which interrelated applications were written. In other cases still more function-specific, non-integrated applications were produced.

Many of the information systems currently used in managing schools around the world are good, well designed systems. Unfortunately, however, some were designed primarily to satisfy the information needs of central education authorities (Tatnall, 1995) and others appear to have been designed on the premise that the designers knew all about schools' information needs and so did not see any need to offer any third-party expansion options. What is more, the use of such a closed, proprietary-like approach means that these systems are also premised on the assumption that the designers alone would be able to modify them to satisfy future needs. It assumes that the designers know what schools will need in the future, and that they will be able to incorporate these changes into their systems. On this premise they construct closed systems that schools cannot add to or change. This creates a problem that Frank and Fulmer (1998, p. 94) put this way: "... it is a common experience that the information systems developer who limits development to working with what is instead of what should be has created a static system that is outdated and serves only to audit a system going nowhere."

The techniques used in the development of organisational information systems of all types are quite transferable, and lessons learned in developing business systems and systems for use in other organisations have relevance to the design of information systems for educational management.

3. INFORMATION SYSTEMS DEVELOPMENT

Creating an information system and getting it working can be considered to comprise three separate phases: systems analysis, systems design, and systems implementation. The purpose of systems analysis is to investigate what is required, then to describe a logical model of the proposed system in non-technical terms, independent of the actual physical implementation. Systems design begins the business of converting this logical model into a usable system, and systems implementation involves the construction of the physical system to the level of hardware acquisition and programming (Tatnall & Davey, 1996).

In systems analysis the system under development is visualised in levels of increasing abstraction. Using techniques of top-down stepwise refinement, attention is first focused on understanding the system as a whole, then on working at increasingly more detailed levels. Systems analysis uses a number of graphical and other tools to describe how a system is laid out, and what it does. It examines the complete system as a series of interacting processes whose purpose is to transform input data into output information. The focus is on *what* the system does, not on how it works or the way in which it is implemented. Further along, systems design looks at *how* the system will work, and in implementation the interacting processes will become program code modules. This standard methodology is a structured one that uses a top-down model of problem solving.

3.1 Process Modelling – Data Flow Diagrams

There are many ways of modelling an information system and many tools to assist in this. Data flow diagrams and function charts are useful in showing *what* happens, while structure charts, structured English and decision tables can be used to show *how* the system works.

Data flow diagrams (DFD) are useful in both analysis and design, in that they are good for documenting both existing and proposed systems. An example showing how a DFD can describe a system to monitor school departmental budgets is presented in Figure 1 below.

Systems theory requires that what is considered to be *outside* the system can have no bearing on the investigation (Emery, 1969) and so it is necessary to define the bounds of the system so that some entities are seen as being within it and others as being outside. Making no attempt to consider the actual hardware or physical implementation, a DFD provides a description of the data elements, showing how data moves from one process to another within an organisational system.

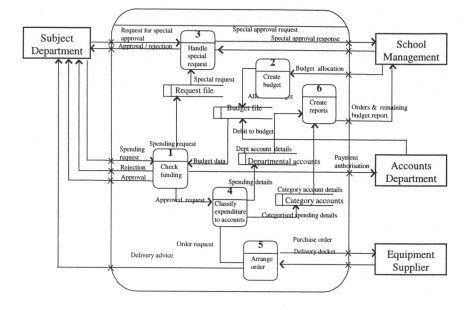

Figure 1. Dat Flow Diagram showing a School Budget Monitoring System

3.2   Data Modelling – Entity Relationship Diagrams

Data modelling describes the data that is used by the system. A tool often used in data modelling is the Entity-Relationship (ER) diagram which shows the entities - things we need to store data about -, and how these entities are related to each other. In the systems design stage, each entity will become a table (or list of items) in a relational database.

The ER diagram shown in Figure 2 below, represents a first attempt at modelling the data required for a school timetable system. It can be read as follows:

- Each teacher occupies a staffroom and undertakes several items of teaching load. (A given staffroom may temporarily be unoccupied by any teacher, and a given teacher may do no teaching which appears on the timetable in a given school term.)
- Each item of teaching load involves a single subject and is scheduled as one or more entries in the timetable. A given subject can appear in several teaching load items, each of which is taught by a given teacher, so that one or more teachers can teach a given subject.
- Each timetable entry describes a class that occupies (a room in) a given school building, and each school building can be used by several timetable entries. Each timetable entry refers to a specific teaching item.

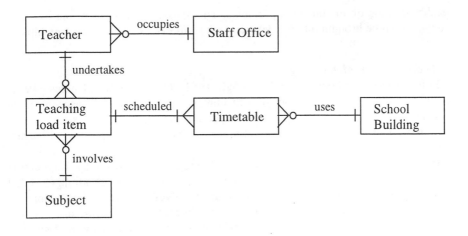

Figure 2. Entity-Relationship Diagram for a Timetable System

The purpose of the ER diagram is to specify precisely the relationship between these entities so that when each is later translated into a table of values, such as a list of teachers, or subjects, or timetable entries, new data can be added and data can be updated without adversely affecting data already entered. Modelling data in this way ensures integrity and eliminates redundancy. ER modelling is a well established information systems development technique.

3.3 Alternative Systems Design Methodologies

In addition to the standard structured development methodology described above a number of alternatives are also in common use. Several of these are discussed below.

3.3.1 Rapid Application Development
The availability of fourth generation languages (4GL) and CASE[1] tools has meant that under some conditions, information systems can be produced quite quickly. Rapid Application Development (RAD) and Joint Application Development (JAD) are two approaches that attempt to do this. RAD and JAD involve a number of common elements:
- The use of CASE, prototyping and 4GL tools.
- An increased involvement of users at all decision-making stages of development.
- Data-oriented approaches to development.

The idea of these techniques is that CASE tools allow much more rapid progress and support through each stage of development, meaning that the analyst is free to

---

[1] Computer Aided Software Engineering

spend more time on the business problems. This means the experts in the business (the users) can be brought into the development team in a more equal partnership.

3.3.2 Soft Systems Methodology

Soft systems methodology (Checkland, 1981; Checkland & Scholes, 1991) attempts to give due recognition to both human and technological aspects of an information system, and is especially useful for the analysis of systems where technological processes and human activities are highly interdependent (Finegan, 1994).

In traditional approaches to systems analysis problems are solved by fragmenting them into separate parts and then deriving a solution for one part at a time (Kendall & Kendall, 1992). Soft systems methodology involves a more holistic approach which is intended to incorporate the human element of such systems into the systems design work. It is claimed to be most appropriate in the analysis of systems that are messy, poorly defined, or especially complex (Finegan, 1994). Checkland (1981) proposed that work organisations should be seen as consisting of a technology system (hard) and a human activity system (soft). Soft systems methodology is then used to analyse and describe the relevant parts of the human activity system and how this interacts with the technology system.

3.3.3 Prototyping

Prototyping is the process of producing small parts of a new system and demonstrating them to the users before further development. It usually concentrates on the user interface and makes use of screen and report generator programs that build small modules in successive iterations. Input from the users is then utilised to fix, improve or enlarge the system. Users are involved at all stages, and user approval provides instant feedback to the developer. A prototyping approach is particularly appropriate if user requirements are unsure as the user is always in a good position to suggest changes.

No matter whether the standard approach or one of these alternative approaches is adopted, however, the faithful use of an appropriate systems development methodology is a well-established procedure that, if followed carefully, has been shown to enhance the chances that the system will be developed successfully.

4. WHO OWNS THE SYSTEM?

All systems development methodologies place considerable importance on the need for the developer to seek the views, and obtain the collaboration of users and, in particular, with the principal user or client. But before the systems requirements can be fully ascertained it is necessary to answer the question: for whom is the system *primarily* being designed? When this question has been answered the developer will have identified the client who is the one to determine the critical systems requirements and how changes to the system may be made. As different clients are likely to have different, and even conflicting requirements, identification of the main client is a crucial step in systems development. In many cases, of course, this identification task is made much easier as the principal client is usually identified with the party that is paying for the systems development.

In designing and building a school management/administration system the task of identifying the principal client is no less important. Perhaps this system is being designed for the central or local education authority, perhaps it is being designed for a single school, or perhaps it is the creature of a single teacher or school administrator. It is important to recognise that each of these groups will have different requirement for what the system should do and how it should do it, and that each will require a system that is different in many ways.

Ownership issues presented a significant problem with the early teacher-developed administrative systems as this teacher, and not the school, was clearly the owner of the system.

In several Australian states (and elsewhere) in the late 1980s, schools' administrative computing systems were built by central educational authorities and issued free (or at low cost) to schools. The primary motivation for doing this was to provide a reporting mechanism from schools back to the centre, and schools' local administrative computing needs were not the main consideration (Tatnall, 1995). The general distribution of these systems meant that schools could then be instructed that they must use them to provide the required reports back to the central authority. While understanding why this approach was adopted, and not wanting to denigrate the information needs of central educational authorities, I would argue that in future it would be much better if individual schools, rather than school systems, were seen as the prime clients by systems developers.

At issue here is who should be seen as the client. Who should the systems developers speak with about the systems requirements? There is a great deal of information systems literature that points to the necessity of involving users in the process of designing information systems (Fuller & William, 1994; Alter, 1996; Lawrence et al., 1997; Lindgaard, 1994) if we want these systems to be used to their full potential. Lawrence et al. (1997) stress the need to consult with users, and Lindgaard (1994) notes that a large body of research has shown that potential users do not make best use of information systems unless they feel that these systems have been designed with their involvement and in their interest. Fuller and Williams (1994) point out that when business users think that central computing departments have been unresponsive to their needs they often take application development into their own hands, 'do their own thing', and ignore the central authority. If the central education authority is seen as the client then it is unlikely that schools will be entirely happy with the end product. It is more likely that they will do as Fuller and Williams suggest and bypass the central system where they can.

There are many examples in business of information systems being designed for both central and local use. These systems can be built to offer the best of both worlds; a secure centralised database, combined with a degree of local autonomy in use. The technology and tools exist so that such systems need not compromise data integrity and security when offering local users some flexibility in how they use the data, and what other third-party systems they allow to be connected. The theoretical advantages of such *integrated* systems (Tatnall & Davey, 1995) have been understood by those building business information systems for many years. A significant problem in building educational systems occurs when system developers look only to the central authority and do not acknowledge that schools have differing information needs.

It should be stressed that the identification of the principal client is crucial, and many systems development projects have gone off the rails because they did not get this right and so did not establish systems requirements properly. No systems can do *everything* for everyone, and answering this question is necessary before commencing the analysis phase.

5.   CATEGORIES OF ORGANISATIONAL INFORMATION SYSTEM

Organisational information systems in business (- sometimes called Management Information Systems[2]) are normally divided into four main types based on the type of operation they perform: transaction processing systems, management reporting systems, decision support systems, and executive information systems. It is also appropriate to use such descriptions in the context of organisational information systems in schools.

5.1   Transaction Processing Systems (TPS)

TPS deal with well-structured routine processes, and support many of the day-to-day operations of the organization. In the business context TPS include order-entry systems, ticketing systems, automatic teller machines, payroll systems and accounts receivable/payable systems (Tatnall et al., 2000).

Many school administrative systems are currently used for day-to-day administration rather than management, and most are examples of Transaction Processing Systems. Such systems include:
- Library borrowing systems.
- Student attendance systems.
- Accounting systems (student receipts and payments, supplier payments etc).
- Student results/performance systems.

While very important in handling data, Transaction Processing Systems are not designed to provide management information, which is the purpose of the next type of information system.

5.2   Management Reporting System (MRS)

These are not concerned with fine operational detail, but rather in providing information to support the management of activities that support these operations

---

[2] The term Management Information System is ambiguous, but is generally taken as synonymous with the overall organisational information system.

(Tatnall et al., 2000). The purpose of an MRS is to condense selected internal data from the TPS and, combining this with relevant external data, to produce regular summary reports on the activities of the organisation.

In the school context Management Reporting Systems are often used to produce printed periodic reports to the central education authority of the district or state, to School Councils (Boards of Governors), to parents' groups and so on.

5.3 Decision Support Systems (DSS)

Unlike the general information support provided by an MRS, a DSS is designed to assist specific managers in solving specific semi-structured problems. (Expert Systems, which are often considered as a special type of DSS are also sometimes used for this purpose.) A DSS operates through the application of a mathematical model specifically designed to solve the problem in question. In business, Decision Support Systems can be used to support the making of decisions such as 'what sale price should be put on a particular product', and 'how many staff would be required for a particular task'. These are often designed to answer *what if ...?* questions such as 'what would be the effect on profitability if we increased prices by 10% accompanied by a 12% increase in staff wages?'

In education most of the use of Decision Support Systems appears to be by central authorities, rather than schools. Examples of their use by central authorities include planning systems to support decisions on where to build new schools (Taylor, 1995) and where to deploy teachers.

5.4 Executive Information Systems (EIS)

An EIS aims to provide senior managers with both summary information on the overall performance of the organization, and also with the ability to 'drill down' to lower levels to see the actual data. The idea is to provide these people with information about *critical success factors*, so facilitating their use of management by exception techniques (Tatnall & Davey, 1995). Rather than attempting to attend to the details of *every* matter, management will often require reports on just those matters that are *not operating normally* - those that are the exceptions. One example is library borrowing. Rather than examining lists of all students who have borrowed books, library management might be more interested in those students who have not returned their books on time (- an exception). Another example is in attendance records - the Deputy Principal may be more interested in all those students who have been present in period 1 and absent in period 2 on a given day (- an exception) rather than those who have been absent (or present) all day.

Decisions made by executives usually have a future orientation and the information used in these decisions is often informal. The idea of an EIS is to allow executives to review critical success factors on a frequent basis to quickly perceive important trends.

In the school context one principal may consider low truancy rates and the incidence of bullying to be important critical success factors, while in another school a different principal may be more concerned with monitoring student test results. In each case an EIS could be set up to provide this summary information on a daily basis, with the facility to drill down to see details of specific students if required. These systems could provide much useful information to school principals and administrators, but few appear to exist in schools at present.

5.5 Function-specific versus Integrated Systems

As businesses have traditionally been organised along functional lines, until about the early 1980s business information systems tended to be *function-specific* - each function such as human resources, bookings, accounts receivable or manufacturing, having its own *independent* information system. Each of these function-specific systems typically stored data items independently, and data collected for use by one system was usually not available to others. Not only is the re-entry of data, required when using such systems, a waste of time and resources, but it also violates one of the main principles of database management (Date, 1983): that data should be stored in one place, and one place only. (It should be noted that there must always be a back-up copy of any database, but that only one copy should be *in use*.) Using function-specific systems that are not integrated with the central database means that there will need to be multiple copies of the student database (for example), each of which must frequently be updated (Tatnall et al., 2000). The difficulty is that when there are two or more different, unrelated student databases any changes, such as new enrolments, changed student details and so on that occur must be made to *each* database *every* time they occur. Human weakness means that with almost complete certainty, there will be a time when this does not occur and not all of the databases are updated. This means that the other databases will then become inaccurate.

Because their designers were usually concerned with only a single application, most early school administrative systems were function-specific. This is also true of a number of current school systems.

The recent trend in business has been towards *integrated* systems where each separate system co-operates by sharing data with the others and providing for the flow of information across all levels and functions. Data need then only be stored once, without redundancy, to support all activities relevant to the organization. The model of an integrated information system shown in Figure 3 should be seen *not* as a single system but as a composite comprising a number of separate but cooperating *sub-systems*, each of which is made up of a suite of custom designed programs.

Many school administrative systems currently available appear to be more function specific than integrated, resulting in a considerable reduction in usability. Schools would be well advised to look at the ways that business makes use of information systems, and to adopt those business approaches that are relevant. Future school systems should be integrated, and should also offer DSS and EIS capabilities, in addition to TPS, so that their use can move from predominantly *administrative* towards *managerial* applications.

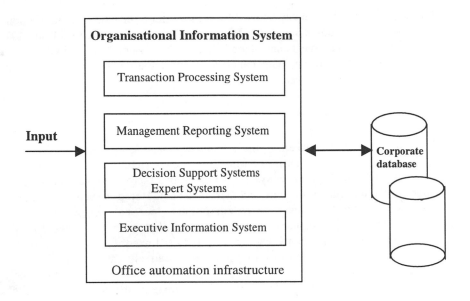

Figure 3. Model of an Integrated Information System

6. SYSTEM DESIGN CONSIDERATIONS

In designing any information system the requirements of the user must be regarded as the most important consideration. The user will, however, often not understand the design implications of some of their requirements, and these will need to be explained by the analyst. In addition to user requirements, important design considerations include: system architecture, database characteristics, data integrity, degree of integration of components and sub-systems, maintainability, expandability, security, usability and backup.

6.1 System Purpose, Nature and Ownership

The starting point of any systems design project must be to ascertain the main purpose and nature of the information system, and this requires the identification of the primary client as it is this client who determines the purpose of the system. Closely related to the system's purpose is its nature. Is the system to be primarily involved in transaction processing? Is it to offer management reporting or decision support facilities? Is it to provide executive information to the principal and senior school administrators?

Of course it is not just the primary client who will use the system, and the other users will also determine the type of system required. If the system has transaction processing facilities then these are most likely to be used by staff from the school administrative office. If the system has management reporting or decision support facilities then these will probably be used by subject and mini-school (a sub-section of the school – e.g., 'Senior Secondary Mini School' might mean years 11 and 12) co-ordinators. The requirements and characteristics of all users should be taken into account in the system design, with over-riding consideration being given to the requirements of the principal user.

6.2 Systems Integration

The main difference between having a number of un-related functional systems and an integrated system is that in the first case, each system has its own database which is not shared with any other system, meaning that there is a great deal of data redundancy. An important issue thus becomes: is the data stored in such a way that it can be accessed by the other sub-systems? This does not necessarily imply *physically* storing all data in a single central database, but more likely would result in data stored in several locations that are *conceptually* linked together into a single database. If a system is set up this way it is comparatively easy to link in other functional systems at a later date.

To get an idea of the magnitude of the problem, imagine that a particular school has function-specific library borrowing, student attendance, student results, and sports meeting systems as well as its central administrative system. As each of these systems involves lists of students there will need to be *five* separate, unrelated copies of the student database maintained and used in the school. When a student transfers into or out of the school or changes their personal or address details, five different databases need to be updated. This can be done by just updating the central system then downloading this data again to each of the other systems but, however it is done, it is a substantial and time wasting task that has lots of potential for going wrong with the result that one or more of the databases becomes corrupted or not updated properly. It does not matter how good the functionality or user-interface of the system if the information given is inaccurate or incorrect due to loss of integrity. Careful choice of additional functional systems that are able to co-operate and share data can reduce this difficulty (Athey, Day & Zmud, 1991; Selwood, 1996), but problems of an inflexible central system still remain.

When systems integration is not considered and *closed* function-specific systems are created that allow no other systems to access their data, except perhaps by download, data integration and the use of a single common database is not possible. The result is data duplication, waste, and possible loss of data integrity.

6.3 System Architecture and Scope

The scope of an information system can vary from the performance of a single function at a single location (e.g., a library borrowing system or a sports meeting result-recording system), to a system spanning a school section, the whole school, a school district, or even the entire school region. The architecture appropriate for the system will depend on its scope and its degree of centralisation and integration. For instance, if a centralised system is to span a complete district or region then a time-share system might be considered with all system and data storage functions performed at a central location on a mini-computer and directed to dumb terminals located in each school. At the other extreme, a completely decentralised system might make use of PCs in each school that are not in any way connected together. But the most likely scenario lies in-between with some type of networked, distributed database or client-server architecture. An important related question is: 'where and how will the data be stored?' The answer to this question is closely tied to decisions on systems architecture and needs to be considered in this context.

A suitable design for a system to link a school authority to its schools may involve a client-server architecture (Davey & Tatnall, 1997; Davey & Reyes, 1998) offering read-only access to some tables of the central database (Tatnall & Tatnall, 1998). The important point is that only one copy of data, such as lists of students and teaching staff, should be kept. If the system is designed as an *open system*, then easy integration of new third-party products, where appropriate, can be facilitated.

Because schools are different, their information needs are also different. As the designers of many central school administrative system have not foreseen any need for schools to use solutions for applications, such as student attendance, other than those that have provided, they do not offer the facility for other systems to connect to theirs. In similar vein there are many other situations in which a systems designer could not possibly come up with a perfect solution that would be suitable for all schools in the future. Perhaps the information system provided to a particular school does not link in with the library borrowing system, perhaps it does not handle school sports and the school wants to add this feature, perhaps it handles lateness in a way that is not appropriate for this particular school, perhaps it needs to do something else that no one has thought of yet.

A good school information system should thus be open to *accredited*, conforming third-party applications to have read/write access to this data, while other (non-conforming) applications should be granted read-only access. Such a system could look like the model shown in Figure 4 below.

As well as the central database, use could be made of a data warehouse that could be set up to allow any users (accredited or not) easy and rapid read-only access to specialised queries on selected data.

For any access like this to be possible, however, the data should be stored in a commonly accessible format. An ODBC format useable by database systems like Microsoft Access, and programming languages like Visual Basic is preferable as it means that users and third-party developers can easily access this data via other custom-designed programs. The data structure must be clearly set out and documented, with information and help for potential school developers. Documentation on the operation and design of the system should be clear, and should be written at a number of different levels suitable for users, school-level developers, and third-party developers.

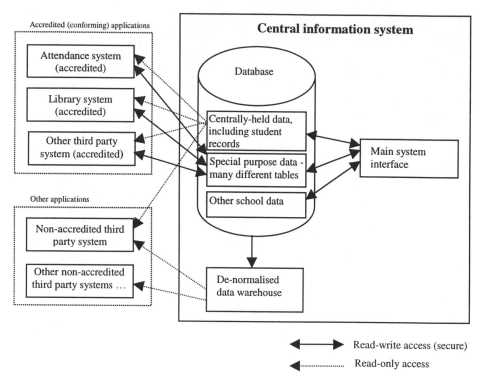

Figure 4. An Architecture for a Client-server System linking Schools to a Central Authority

6.4 Security, Integrity and Backup

While security of access to school information systems is an important issue, some systems go to such lengths to achieve security as to make the system less usable than it should be. Keeping some important data private and confidentiality is essential, but other data items do not need to have the same constraints. A balance must inevitably be found between security and ease of access, and this will probably involve some decisions on just which items of the data that is stored really need to be kept confidential and secure. It is technically quite possible to build different levels of user access into an information system, and to prevent some users from seeing some data at all, and other users from changing certain data.

System integrity, on the other hand, must never be compromised. Integrity demands than any given item of data is stored consistently and accurately. The best way to achieve this is to have a well-designed database schema and to ensure that each data item is stored only once (plus a back-up copy of course). Many current school administrative systems do not obey this rule and use several unrelated copies of, for example, the student table. Doing so violates the most fundamental rules of database theory and may result in insertion, update and deletion anomalies. Database replication, under strict conditions, can be allowable, but should be avoided where possible.

As anyone who has stored any important data knows well, accidents do happen, and having a procedure for backup of data is important. Backup procedures should be written into systems operations as a normal and regular part of these operations that require no special initiatives to be undertaken. Whether data backup is performed weekly, daily, or with some other frequency is a matter for each individual systems designer to consider. In short, however, frequency of backup is determined by how much data the user can afford to lose if the system crashes.

6.5 Maintenance, Expandability and Upgrading

No matter how well designed an information system is for the needs of *today's* schools and their *anticipated* needs into the future, no system will ever perfectly meet the needs of all schools at all times. There will always be some schools that will want to make modifications or additions, and no developer can anticipate all these requirements. New technologies and changing needs mean that systems will always potentially need to be upgraded.

If the school information system is designed as an *open system* in which the specifications and documentation are easily accessible, it will be possible for schools to make or commission changes to suit their own requirements. The alternative is to force all schools to use a centrally-designed system and adjust their procedures to those of this system.

Other design issues such as a well-constructed user interface, intuitive system operation, good documentation and ease of use should hardly need mentioning now as consideration of such matters has become routine in systems design.

7. CONCLUSIONS

Early school information systems were often designed by teachers themselves (Visscher, 1995), but more recent systems have usually been built by organisations or companies specialising in this task. It is tempting to just presume that the professionals designing these systems know what they are doing, and to leave this task to them. Such an approach, however, risks the creation of systems that are not readily useable to perform the changing tasks required of them. It is important that a wide range of views be considered, and input is needed from many different actors.

Of course all systems should be easy to use. They should be robust and should operate as required by their users with complete data integrity: today we would expect this. But a system will only perform the tasks required by its users if the developer understands who the users are, and is able to prioritise their needs appropriately. The first, and probably most important, consideration in the design of a school information system is who are the users? A number of current systems have been designed on criteria proposed by central education authorities, or companies trying to develop one product to suit many purposes. If individual schools are to get maximum advantage from their systems then these systems should be designed after consultation with these schools and be adaptable to meet their individual needs.

Many current school administrative applications are based around transaction processing and management reporting, but increased use could well be made of decision support and executive information systems.

An important issue in building school administrative systems is the degree of integration between the applications, and whether each has its own separate database. New systems should be built as integrated systems with an architecture designed to minimise data redundancy.

As it is impossible for even the most forward looking developers to predict all future trends and to cater for the needs of every school, new systems should be built as open systems. They should then come with published systems documentation so that making changes is possible for individual schools. If these systems are designed to be open systems then it will be possible to allow a number of accredited developers to be authorised to make additions and changes to the system to suit individual requirements. This can be done, consistent with the need to maintain a high level of system security.

The discipline of Information Systems has developed a number of tools, techniques and methodologies suitable for the design of business information systems. Although schools are not businesses, they are organisations that use information, and their information needs are not fundamentally different to those of other organisations. Many of the strategies available to assist in the design of organisational information systems are thus quite suitable for use in building school systems, and maximum use should be made of these.

REFERENCES

Alter, S. (1996). *Information Systems: a Management Perspective* (2nd edition). Menlo Park, CA: Benjamin/Cummins.

Athey, T.H., Day, J.C. & Zmud, R.W. (1991). *Computers and End-User Software*. New York: Harper Collins.

Checkland, P. (1981). *Systems Thinking, Systems Practice*. Chichester: Wiley.

Checkland, P.& Scholes, J. (1991). *Soft Systems Methodology in Action*. Chichester: Wiley.

Date, C.J. (1983). *Database: A Primer*. USA: Addison Wesley.

Davey, B. & Reyes, G. (1998). Overcoming Resistance to Integration: Using Client-Server Systems and Data Warehousing. In Fulmer, C.L., Barta, B.Z., and Nolan, P. (Eds.*), The Integration of Information for Educational Mangement*. Whitefield, Maine: Felicity Press/International Federation for Information Processing.

Davey, B. & Tatnall, A. (1997). Distributed ITEM for the Future: Moving Towards Client-Server Systems. In Fung, A.C.W., Visscher, A.J., Barta, B.Z. & Teather, D.C.B. (Eds.), *Information Technology in Educational Management for the Schools of the Future*. London: Chapman & Hall/IFIP.

Emery, F.E. (1969). *Systems Thinking*. Middlesex: Penguin.

Finegan, A (1994). *Soft Systems Methodology: an Alternative Approach to Knowledge Elicitation in Complex and Poorly Defined Systems*. RMIT Centre for Remote Sensing and Land Information: http://www.csu.edu.au/ci/vol1/Andrew.Finegan/paper.html, 15 Nov. 1998.

Frank, F.P. & Fulmer, C.L. (1998). The Dysfunctional Side of Educational Organizations: Themes from Clinical Information Systems Development. In Fulmer, C.L., Barta, B.Z. & Nolan, P. (Eds.), *The Integration of Information for Educational Management*. Whitefield, Maine: Felicity Press/International Federation for Information Processing.

Fuller, F. & Williams, M. (1994). *Computers and Information Processing*. Massachusetts: Boyd & Fraser.

Kendall, K.E. and Kendall, J.E. (1992). *Systems Analysis and Design* (2nd edition). New Jersey: Prentice Hall.

Lawrence, D.R., Shah, H.U. & Golder, P.A. (1997). Business Users and the Information Systems Development Process. In Barta, B.Z., Tatnall, A. and Juliff, P. (Eds.), *The Place of Information Technology in Management and Business Education*. London: Chapman & Hall.

Lindgaard, G. (1994). *Usability Testing and System Evaluation*. London: Chapman & Hall.

Selwood, I.D. (1996). Information Technology to Record and Monitor School Attendance. In Fung, A.C.W., Visscher, A.J., Barta, B.Z. & Teather, D.C.B. (Eds.), *Information Technology in Educational Management for the Schools of the Future*. London: Chapman & Hall/IFIP.

Tatnall, A. (1995). Information Technology and the Management of Victorian Schools – Providing Flexibility or Enabling Better Central Control? In Barta, B.Z., Telem, M., and Gev, Y. (Eds.), *Information Technology in Educational Management*. London: Chapman & Hall/IFIP.

Tatnall, A., Davey, B, Burgess, S., Davison, A. & Fisher, J. (2000). *Management Information Systems – concepts, issues, tools and applications* (2nd edition). Melbourne: Data Publishing.

Tatnall, A. & Davey, B. (1995). Executive Information Systems in School Management: a Research Perspective. In Tinsley, J.D. and van Weert, T.J. (Eds.), *World Conference on Computers in Education VI. WCCE'95. Liberating the Learner*. London: Chapman & Hall.

Tatnall, A. & Davey, B. (1996). Implementing New ITEM Systems: Strategies for Systems Development. In Fung, A.C.W., Visscher, A.J., Barta, B.Z. & Teather, D.C.B. (Eds.), *Information Technology in Educational Management for Schools of the Future*. London: Chapman & Hall/IFIP.

Tatnall, A. & Tatnall, B. (1998). Data Integration in a Training Institute – Modelling a Client-Server Solution. In Fulmer, C.L., Barta, B.Z., and Nolan, P. (Eds.), *The Integration of Information for Educational Management*. Whitefield, Maine: Felicity Press/International Federation for Information Processing.

Taylor, R.G. (1995). Geographic Information and School Facility Planning. In Barta, B.Z., Telem, M., and Giv, Y. (Eds.), *Information Technology in Educational Management*. London: Chapman & Hall/IFIP.

Visscher, A.J. (1994). A Fundamental Methodology for Designing Information Systems for Schools. *Journal of Research on Computers in Education*, 27(2), p. 231-249.

Visscher, A.J. (1995). Computer Assisted School Administration and Management: Where Are We and Where Should We Go? In Barta, B.Z., Telem, M., and Gev, Y. (Eds.), *Information Technology in Educational Management*. London: Chapman & Hall.

CHAPTER 7

IMPERATIVES FOR SUCCESSFUL IMPLEMENTATION OF SCHOOL INFORMATION SYSTEMS

Adrie J. Visscher[1] & Alex C.W. Fung[2]
[1]University of Twente, The Netherlands
[2]Hong Kong Baptist University, China

1. INTRODUCTION

Figure 2 in chapter five presents an overview of the groups of factors that are supposed to influence the success of implementing SISs (blocks A-E). In chapter six Tatnall elaborated on effective strategies for designing SISs. As such he addressed the blocks A (design strategies) and B (the SIS-quality resulting from a followed design strategy) in Figure 2 in chapter five.

This seventh chapter focuses on the prerequisites for implementing a SIS, thereby taking account of what is known about the nature of schools as organizations (block D in Figure 2 in chapter 5), as well as the experienced pros and cons of various implementation activities (block C in Figure 2).

Successful implementation in the case of a SIS means that the SIS is fully utilized with, hopefully, maximum intended effects and minimum unintended effects. Therefore, in section 2 a brief description is given of the research that has been carried out on the magnitude and nature of SIS-usage and its effects (blocks E and F in Figure 2 in chapter 5).

The body of knowledge concerning the effectiveness of implementation activities is then presented (block C) in section 3.

Thereafter, in section 4 the scientific literature is analyzed to illicit the characteristics of schools as organizations and school managers as 'information processors' that can help in formulating strategies for promoting greater use of SIS to assist higher order managerial activities (block D). In the case of a mismatch between the nature of SISs and the information processing characteristics of school staff, ways to overcome them will be explored.

2. THE USAGE OF SCHOOL INFORMATION SYSTEMS

For a long time only exploratory studies on the degree to which SISs are being used by target users were available (e.g., Visscher & Spuck, 1991). However large-

A.J. Visscher et al. (eds.), Information Technology in Educational Management, 115–133.
© 2001 *Kluwer Academic Publishers. Printed in the Netherlands.*

scale, empirical research on the magnitude and nature of SIS-usage has now been carried out in Hong Kong (Visscher et al., 1999), the Netherlands (Visscher & Bloemen, 1999), and in the United Kingdom (Wild and Smith, 2000). The results of these studies overall show that available SISs are being used to varying degrees in schools and mainly for routine, clerical work such as registration and processing of student test scores, examination scores, and financial data. In terms of the computer functions described in chapter 1, school office staff and teachers as school managers, spending much of their time on clerical activities, benefit most from the functions 'updating the database', 'information retrieval and document production', and 'communication' (Visscher, 1995; Visscher & Bloemen, 1999). In some countries even this 'lower order' type of SIS use remains relatively limited several years after SIS implementation.

The computer function 'autonomous decision-making' has not been utilized much in schools because little software is available that enables this type of support.

'Decision-making support' is a type of support SISs can offer that is strongly under-utilized. In quite a few countries the computer does help in finding solutions for *structured* problems like school timetabling and student-lesson group allocations. However, even if powerful SISs with enormous support capacities are at hand, the various possibilities of assistance in solving more *ill-structured* problems (in which case problems, relevant factors and remedies are much more uncertain; see chapter 1) are provided at a very low level (Visscher & Bloemen, 1999; Visscher et al., 1999). We will elaborate on the reasons for this in section 4.

As previously mentioned, successful implementation implies that the intended effects of SIS-usage are achieved and that negative unintended effects are as small as possible. The large-scale research (Visscher et al., 1999; Visscher & Bloemen, 1999) shows that, in the perception of the SIS-users, the use of SISs has lead to positive effects such as:

• better insight into how the school functions;
• better evaluation of school performance;
• better use of school resources;
• better information for curriculum planning;
• better internal communication.

Some negative effects are also experienced by school staff:
• increased monotony of clerical work;
• more time needed for and less ease of duties;
• limited assistance from the SIS to clerical staff.

These negative effects vary in strength between the studies and between the respondent groups of teachers, principals and clerks.

In section 3 we analyse what we have learned so far on the ways to promote the use of SISs in schools as planned by the innovators.

3. HOW TO IMPLEMENT SCHOOL INFORMATION SYSTEMS?

Implementation is a concept used in the literature on educational change to describe the process of introducing an innovation into an educational institution. One has to be careful to interpret the use of the term in different contexts, as it is used at times to represent the whole change process and at other times to indicate only one specific stage in the change process. For example, the former would be the case in Fullan's definition of implementation as "the process of putting into practice an idea, program, or set of activities and structures new to the people attempting or expected to change" (1991). In case of the latter, a distinction is made between the 'initiation', 'implementation', and 'institutionalisation' stages of innovation processes.

Our discussion in this chapter will concentrate at the *school* level of implementation. Implementation is considered here to concern the introduction of an externally developed SIS into a school in the way considered ideal by those who implement a SIS. Even for a single school, such a process is often a quite complex one, as Nolan et al. (1996) conclude on the base of three case studies:

> "The results of the case studies suggest that implementation of a computerized information system, like any innovation, can be both problematic and complex. It is problematic because implementation challenged the staff in all three schools to modify, and in some cases abandon, tried and seemingly true ways of doing things. The result is alternative and new methods, systems, and ways of thinking. Implementation is complex because the change process, of which implementation is one stage, occurred at different institutional levels and at different rates simultaneously. The complexity was frequently compounded by factors such as competing institutional demands on time, energy, and resources and differing degrees of staff readiness to entertain and embark upon change." (p. 346).

In chapter 5 (Figure 2, block C) the role of implementation processes has been stressed based on experience. From this it is clear that sophisticated and high quality SISs cannot be introduced into schools assuming automatic success. Visscher and Spuck (1991) also stressed this, based on an analysis of the implementation of SISs in England, Hong Kong, the USA, Israel, The Netherlands, Mexico and Australia:

> "A number of variables proves to be of importance in every country that is active in the field of computer-assisted school administration and management. However, it is remarkable that almost all of the variables that are emphasised as important in the country-specific articles are aspects of the implementation process." (p.158)

Aspects of the implementation process Visscher and Spuck point to concern what they call 'people variables' like the motivation for and attitude towards the SIS-innovation, and the degree of user influence on how SISs are introduced into their organisations. They also hold a plea for a careful management of the innovation process; clear innovation goals and a realistic innovation process are required. The innovation process must include time for schools to assimilate a computer application into their administrative functioning. Therefore, a 'stepping stone' implementation of a modular SIS is recommended.

A 'project champion' and a principal encouraging the SIS-innovation are also considered important. The project champion should possess sufficient expertise and authority to manage the SIS and innovation process and have an important user support role, especially for users facing problems with the SIS. Visscher and Spuck observed in the case studies that if the principal does not stimulate the introduction and usage of the SIS its usage is very unlikely.

Visscher and Spuck also note that although users in many cases receive some degree of training when a SIS is being introduced into their school, their training is often limited in magnitude, too technical and focussing on hardware and non-relevant software matters and does not clarify how users can interpret and use the information they retrieve from the SIS in day-to-day support and in school policy making. As the 'people factor' is so important in innovations of this kind user training should also address user questions concerning the benefits of SIS usage. Ideally users, as a result of such a training course, become convinced that it is in their own interest to invest in the innovation.

Nolan et al. (1996) on the basis of case studies in New Zealand schools using MUSAC (see chapter 4 for details on MUSAC) stress that top-down SIS-implementation approaches should be avoided. They hold a plea for a so-called 'bottom-up, grass roots' strategy:

> "Effective implementation of the MUSAC system has depended largely on existing management expertise within the schools, the ability of the schools, themselves, to organize implementation strategies of their own, and the emergence of agencies in the community which now provide schools with the back-up, training, and support services that they want." (p. 336)

3.1   Implementation Levels

3.1.1   The Level of Use Perspective

Nolan et al. (1996) present a different approach to the implementation of school information systems by using the conceptual framework shown in Table 1. They do not study directly which factors are correlated with the degree of SIS-use and therefore require careful attention of those who implement SISs. As an alternative they have developed a scale for measuring the degree to which SIS-implementation has progressed in a specific school. For this purpose Nolan et al. link the 'Levels of Use' perspective from the Concerns Based Adoption model (CBAM), (Hall et al., 1973) with three generally accepted innovation stages (the adoption, implementation and utilisation stage).

Table 1. Levels of SIS-usage

Level of Use		Innovation stages
0	Non-use	
I	Orientation	Adoption
II	Preparation	
III	Mechanical use	Implementation
IV a	Routine use	
IV b	Refinement	
V	Integration	Utilisation
IV	Renewal	

According to Nolan et al. innovation <u>adoption</u> includes the development of an awareness that a situation needs to be addressed, followed by *orientation* activities which predispose decision-makers to take a particular course of action (Hall et al., 1973). Together, awareness and orientation lay the foundation for implementation.

The <u>implementation stage</u> in Table 1 covers *orientation*, *preparation*, and the *mechanical* Levels of Use. This illustrates that while key decision-makers in the adoption stage may have successfully oriented themselves towards the SIS-innovation, those staff who are starting at the level of non-use will require orientation in order to accept the innovation. At the *preparation* Level of Use, staff are engaged in setting up the SIS for practical use. Typically, such activities include the acquisition and installation of the system, the determination of locations (e.g., where to place the file server and remote networked terminals?), the assignment of staff roles and responsibilities, and the initiation of staff training. The final implementation step concerns *mechanical use*, when staff are involved in learning to use the system. Implementation ends when everyone who the school identifies as needing to use the system or part of it, has mastered the program(s), and is using it to carry out day-to-day tasks.

The final stage of <u>utilization</u> is characterized by the remaining four Levels of Use of routine use, refinement, integration and renewal. Here, the users evaluate the quality of the innovation and examine new developments with a view to setting new goals. Once integrated into a school's day-to-day operating procedures the quality of SIS-use is evaluated in terms of outcomes. In the case of favorable evaluations a school may decide to expand SIS use by introducing a new component. Implementation can then be seen as typically on going and incremental.

3.1.2 The six-A Model

Fung (1995) like Nolan et al. distinguishes between various stages of introducing a SIS. He, however, goes one step further as he also analyzes, from the standpoint of a change facilitator, the best way to stimulate the SIS-innovation process.

His model focuses on how to help individual schools to utilize a SIS created and developed externally. Fung developed a model that is of value to practitioners in the sense that it can be used as a kind of reference guide for a change facilitator to follow in the process of helping the user organisation assimilate a SIS successfully. In the 'Six-A' model shown in Figure 1, the whole implementation process is considered to be a non-linear process consisting of re-cycling loops channelling through six broad stages: (1) Awareness, (2) Attitude Formation, (3) Adoption, (4) Adaptation, (5) Action, and (6) Application.

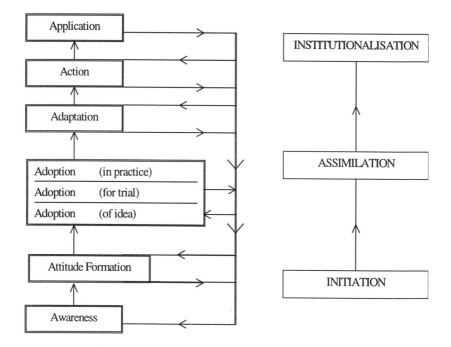

Figure 1. The Six-A Model of SIS-implementation

The six "A" stages are interrelated and overlapping, and can be grouped roughly into three main phases. The *initiation* phase encompasses awareness, attitude formation, and adoption. The *assimilation* phase includes adaptation and action; and the third and final phase is that of *institutionalization* which includes action and application. The cybernetic loops among the different stages indicate that these stages, although shown as discrete and sequential, are considered to 'interact' with one another. For instance, trial of an innovation will bring awareness and understanding about the innovation to a different level compared to that at the start. Different attitudes will probably also be formed as a result of the trial which might affect decisions for subsequent actions depending on whether the attitudes formed towards the innovation are positive or negative. We will have a closer look at each of the three phases now.

The initiation phase

The initiation phase concerns the transition from a state of knowing that an innovation exists to the state of making a decision for adoption or rejection. During the initiation phase, the change facilitator in the view of Fung should be working in a cyclic process involving awareness and attitudinal changes of actors participating in the innovation. According to Fung the key feature of this phase is that it follows the action approach (Silverman, 1970), or the phenomenological approach (Fullan, 1991). The working target of the change facilitator in this phase is on the meaning of the innovation to the actors concerned such as teachers and clerical staff.

Fung states that the primary task is to reach the stage of decision for adoption and that a change facilitator can consider taking the following strategy:

Step 1: Defining the 'Relevant System in Focus' (RSF);
Step 2: Searching and communicating information to raise the RSF's level of awareness about the innovation; and
Step 3: Building common grounds of worth for the RSF.

Fung also points to the fact that even for innovations at the individual school level, the user system consists often of a large number of subsystems. He considers it impractical for a change facilitator to attempt to manage the entire user system as a single entity during the change process. Fung prefers the definition of a span of focus at a certain time for a certain situation (or phase) during the change process. In other words, the change facilitator, with a 'dynamic systems view', is situational in defining the system boundary with relevance to the objective(s) at different phases. School staff identified as key persons at different stages form the 'Relevant System in Focus' (RSF), that is, the 'working system' isolated for attention by the change facilitator.

Any innovation will carry different meanings to different user subsystems. Dalin (1978) has pointed out that whether an innovation is beneficial or not depends on the answer to the question 'to whom?'. It is argued that successful assimilation of a SIS requires that relevant subsystems involved in the user organisation see some worth of the innovation from their standpoint in this initiation phase of the change process. The major task of the change facilitator at this stage is to help merge the initial, perhaps incongruent, sets of needs or purposes held by various actors in the school;

or to make overlaps amongst the different sets of goals as large as possible where congruence is impossible to achieve.

The term awareness used in this context includes information, knowledge, and understanding of the SIS on the part of the RSF. Different levels of awareness will lead to different attitudes of the actors (staff in the school) concerned, subsequently leading to adoption (or rejection) of the innovation, as well as to different degrees of ownership. The role of the change facilitator during the initiation phase according to Fung is therefore one of transmitting knowledge, raising concern, and communicating information among the subsystems in the RSF. The provision of information about the innovation system to the participants is particularly important at this stage.

During the initiation phase, it can be said that the focus of the change facilitator is more on knowledge acquisition than on acquiring skills and providing support. For the assimilation phase, however, the emphasis would be on skills training and support rather than on basic knowledge about the SIS.

The adoption stage marks vaguely the beginning of the assimilation phase. For major changes, it is simply sensible and natural to assimilate the new 'thing' by adopting it on a trial basis before putting into real practice. Thus adoption of a SIS may be sub-divided into three levels:

1. Level 1: the adoption of an idea about the new SIS, with a decision to search for more information, knowledge, and understanding for further consideration;
2. Level 2: the adoption of the SIS on trial;
3. Level 3: the adoption of the SIS in practice, i.e., by gaining enough confidence, knowledge and skill, the innovation is put into action in real practice.

For large and complex SISs, adoption in practice is usually preceded by pilot runs or trials. This is a more secure way to step into the unknown without risking too much. In case the impact of the SIS on the user system is too undesirable, or if the adaptation is too costly, the user system can still revert to its original state.

The assimilation phase

The term 'assimilation' spells out clearly the concept of an innovation being absorbed into a system, with a change facilitator catalyzing or managing the process, rather than the traditional view of an innovation being implemented into an organization by a change agent.

The assimilation phase includes adaptation and action by the user system. It is immaterial whether adaptation precedes action, or the reverse. Assimilation is a cycle of events after the user system has adopted the innovation for trial. It is in essence a phase of experimentation and learning for the user system. In the view of Fung, when a SIS is used in a school, feedback from different school-subsystems can lead to two kinds of adaptation:

1. adapting the SIS to meet user system requirements, i.e., tailoring or modifying the innovation to meet the organization's need, or,
2. adaptation on the side of the user system to suit the innovation, i.e., modifying existing subsystems within the organization (such as structures, tasks, habits, etc.) to achieve compatibility with the SIS.

These two kinds of adaptation are not mutually exclusive and according to Fung often both are required together. In other words, effort may be required to manage the relationship between the target of change and the other sub-systems of an organization. It is worth mentioning that feedback during the assimilation phase is not limited only to the adaptations and actions taken. In effect, the degree of awareness and attitudes of people in the user system are also unavoidably affected as a result of assimilation. Thus, the whole process of innovation is considered an interrelated one, although a breakdown of it into component stages is required for the discussion here.

The role of the change facilitator during this phase of change is one of training, support, and problem-solving in practice. The primary objective is to help and guide the user system in assimilating the innovation, i.e., in getting accustomed to using the innovation, gaining confidence and achieving with it. With enough experience and learning through action while using the SIS, the innovation can be fully applied with confidence.

Fung stresses that commitment of the potential SIS-users is necessary and that their perception of the overall benefits of innovating is essential. This is what the initiation phase in an innovation process is all about. However, it is argued that willingness to change is one thing, and whether the potential SIS-users are able to do so is another. This last question is exactly what assimilation should address. During the assimilation phase potential users need to become effective users of the SIS. Training and support for the parties concerned are most crucial to overcome general feelings of insecurity and temporary incompetence. During this period of uncertainty, acquisition of technical skills and subsequent transfer to the workplace on the part of school staff is the prime objective of the assimilation phase. In this regard, the theory-demonstration-practice-feedback approach of Joyce and Weil (1986) in training teachers has much to be borrowed. These authors have identified a four-step approach, working in an adequate time frame, to be both necessary to, and sufficient for, the development of job-related skills in most vocations and professions.

Institutionalisation

With successful initiation and assimilation, staff in the user system are expected to be able to master the skills required for the SIS with confidence, gaining the full, intended benefits of the innovation. The SIS will then no longer be something new to the organization, and its application will become a matter of routine. In other words, the SIS by then will have been incorporated as a subsystem into the organization and thus the assimilation phase reaches a sustainable stage. This end state of the innovation process is the stage of application, when the mission of the change facilitator is accomplished. Institutionalisation is then reached, marking the end of the whole SIS-implementation process.

3.2 *Empirically verified Implementation Promoting Factors*

Recapitulating the previous, various authors have pointed to variables and strategies (e.g., Fung Six-A model) they consider important for successful SIS-implementation. Most of these ideas have been developed by them during the process of introducing SISs in a small number of schools. The empirical proof of the associations between the variables and SIS-implementation as well as the effectiveness of the Six-A strategy was lacking. In other words, although many of the discussed variables and strategies sound plausible it was uncertain whether they really matter.

In the late 1990s this observation stimulated Fung, Visscher and Wild to compose the theoretical framework presented in chapter 5 and use it as a basis for large-scale empirical research in Hong Kong, The Netherlands and The United Kingdom (the levels of use as discussed by Nolan et al. actually concern an approach that can be applied for measuring SIS-use more accurately). Their review of the literature resulted in the selection of 12 implementation process characteristics they expected to be associated with SIS-usage:
1. the amount of internal training
2. the amount of external training
3. the satisfaction with internal training
4. the satisfaction with external training
5. the training contents
6. the sources of help
7. the satisfaction on ease of help
8. the introduction pace
9. the encouragement by principal
10. the encouragement by SIS-administrator
11. the clarity of innovation goals
12. the clarity of innovation means

The empirical findings of their studies (Visscher & Bloemen, 1999; Visscher et al., 1999; Wild & Smith, 2001) showed that four variables explained variance in SIS-usage indices:
*   the amount of internal training;
*   the amount of external training;
*   the degree to which the goals of the SIS-innovation are clear to users;
*   the extent to which the means for accomplishing the SIS-innovation are clear to users.

In other words, so far no empirical proof has been found for eight of the variables in Block C of Figure 2 in chapter five:
*   the satisfaction with internal training
*   the satisfaction with external training
*   the training contents
*   the encouragement by the principal

- the encouragement by the SIS-administrator
- the introduction pace
- the sources of help
- the satisfaction on ease of help

The large scale research is an important step forward as it starts to indicate what really matters when SISs were implemented. As the correlations between SIS-usage and other factors strongly depend on the degree of variance in respondents' answers more research in other implementation contexts is needed to further refine our insight into the features of these innovation processes. This will then lead to knowledge of how we can manipulate in order to make the probability of successful SIS innovations as large as possible. Research is needed to determine whether one strategy for managing SIS implementation is indeed more effective than alternative strategies.

In the next section, we will look at the features of schools as 'information processors' in order to discover reasons for the limited degree of managerial support from SISs to help develop strategies for improvement.

4. THE ROLE OF THE NATURE OF SCHOOLS AS ORGANIZATIONS[1]

Block D in Figure 2 of chapter 5 includes the school organizational characteristics that are supposed to influence the intensity of SIS-usage and the way it is used. The first two D-variables refer to the attitude of potential SIS-users towards the system, in particular in their expectations of it and how motivated they are to use it. Bennet and Lancaster (1986) state that if the innovator does not have the commitment and trust of the staff of the organization the innovation is introduced into dysfunctional behavior, which is obvious. According to O'Brien et al. (1989) the innovation has to fit with the existing values and attitudes, and a certain need for the innovation should exist (cf. Piercy, 1987; Bird, 1984; Fullan, 1982). It seems logical that if users have a more positive attitude towards the SIS they will probably use it more.

The same goes for variable D-3; staff having more experience with, and being more familiar with computers will probably use SISs more. These three characteristics of schools seem very straightforward in their relationship with the use of SISs.

The evaluation of the implementation of the computer-assisted SAMS in Hong Kong (Visscher et al., 1999) provided strong empirical evidence for these variables: variation in the start motivation of school staff and their computer knowledge before the introduction of the SIS, quite strongly explained variance in SAMS-use.

---

[1] Part of this section was published in A. Visscher (1996). The implications of how school staff handle information for the usage of school information systems. *International Journal of Educational Research*, 25 (4), pp. 323-334.

As explained in chapter 5 the goals of introducing SISs into schools as perceived by target users may influence their eagerness to accept a SIS because they consider certain innovation goals, such as better evaluation and control of teachers, as threatening to their classroom autonomy.

The fifth variable in the D-block of Figure 2 relates more to the characteristics of school organizations as elaborated in the theoretical literature on organization. In that literature organizational structures, relationships between staff, relationships between divisions and the distribution of organizational power (cf. Visscher, 1992 & 1999) are important topics.

In section 4.1 we will concentrate on the last variable in block D, i.e., the policy-making capacity of school staff. This is extremely relevant for the introduction of school information systems with the capacity to assist in the development of school policies.

4.1   The Decision-making Capacity of Schools

The congruence between an information system (IS) and its organisational context influences the impact of an IS (Iivari, 1992). This also applies to schools because how they function as organisations, especially in terms of their decision-making capacity, affects the use of SISs in policy-making processes.

As indicated in chapter 5, in the literature schools are portrayed as weak policy-makers. Decisions are often put off, or only decisions are taken that neither threaten any participant, nor solve any problem.

Weick (1982) also points to the fact that the link between decisions and their execution is not strong and many decisions are not, or only partially, executed.

A further difficulty in the case of school organisational problems is that it is often difficult to determine cause, effect and remedies, which will further exacerbate the decision making capacity. For example, the course and outcomes of the teaching-learning process are affected by many factors such as the features of students, teachers, home situations and societal patterns, of which the precise influence is difficult to determine. Although we may find relations between factors, in most cases it will be very difficult to determine 'what causes what', or what should be done to achieve a solution.

Restated briefly, policy-making at school level is limited as a result of political interests of participants, the partial execution of decisions and the difficulty to determine cause of and remedy for organisational problems.

Until now we have determined some general features of schools with regard to decision-making. However, among others Marx (1975) and Visscher (1992) have demonstrated that 'the' school does not exist as they all vary in their policy-making capacity. They have also shown that a school can be more able to develop school policy in some specific areas of policy-making, such as allocation of resources, than in others, such as in teaching related areas.

Two of the five school organisational types Marx and Visscher distinguish are presented now to give an impression of this perspective. According to the authors many schools possess the features of the *'segmental' (departmentalised) school* in which teachers operate as loose segments, taking care of their teaching task by co-operating little or not at all with colleagues. There is very little consultation and policy-making in this type of school. If it is done it mainly occurs at management level and concerns the development of a resources policy. School policy-making in other areas is rare.

In the *'fraternal' (collaborative) school* consultation among staff is intense at all school levels of organisational infrastructure. Within this subject departments are solid co-operative teacher groups fulfilling a pivotal function and actively developing instructional policy, which is also strongly stimulated by school management who itself develops supporting policy in related areas.

Although a school never fully possesses the features of only one of these two school types the models point to the fact that schools can differ greatly in their policy-making abilities.

The impact of introducing SISs on school policy-making will vary in relation to the degree to which the prerequisites for policy-making are fulfilled in a school. In schools capable of developing school policy before the computer becomes available, the impact of a SIS may be enormous. These schools may be able to use computer-information in all areas and at all school organisational levels to support their decision-making. In schools that have little policy-making capacity, a pre-condition for increased policy-making is the alleviation of the root cause through organisational development.

4.2 Features of Information Management at Two School Levels

This section presents a review of the research about the kind of information school managers collect and use.

4.2.1 Information Management by School Managers

Mintzberg (1989) typifies managers as sophisticated *nerve centres* of organisational information, looking for internal and external informers and disseminating information. They receive information from many different sources, among others from specific staff to whom only they have access as a result of their organisational position. It concerns information on internal organisational operations, external events, analyses in reports, ideas and trends, pressures from consumers or interest groups, etc. They restructure information for using it in decision-making and build their own models of how the organisation functions.

According to Mintzberg managers seek and use information that is current and comes in the form of triggers. 'Hot' information that moves quickly like a rumour is more important than absolutely right information. Triggering information concerns concrete stimuli, no aggregations, but tangible detail that pieced together in the manager mind illuminates issues. Mail information is not appreciated since it contains formal, lengthy, general, non-current information and does not trigger immediate management action. Since managers appear to verbally communicate 70-

80% of their time they prefer information that is transmitted by verbal media like telephone and meetings.

They do not operate as reflective planners, but as adaptive information manipulators. We are often inclined to think of managers in terms of the stereotype rational problem solvers, receiving relevant information from management information systems and other sources and taking decisions on that basis. However, this image proves to be a fairy tale (McPherson et al., 1986). Time consuming, profound problem analysis, the subsequent generation of alternative solutions, and elaborating the most suitable solution, is rare. Sproull (1981) states that managers lack the time and inclination to dig through data and that they tend to read or hear information only once. Riehl et al. (1992) have reviewed the literature on how principals value certain types of information and how this influences their information use. In particular, they argue that the nature of the conditions under which principals work, with days filled with many brief episodes of unpredictable interactions with others, affects how they use information.

Principals can only devote short periods of time to the many different topics and situations which fall within their responsibility. They have to react rapidly, need information quickly and therefore receive most of it in informal ways through opinions, advice, anecdotes, hearsay, speculation and even gossip. Although school life is complex, they desire 'simple' information they understand and (think they) can rely on. As a result of their work place constraints and the limitations of the human information processing capacity they are inclined to use information that is communicated informally, verbally, in face-to-face interactions, quickly, accompanied by an interpretation, and consistent with their understanding of and orientation to their administrative role. The collection and processing of formal information often takes too much time. Quantitative, aggregated reports are therefore only used to a small degree (Sproull, 1981; Mintzberg, 1989). These findings imply that managers often take decisions based on insufficient information. However, taking decisions in that way is preferred to not taking decisions, since then at least something is done (Mintzberg, 1989).

According to Shangraw (1986) managers rely less on computer-output than on other printed information. They prefer summary reports showing a bottom line, even when more detailed information is available, and prove to make fewer interpretation errors, when using these summaries.

Although managers do not use computer data very intensively Leithwood and Montgomery (1982) have shown that principals who frequently quantitatively analyse student and teacher performance, which nowadays can now be computer-assisted, run more effective schools.

Principals experience difficulties in using quantitative/statistical data because they are untrained and inexperienced with the use of this type of data, which makes it difficult for them to determine the quality of this information, and to interpret and use it for school improvement. This is in line with Riehl et al. (1992) arguing that principals who are comfortable with quantitative data on student outcomes, who trust them and are trained to interpret them are more likely to use these data.

In the opinion of Mintzberg (1989) the characteristics of the information managers rely on are in conflict with most formal ISs producing aggregated, precise, internal, historical information. According to him managers do not use all the formal information ISs produce for *rational* problem solving because of:

1. The poorness of formal ISs: A lot of qualitative information such as politics and personality features and formally non-transferrable information like gestures and tone is missing. Aggregated information is too general. Formal information often comes too late, and its processing makes the required quick responses impossible. Moreover, it is often difficult to draw conclusions and base actions on the basis of formal information. For instance, what statistics on the number of students passing the examinations say about the quality of teaching is not clear.

2. Problems of organizational functioning: Rigid organisational goals can result in inadequate organisational behaviour, like trying to raise profit figures without paying attention to other matters that are important on the long run. In addition, people may distort information for political reasons and only use information that strengthens their own position.

3. The limitations of the human mind: Humans can only take a limited number of relevant information elements into account in decision-making. Moreover, the human brain often filters information in such a way that it fits with personal perception. The marketing division for instance interprets information in such a way that a problem becomes a marketing problem. As a result, some relevant information may be neglected.

ISs contain only a small part of all available and relevant information, of which the manager receives a subset, of which the brain only absorbs a subset and of which only part is precise and relevant! Much of the relevant information is in human instead of in computerised memories, which implies that as well as printed/written information, verbal information channels have to be used.

4.3 *Proposals for Promoting more intensive SIS-usage for Decision-support*

Summarising the findings of the review of the research on information handling by school managers the following picture emerges. They have to take many decisions in uncertainty, are burdened with information and have little time to process information and reflect on it. As a consequence, they reduce their need for information and information processing and use information selectively. Full rational behaviour, in terms of choosing the best mode of operation for achieving explicit goals, after having processed all relevant information, is rare. Many actions are uninformed or based on inaccurate information. The perceived quality of a piece of information is more decisive for its usage than its objective quality. There is a strong preference for up-to-date, quickly available and directly usable, informal, clear and action triggering information.

The fact that managers and other school staff involved in school decision-making processes benefit little from SISs does not mean that we should not try, where possible, to increase the degree of rationality in their behaviour. Some ways of increasing decision-making support need to be considered:

1. Since the user-perception of the value of certain information is crucial for its use it is very important to show school managers how useful SIS-information can be in school policy-making. Just as millions of people use computers for office work because they experience the advantages of doing so, experiencing the added value of computer-assisted decision-making will probably stimulate school leaders to use SISs for working on complex problems (cf. Visscher & Bloemen, 2001). The best strategy to do so may be to start with small projects with a high success probability. If a school's functioning for instance improves as a result of computer produced information this will lead to school staff feeling encouraged to invest more time and energy in using these tools. In other words, success breeds success.

The view so far is that carefully designed training courses can fulfil an important role in supporting success and Visscher and Branderhorst (2001) have set up a project to investigate whether deliberate training courses can change the under utilisation of SISs by school managers for decision-support. A review of the literature indicated that such a training course should have the following characteristics:

*   involvement of representatives of the target group in the design of the course;
*   voluntary participation;
*   potential participants should be informed on the main features of the course;
*   individual intake to determine the level and needs of participants;
*   set clear, specified and measurable training goals;
*   match the nature of the training course with the know-how and skills of participants, starting with problems that they face in their professional practice;
*   make the probability that participants will soon experience success as high as possible, by providing training content that they can apply immediately;
*   teach participants to determine what kind of information they need, and how to select, retrieve, interpret and use it in school policy-making;
*   use various instructional strategies such as active learning, self-study, group assignments, etc;
*   explicitly pay attention to the various stages of a learning process with experiential learning, reflection, theory and experimentation;
*   transfer what has been learned to professional practice by having participants write an action plan, offer 'on the job' support, involve their colleagues in the training course and guarantee follow-up training activities.

More specifically Visscher and Branderhorst (2001) propose a training course with the following structure:

*   inform the target group on the training course;
*   individual intake of participants;
*   5 days 'off the job' training;
*   2 days 'on the job' training.

Twelve is the maximum number of participants in the training course. Based on the previous characteristics the effectiveness of this strategy can be evaluated in a pre-test post-test, experimental and control group study.

2. Simon (1993) stresses that information is not a scarce resource, but that the human attention and information processing capacity is limited. If we let computers produce all the information they can produce, the school staff will be unable to function efficiently as a result of information pollution. The review on information handling within schools has shown that the contents and nature of information influences its usage. SISs should operate intelligently, be selective, and only output information that is interesting and has the potential to improve school quality.

Computer output must also be appealing, easily retrieved, readily analysed, and trigger actions. Current SISs often do not meet these requirements. It therefore would help if output is manipulated by school staff with a specific information handling task, before it is distributed among other school staff, in such a way that it meets the 'promotors of information use' criteria. Preferably we would build SISs that make it easy to retrieve all kinds of data and that produce information that is easily understood. The barriers for retrieving and processing valuable SIS data should be made as small as possible, and hence the probability that this information is used will be as great as possible.

3. The description of the decision-making capacity of schools showed that although schools differ in their policy-making capacity, they are not in general considered to be very forceful policy developers and evaluators.

Computer-assisted policy-making and evaluation touches the whole school organisation. In many schools integrating SISs fully in their policy-development requires fundamental *organisational development,* demanding a lot of energy from school staff. Organisational innovation and evolution should bring them to a level of organisational functioning that enables them to:

- decide which SIS-information they need for decision-making;
- retrieve (part of) the information they need from a SIS;
- interpret the data in such a way that it can be used for decision-making;
- use the information for developing, implementing and evaluating new school policies

4.4 Resume

This chapter has shown the complexity of change associated with benefiting from computer-assisted SISs, especially where decision-making support is concerned. Achieving full system utilisation resulting in school performance improvement is proving to be enormously difficult, even when a high quality SIS is available. Decisive for success is the degree to which we will be able to design and implement SISs that produce interesting, valuable and accessible information, that match the nature of schools. School staff need to become convinced of the added-value of these systems, and we need to find ways to prepare them for full system use through training, support, clear innovation goals, clear implementation processes and a feasible implementation pace. If we accomplish this we may be able to change the nature of schooling in an important way.

REFERENCES

Bennet, J., & Lancaster, D. (1986). Management Information Systems in Further Education: some observations on design and implementation. *Journal of Further and Higher Education*, 10(3), 35-49.

Bird, P. (1984). *Micro computers in school administration*. London: Hutchinson.

Dalin, P. (1978). *The Limits of Educational Change*. London: Macmillan.

Fullan, M. (1982). *The meaning of educational change*. New York: Teachers College Press.

Fullan, M. (1991). *The New Meaning of Educational Change*. London: Cassell.

Fung, A.C.W. (1995). Managing change in ITEM. In Barta, B.Z., Telem, M. and Gev, Y. (Eds.), *Information Technology in Educational Management*. London: Chapman & Hall.

Hall, G.E., Wallace, R.C. & Dosset, W.A. (1993). *A developmental conceptualisation of the adoption process with educational institutions*. Austin: The University of Texas.

Iivari, J. (1992). The organizational fit of information systems. *Journal of Information Systems*, 2(1), 3-29.

Joyce, B., & Weil, M. (1986) *Models of Teaching*. Prentice-Hall International, 3rd edition.

Leithwood, K.A. & Montgomery, D.J. (1982). The role of the elementary school principal in program improvement. *Review of Educational Research, 52*, 309-339.

Marx, E.C.H. (1975). *De organisatie van scholengemeenschappen in onderwijskundige optiek*. [The organisation of comprehensive schools from an educational point of view]. Groningen: Wolters-Noordhoff.

Mintzberg, H. (1989). *Mintzberg on management*. New York: Free Press.

Nolan, C.J.P., Ayres, D.A., Dunn, S., & McKinnon, D.H. (1996). Implementing computerized school information systems: Case studies from New Zealand. *International Journal of Educational Research,* Vol. 25, 4, 335-349.

O'Brien, C.J., Merriam, E., Rule, D.L., & Chapman, D.W. (1989). *Information Systems Adoption: a study in implementation*. New York: University at Albany.

Piercy, N. (Ed.) (1987). *Management Information Systems*. New York: Nichols Publishing Company.

Riehl, C., Pallas, G. & Natriello, G. (1992). *More responsive high schools student information and problem-solving*. Paper presented at AERA conference in San-Francisco.

Shangraw, R.F. (1986). How public managers use information: An experiment examining choices of computer and printed information. *Public Administration Review, 46*, 506-515.

Silverman, D. (1970). *The Theory of Organisations*. London: Heinemann Educational Books.

Simon, H.A. (1993). Decision Making: Rational, Non-rational, and Irrational. *Educational Administration Quarterly, 29*(3), 392-411.

Sproull, L.S. (1981). Managing education programs: A micro-behavioral analysis. *Human Organization*, 40(2), 113-122.

Visscher, A.J. (1992). *Design and evaluation of a computer-assisted management information system for secondary schools* (Ph.D. dissertation). Enschede: University of Twente.

Visscher, A.J. (1995). Computer-assisted school administration and management: where are we and where should we go? In Barta, B.Z., Telem, M. and Gev, Y. (Eds.), *Information Technology in Educational Management*. London: Chapman & Hall, pp. 15-26.

Visscher, A.J. (1999). *Managing schools towards high performance; Linking school management theory to the school effectiveness knowledge base*. Swets and Zeitlinger Publishers; Lisse/Tokyo.

Visscher, A.J. & Bloemen, P.P.M. (1999). Evaluation and use of computer-assisted management information systems in Dutch schools. *Journal of Research on Computing in Education, 32(1), 172-188*.

Visscher, A.J. & Bloemen, P.P.M. (2001). School managerial usage of computer-assisted school information systems: a comparison of good practice and bad practice school. In Nolan, P. and Fung, A. (Eds.) *Institutional Improvement through IT in Educational Management*. London: Kluwer.

Visscher, A.J. & Branderhorst, M. (2001). How should school managers be trained for managerial school information system usage? In Nolan, P. and Fung, A. (Eds.) *Institutional Improvement through IT in Educational Management*. London: Kluwer.

Visscher, A.J. & Spuck, D.W. (1991). Computer-Assisted School Administration and Management: the State of the Art in Seven Nations. *Journal of Research on Computing in Education*, 24 (1), 146-168.

Visscher, A.J., Fung, A. & Wild, P. (1999). The evaluation of the large scale implementation of a computer-assisted management information system in Hong Kong schools. *Studies in Educational Evaluation,* 25, 11-31.

Wild, P. & Smith, D. (2001). Has a Decade of Computerisation Made a Difference in School Management? In Nolan, P. and Fung, A. (Eds.) *Institutional Improvement through IT in Educational Management*. London: Kluwer.

SECTION III

Future directions

CHAPTER 8

THE FUTURE OF SCHOOL INFORMATION SYSTEMS

Debbi Smith & Phil Wild
Loughborough University, United Kingdom

1. INTRODUCTION

This chapter addresses the future of school information systems, some of it speculative, with views included from representatives from governments, non-governmental organisations, vendors and end-users. In addition widely published international experts in the field, Bill Davey (Australia), Alex Fung (Hong Kong), Pieter Hogenbirk (Netherlands), Toshio Okamoto and Alexandra Cristea (Japan), Arthur Tatnall (Australia), Ray Taylor (USA) and Brent E. Wholeben (USA) were asked for their views which have been incorporated in this chapter to provide a broad range of opinions, ideas and perspectives from a number of different countries.

The changing demands of the 21st century give rise to a number of common strands in the contributions to the chapter, in particular the impact of these demands on productivity, accountability and community in schools of the future and the question of how IT developments and changing technology will be used to address this in terms of functionality and design. The convergence of school administration systems and curricula IT and how it will result in inextricable links between these two formerly discreet areas is also addressed.

In this chapter we discuss the school of the future, the ways in which the school as an organisation will change and how emerging technologies will impact on educational organisation and management. This is contextualised by commentary on the national and international perspectives on education in the 21st century from governments, vendors and end users of IT in Education Management (ITEM).

In collecting together these materials we attempt to provide an indication of some of the foreseeable needs and directions of school information systems (SISs) in the 21st century. If the technology can be shown to be beneficial and improve administrative systems to enhance school effectiveness it will be used and, however, reticent teachers are now they will have to adopt the new technologies

2. SCHOOLS OF THE FUTURE

One cannot easily describe *the* School of the Future. There are too many uncertainties that will affect the way education will evolve to a new paradigm.

A.J. Visscher et al. (eds.), Information Technology in Educational Management, 137–160.
© 2001 *Kluwer Academic Publishers. Printed in the Netherlands.*

Nevertheless it is to be foreseen that education and the educational environment will change, because of the mere fact that society is changing. Information and Communication Technology (ICT) will at least support these changes but more likely will act as a catalyst.

If schools are to become more effective institutions in the information age, they should perhaps model themselves on the businesses and institutions which have successfully 're-engineered' themselves to take full opportunity of the potential created by the information society.

When the full potential of ICT is finally realised in schools, the traditional, 'one teacher to a class of thirty students/ nine to three-thirty/five days a week' system of operation might give way to a more flexible system where teachers are effectively learning consultants, planning and assessing individual and collaborative programmes of learning for students, both in and out of school, involving the use of learning associates and learning assistants. These ICT-rich environments would be open from early morning till late at night, seven days a week, serving the learning needs of the community, staffed by a range of education professionals. Schools will progressively evolve and become the hubs of learning networks, effectively neighbourhood learning centres, providing learning facilities and support for learners of all ages.

In this potential scenario, the present hierarchical management structures within schools will need to alter to serve the learning needs of twenty-first century students. Leadership will need to be distributed throughout the school, and each school will need to become more of a 'learning organisation' than present structural conditions permit or encourage. More control will be placed in the hands of the learner, with consequences for the roles of the staff who support the learning activities (Long, 2000).

The learning process will be more student centred and less teacher centred. In essence this change is about responsibility. In a traditional paradigm the teacher is bound to his or her curriculum. He chooses the learning environment (book, working guide, practical tools), he plans the teaching process so that *he* finishes the book in the available time. He monitors the pupils' achievements and helps them to complete their exercises. Finally he designs the test and gives the pupils their grades.

In the new paradigm pupils are given the main responsibility for their own learning processes which will eventually become an activity under full control and responsibility of the pupils. An example of this is illustrated by Hogenbirk (2001):

"Alice Springfield goes to the computer in the working room at home. She connects to the national educational network and logs in on the network of her school. She gives her password and the computer reacts friendly: he recognises her! A message appears: *There will be no History class tomorrow; instead there will be an opportunity to attend the study class in the Open Learning Centre. Mr. Gore will be available for assistance.*

Alice goes to *Planning* and changes the date for delivering the history project results. She confirms to Mr. Gore that she will attend the study class. She is delighted because Mr Gore is also her mentor. For the English course she marks assignments 3 to 11 from chapter 12 as *done*. Then she passes through the rest of her planning. For Mathematics a message from Miss Maple appears: *Could she do her test on chapter 3 next Thursday in room 3-12?* Alice types: *Ok.*

She mails one question on break-even-points for Mr Hardman of economics. For French she makes a reservation in the Language Lab.

She then quits *Planning* and goes to *Testing* to make a pre-test for Mathematics on chapter 3. She performs the test quite well, but one item is wrongly answered; she will ask Miss Maple tomorrow for more explanation. After one and a half hours of working Alice is ready. She prints her weekly agenda and goes to the chat room to see if her friends are ready as well."

This scenario represents a much less clearly defined distinction between the roles of teacher, guide, expert and learner. It also seems likely that there will be a dispersion of the educative function, with telecommunications and computer technology ensuring that much learning, which currently occurs in schools or in institutions of higher education, will occur at home and in the workplace. Computer networks will make all intellectual resources available at any place at any time. The basics of education will be expanded to include problem-solving, creativity and a capacity for life-long learning and re-learning. This suggests that the school of the 21st century may look very different as an organisation to that of the 20th century. The image of the ladder of grades with students climbing upward and leaving on reaching a particular age may no longer apply. It is possible that a learning community will be envisaged with its youngest children entering the centre, then moving outward as they grow through a series of concentric circles, with parents, teachers, and other adults ringed around them, and with lines of interactive electronic communication linking all from the centre of these circles out to the full range of cultural institutions and specialized resources of the society. If this were to be the case, the SIS of the 21st century will need to be completely reassessed to accommodate these changes.

3.   THE CHANGING FACE OF EDUCATIONAL MANAGEMENT AND ORGANISATION

In the 21st century productivity demands on educational management will increase. In reacting to the productivity imperative, schools and educational management will have to improve their organisation's primary function and process of teaching & learning. Increased efficiency will be demanded in:

*   Managing resources, including human resources;
*   Managing the curriculum;
*   Managing the learning progress of students, or 'learning management', viz. individualized learning (e.g., e-portfolios, smart cards).

The requirement for accountability will increase. Schools will need an in-built quality assurance mechanism aiming at continual improvement through school-based self-evaluation (equivalent to school-based action research) and proactive initiatives. A good SIS would be expected to assist schools in such cyclic activities of data collection, data analysis and interpretation to generate 'intelligence' (school management information'), for action planning, implementation, monitoring, and evaluation. The SIS will also be expected to assist in wide information sharing, to fulfil growing accountability requirements, in appropriate formats and access levels to interested parties such as students, teachers, parents and Government.

The wider demands of the community will become an imperative influence on educational management. The role of SISs in supporting the development of professional learning communities, both within and across schools (e.g., Teacher Support Systems), staff development online, global collaborations on the internet and cross-cultural exchange will all become commonplace (Fung, 2001). In a changing social climate schools will need to understand who their clients are and how they learn best so they can be effectively served. They must develop a vision that is shared by all members of the learning organisation and a plan that is the action to achieve the vision. They will have to gather and analyse multiple measures of data in order to replace hunches and hypotheses about how the school operates with facts to make informed decisions. They must then study the results they are getting to understand what they need to change to get different results and study new approaches to meeting their students' needs. They will need to plan for partnerships with parents, business, and communities, to help with student attainment of essential learning, to align all aspects of their learning organisations in order to attain and maintain systemic reform; and to achieve student learning increases. Public pressure is continuously being exerted to improve all aspects of the learning organisation on an on-going basis.

Wholeben (2001) proposes that education managers will have to see the focal nexus between the three levels of functioning in the school: academic, administrative, and auxiliary. In this proposal, teachers see SIS as a magic remedy for ineffective teaching in the form of computer-assisted (CAI) and computer-managed (CMI) instruction. Administrators view SIS similarly as a way to mechanize what is seen as the drudgery of educational management. Staff responsible for auxiliary services (facility maintenance, supply and material logistics and transportation), accept SIS as a way to increase available time for other hands-on endeavours. Trust for, and understanding of, technological, data-oriented support systems must be overcome through resource capability and machinery availability. For the true, lasting investiture of computerized SIS in education, SIS must *first* be viewed not as a substitute for manual functioning, rather as a catalyst for augmenting, supplementing, and enhancing what might otherwise not be possible manually. Secondly, SIS must be viewed as a triangulated relationship between each of academics (teaching), administration (supervising), and auxiliary (logistical) services. SIS will only reach its potential by linking each of these three points of responsibility. Thirdly, a successful SIS must be a collaborative effort between provider and user for both trust and understanding to occur (Wholeben, 2001).

The future development of educational management theory and practice is profoundly influenced by the global context within which they occur. Commentators agree that the effects of global forces are not simple and unmediated, but are affected by nation state interventions into economic affairs, the social lives of citizens, and the educational institutions of these states. This means that educational managers can expect to be more, rather than less, directed by national legislation, and that the strategies and policies devised at national level, primarily aimed at providing a national advantage within a global market, may mean that schools and educational institutions will be expected to follow increasingly nationalistic rather than global paths. Indeed it is true that across much of the westernised world, various pressures have transformed the context of public education and educational administration. The changing world economy, declining confidence in the welfare state, and adverse social trends have generated strong pressures for change in education systems, and for nothing less than a paradigm shift in educational management. Together, these social forces have produced three interconnected imperatives for educational administrators: a productivity imperative, an accountability imperative, and a community imperative. Efforts to respond to these imperatives generate tensions between competing paradigms in educational management. We can predict from current trends that there will be a powerful but sharply focused role for central authorities, especially in respect to formulating goals, setting priorities, and building frameworks for accountability in education. National and global considerations will become increasingly important, especially in respect to curriculum and an education system that is responsive to national needs within a global economy. Within centrally determined frameworks, government (public) schools will become largely self-managing, and distinctions between government and non-government (private) schools will narrow.

Taylor (2001) informs us that, in his experience, the techniques of management in education have always lagged behind industry. A very clear example of this is in the field of operations research or management science. Nearly all MBA students for the past two decades have received at least one course in quantitative analysis wherein they become at least familiar, if not adept, at applying the tools of operations research to their future work. But a similar pattern has not been seen in the education of future educational adminstrators. In fact, most educational administrators with doctoral degrees have never even heard of linear programming optimizations, stochastic processes, network models, or even the relatively simple planning tools that have long been commonplace in business and industry.

Operations research as an academic discipline involves the creation and use of mathematical models for the purpose of assisting decision-making. Although each title has its own nuances for professional operations researchers, the field is sometimes known as Management Science, Decision Science, Operations Management, or Management Operations. Until very recently, it made few inroads into public and health administration, but that is quickly changing. Public managers, and especially educational administrators, appear to be among the last to study and consider the powerful advantages of operations research technologies.

Within the public sector, managers are attempting to cope with diminishing resources and, often, with diminishing institutional performance. The few resources they do control are under pressure from multiple, competing demands. Their decisions are fraught with risk and uncertainty. They adopt policies without the benefit of adequate analysis. If any organizations ever needed the tools of modern management science, public institutions, including schools, are top contenders.

When one speaks of this need to operations research professionals, their initial response is usually that they see little connection between operations research and education. Operations research experts, who have any interest at all in messy applications, seem to see the running of public schools as a singularly unsophisticated matter, and the training of educators in our institutions of higher education as a still more unsophisticated matter. Educators, they reason, do not have the mathematical background or the skills in computer usage requisite for learning operations research or for making good use of it. MBA students, maybe; engineers, certainly; but not elementary and secondary school principals or superintendents of public school systems.

There are at least three current sets of conditions that will help to bring operations research to the forefront of management technology in education:

- The advent of friendly microcomputer software, and textbooks that have a more modest mathematical orientation, it is possible to give graduate students and practitioners of educational administration a sound appreciation of operations research in graphic and intuitive forms.
- There are obvious applications of operations research to the public sector that simply parallel the applications already fully developed for management in general: capital budgeting, purchasing, inventory management, and so on.
- There are specialized applications to public management which are not so obvious but which, if undertaken, could be of enormous benefit to public institutions and of considerable intellectual interest to operations research professionals.

It is no secret that the field of operations research is changing rapidly, becoming much more sophisticated on its frontier, and at the same time, becoming more available and less abstruse at its core. The proliferation of MBA programs, the competition for students (not all of whom are well-schooled in the mathematics), and thus the market for texts and software that are modest in rigor, have provided a means and an opportunity to advance the use of operations research in a broad spectrum of management-oriented disciplines, including education.

By 1992, several inexpensive micro software packages arrived on the market. By 1997, all but the most specialized routines were readily available for the desktop computer. As a result there is increased accessibility to operations research and its fundamental operations are rapidly becoming less recondite. Notwithstanding the concerns of some operations research professionals who believe that a little knowledge is a dangerous thing, the accessibility and demystifying of operations research holds great promise for the work of educational administrators.

A specific example of this is how desktop cartography and linear programming can come to the aid of school management at a district level is in an attempt to attain racial balance within their individual schools. By dividing the district into a large number of small geographical planning segments, each containing about 50-100 students, an optimal boundary can be found which minimizes transportation while meeting such constraints as building capacity and racial balance. Working from the student information management record, the address of each student is converted into a geographic coordinate. (If the district has a transportation management system with route optimisation, the address coordinates may already be available.) Each polygon defined by roads over which school buses can pass is a candidate for becoming a planning segment. They stand alone as planning segments if they have at least 50 students, otherwise they are combined with adjacent segments until such a size is reached. Distances from the centroid of each segment to each school are calculated, and a zero-one linear programming model makes the optimal assignment of segments to schools. A great deal of the tedium of this work can be reduced by a quality cartography program which is capable of finding the segment centroids and the rectilinear, or over-the-road, distances from each segment to each school and which can produce attractive maps.

Other possible examples of the Operations Research/Education partnership are: the distribution of merit pay (linear programming), the analysis of impending teacher shortages (Markov analysis), optimal sequence of teachers for a given group of children (dynamic programming), enrolment projections (with an empirical gradient search for optimal parameters), numerous multiple objective and goal programming problems, comparative dropout studies (absorbing Markov analysis) and policy analyses (Bayesian rules, simulation). These and other important problems are awaiting a stronger partnership between operations research and education (Taylor, 2001). Such a partnership will, in time, contribute more widely to education management.

Tatnall (2001) suggests that there will be limitations to the process of change despite the fact that using new management techniques and theories in education will be inevitable in the future as the demands on the education systems change and become more sophisticated. Changes in the organisational arrangements within a school, between it and other schools, and between it and the central education authority are likely to have an effect on whether the school sees any advantage in making use of IT in educational management. Such change may also determine how IT is used. If current organisational arrangements do not favour the use of technology, then organisational change will be needed before its use becomes significant.

Within a given school the construction of a new building, for example, might make the use of a particular kind of computer network attractive, and another type impossible to use. The creation of a new teaching department might produce a need for improved data storage, and hence require different technology to that currently used. Even the gain, or loss, of a teacher experienced in the use of IT may be significant. In the wider education community, management aspects of organisational changes such as new reporting structures, changes in assessment regimes, changes in Government regulations and additional funds (or new funding constraints) will also affect how schools use information technology in administration and management. In one example a Government crackdown on truancy might make computer-based student attendance systems more important for schools to install. In another example, changes in the way that an education authority handles student assessment and university entrance requirements may force the use of student records databases (Tatnall, 2001).

4. IMPACT OF EMERGING TECHNOLOGIES

A great deal of research has been done on how innovation occurs, and a large body of theory exists on how and why technological innovations are adopted (Latour, 1986; Rogers, 1995; Vidgen & McMaster, 1996; Tatnall, 2000). It is clear from this research that just because it becomes available does not mean that a particular item of technology will be used (Franklin, 1990). There are many examples of technology that has not been adopted because people, at the time, could not relate to it or see any useful place for it.

Bearing this in mind, the future of ITEM will be coloured by two emerging enabling technologies. First there is the emergence of unfettered communication made possible by common platforms such as the web, by communication lines such as the internet and WAP and by increases in computing power that make normal media such as video available as a computer delivered tool. Secondly there is the development of techniques for organisation of data and the algorithms to support these techniques that allow manipulation, storage and searching of complex, unstructured data sets and provide possibilities for machine learning. These technologies will be used in the context of a seamless environment in education satisfying the demands of school administration and management and teaching and learning processes.

Let us examine some of these technologies and consider some ITEM based examples of where their use would be appropriate. The existence of platform independent communication means that data can now be gathered and information distributed between any two points within an educational environment. We do not know what the classroom of the future will look like. We can be sure it will be one involving flexible delivery of learning experiences. We can be sure that programs, will be temporally and geographically distributed and that SIS developers will be required to provide management of a far more complex interaction between learners and the system. Distributed systems will be able to provide a detail in captured data greater than that currently underlying SISs. Systems originally based on data being paper based then retyped should be on the way out. SIS developers have the communication technology to capture data as directly as a supermarket reads bar codes for each grocery item sold. However, the SIS developer can no longer assume that all education transactions will take place in a large brick education supermarket. The challenge is to use the technology effectively to encourage a wider information use in education decisions.

More important than the ability to move information to the parts of an educational system is the ability to create new types of information. We can see from industry and commerce that the richness of information and the meta-nature of the information being used has developed to a new level. One can consider the type of information retrieved from a relational database as being flat, historic and summative. The information required to manage future educational systems must find new patterns within the inputs, deliver timely information in advance of problems occurring and provide direct support for the learning process itself. Fields such as expert systems, artificial intelligence and natural language processing have emerged as useful technologies within many industries and examples are available that have obvious relevance to the SIS developer.

Let us take a simple example: How does the educational manager of the future allow for changing needs? A simple algorithm that compares birth rates and population movements with building capacity is not going to be sufficient in a society that expects to have course development lead times in weeks, that can access educational offerings on a global basis and has telecommuting as part of the breadwinner's everyday lifestyle. We would expect the SIS to be aware of a wide range of inputs. This would include behaviours and expectations of the current school population, but would also include constant monitoring of the press (in whatever form that becomes), industry trends for educational requirements of school leavers, and educational research outputs. One could hypothesise a SIS conceptually starting with a software agent constantly monitoring a range of sources and returning filtered information on emerging requirements for the education system. The educational manager would then be aware, not only of the detailed progress of current students, but of the possible future pressures on the educational system. The technologies for this type of planning are available now and being used in other industries for forward planning (Taylor, 2001). Taylor et al. (1997) describe how the technology associated with virtual organisations and their intellectual agents could impinge on education institutions in the future, making the need for a physical presence, such as large buildings, redundant and financially obsolete.

The WWW makes possible new types of content and new means of publishing, distribution, and learning. It gives the ability for authors to create their own content and publish themselves on the Web, and the ability for publishers to update their content as well as to package and distribute information in new ways. The resources will continue to grow as the internet is increasingly seen as an ideal publishing medium for references, instructional materials, and thin-market material. Filters, guides, knowbots, and automated accountants will make finding and selecting appropriate materials easier while controlling costs. This has clear implications on the dissemination of information from central sources that impact upon schools administration and makes a centralised 'chain of command' much easier to manage. Increasingly also, educational material will appear first in electronic form and the legal implications to access this data will need to be considered nationally and internationally as international awareness of the issues of exploitation grow. The strategic development of national data resources such as the Distributed National Electronic Resource in the UK is already becoming established (JISC UK, 2000).

The deployment of higher speed networks is integral to such developments and to further more complex information sharing scenarios. In the US for example, large-scale multi-user virtual reality systems are being developed which can be shared between organisations to allow simulations of complex many person events. The capacity to support major multiple transmissions of quality video and sound will be taken up with increasing rapidity in the education field. This will require more bandwidth, extra resilience, and a co-ordinated approach from the Research Councils in all participating countries together with local infrastructure work. The ability to redirect peak bandwidth to specific sites for short periods of time is also required.

   Virtual reality rendering through laser precision, virtual optical rendering (VOR) will provide the vehicle for students to explore geographic locations in their own classroom. Students could walk through a pyramid's catacomb passages, experience the gladiatorial games of ancient Rome in the Coliseum, or simulate physical science experiments that would otherwise be too expensive or dangerous outside of virtual reality. Student applicants in higher education could visit the various campuses of their choice. Upcoming graduates could practice interviewing skills in a progressively more difficult interview setting with several alternative strategies. Such learning environments will provide their own measures of student competence and achievement which SISs will have to capture as part of the student learning profile.

   Artificial intelligence paradigm (AIP) provides a regenerative programming context to fit the individual development cycles of a particular user. As the user makes certain choices within a particular episode, AIP begins to model that user's choices as trends, and thus present settings that are adaptive to that particular user's needs, capabilities, and potential. For example, as a staff member makes certain choices associated with in-service training activities, AIP would develop a progressively more difficult, but achievable, set of goals for the user to attempt. AIP provides the best approach for insuring individual progress based upon performance testing. A likely outcome of AIP is the redesign of the traditional management information system (MIS) into alternatives' assessment and priority selection protocol. Instead of the MIS simply providing information from which an administrator may make a decision, a decision support system (DSS) would take the MIS output, analyse it according to various needs and AIP history, and provide a priority listing of usable alternatives to select a workable solution. DSS provides a reasonable solution when multiple alternatives exist, and a mix of such alternatives would likely provide the optimal approach to problem solving. This might appear rather futuristic to many readers but much of what we now do was futuristic to readers not many years ago.

   Digital service links (DSL) are the latest marriage between digital technology and common household appliances (television, radio, personal computer). DSL provide the best opportunity for distance learning, using the pre-existing family television with an inexpensive keyboard. With direct ROM storage capabilities, DSL could eventually insure continuous, uninterrupted learning, regardless of illness, weather, or disciplinary status.

   In order to understand how these developments can and should influence the future education environments, we must look at the needs that exist and how the design and implementation of computerized school information systems will answer these needs. As the number of these innovations is large, we will concentrate here mainly on the latest, i.e., the internet. In other words, what are the advantages of using new technologies, and especially, the latest addition, the internet?

   The main advantages of distance learning over the web are the 'from and to' any place, at any time attributes. Often, the free education aspect also appears, although much of the educational software offered today is not free, and many educational institutions offer (distance) learning programmes at a price.

Plain, text-based course materials are not enough anymore. The recent increases in bandwidth have provided new modes of electronic communication, images on the internet are commonplace, sound tracks and videos are used more frequently and other multimedia types such as animation have evolved. Based on learner modelling adapting teaching strategies and (intelligent) user adaptation, Intelligent Tutoring Systems are being developed (Paiva, 1996; Woods & Warren, 1996). More recently the field of adaptive hypermedia has emerged at the crossroads of hypermedia and user modelling (De Bra et al., 1999). This employs adaptive presentation of the educational, management and administration material and implies providing prerequisite, additional or comparative explanations, conditional inclusion of fragments, stretch-text, providing explanation variants and reordering information. Adaptive navigation support is also integral in this concept and can imply a combination of links manipulation including annotation, hiding, disabling, removal and map adaptation (Brusilovsky, 1996).

An important issue is that the imitation of the typical classroom is not always desirable for computerized educational systems, as was initially thought. This imitation tendency will disappear in time. At the present development state of the distance education environments it may help in the transition process towards Web-based education. As many researchers note (for example, Synnes et al., 1999), it makes no sense to try to recreate the classical education process, which might just lead to bad results due to the fact that it would be an incomplete copy. A better approach is to try to make use of the advantages that the new environment brings. Specific advantages over classical classroom teaching are lack of time limitation and the possibility of (guided) learning in an asynchronous mode. Moreover, a teacher has to speak so that most students understand what is being said, producing a tendency to always address the average pupil. Addressing each student separately is, of course, better tailored to the student's needs, but in a classroom situation this can result in idle periods for the other students. Therefore, adaptive, customized teaching environments can become superior to the standard classroom method. Use of the wide range of media can also enhance the human aspect of the course contents, smoothing the transfer from face-to-face teaching and learning to learning in front of the computer. A classical teaching environment leads to 'learning by memorizing' teaching strategy. Interactive learning environments can provide a modality of externalised knowledge-acquisition and knowledge-sharing, via the communication process, and support learning methods such as 'learning by asking', 'learning by showing', 'learning by observing', 'learning by exploring' and 'learning by teaching/explaining'. Among the possible learning advantages supported and promoted by the modern educational system will be meta-cognition and distributed cognition, such as reflective thinking and self-monitoring.

Although many internet based solutions have already been built and although their real potential is much larger than presently seen, their actual implementation and smooth functioning in the classroom is not so easy. When trying to implement such systems for use in the classroom, most of the time is spent building the infrastructure of computer and network hardware and software, laboratory and classroom renovation, supporting personnel, repair and maintenance and training the teachers and students to use the new technologies. Very little time is spent on developing new pedagogical styles and even less time on the automatic collection of performance data to inform management systems.

Computer scientists now have to explore how to contribute to the new developments from the system developer's point of view. For the information accessible via this infrastructure to be useful and to be transformed into knowledge, large databases and the tools for managing them must be developed. Knowledge management plays an important role in handling not only raw data but also different levels of meta data. System developers should try to combine adaptive technologies, especially user modelling and collaborative technologies, to allow users to communicate, learn and work together in a networked environment. They should have at their disposal large databases of educational cases from which to draw conclusions. They should also have automatic helpers to assist them in their choices (Okamoto, 2001). This view of the future is very close to that expounded by Taylor et al (1997) when describing virtual organisations and their use of intellectual agents.

Some general trends are already emerging in technology developments. For example, centralised batch processing using mainframe computers, with slow turn-around time are being superseded by decentralised, distributed data processing using microcomputers and LANs and centralised *and* distributed processing using Web-based technology and the internet. The vision is one using the ASP (Application Services Provider) model where a portal (at a 'Data-Centre') will provide SIS service applications for member schools. School users need only be equipped with an internet-connected browser to interact with the portal SIS. The portal server will do most of the processing, with some data processing delegated to the user's PC. The cost-benefits of this scenario, in terms of savings in hardware, maintenance on the part of users, and training and support make it a very attractive proposition. Such a portal was launched in December 2000 in Hong Kong providing schools with a few application services at this embryonic stage. Plans are being made to add on other functions and applications such as school self-evaluation tools for managerial decision-making support in the future. Other administrative record-keeping functions will be incorporated when required (Fung, 2000).

Other technologies that will be employed in school information systems as in other management systems in the near future are Smart Objects that explain their own functioning and help to create "articulate" educational environments. Information infrastructures provide access to experts, interlinked archival resources, distributed investigations, and virtual communities and through illusion, Shared Synthetic Environments aid better understanding and appreciating reality. Personal digital assistants (PDAs) will become a popular class of computers configured as network clients to overcome their inherent limitations. This means that the entire content of the networked world could be in every manager, administrator, teacher and students hand, with implications that go far. Generally, improvements in client software and applets will cause networking to become highly interactive and responsive. This will give users easy access to inquiry tools such as spreadsheets, graphics, symbolic processors, and all kinds of simulations. Scaffolding applications will help beginning users organise their inquiries. Collaborative working will take many forms and will allow sharing of information over the network. This will grow to include worldwide collaboration in education communities and allow SIS developers access to ever more data and provide management information that is increasingly timely and relevant to the education and planning processes.

Data storage capacity and PC hard-disk capacities will continue to increase while their prices reduce. This greatly increased data storage capacity means that huge amounts of data can now be retained, and so *will be* retained. What is more, most of the administrative data that a school needs can be stored 'on-line' on a normal PC hard disk in a format ready to use: the average PC hard disk has the capacity to store all of a typical school's student records data for the last ten years or more. This large data storage capacity opens the possibility of data warehousing and data mining for student records, and other data at the local school level. Data mining software can be used to look for patterns in student data and, what is more, the software can look for patterns that we do not suspect exist and have not yet considered. This offers important information for decision support for school-level managers. The technologies of data warehousing and data mining are growing in importance in business IT and are likely to become more important in future schools.

In almost every application, when compared to the software in existence ten years ago, today's software is much improved: it is easier to use, more powerful and has more features. This is also true for educational administration and management software. A factor that is likely to lead to further improvement is the greater level of professionalism apparent in design as more and more is now being developed by people who understand schools and how they operate. This has not always been the case in the past. Improvements in database software also mean that schools will be less reliant on pre-designed reports, providing enhance information selection and focus.

At present it is quite difficult for a teacher to access student data outside of the school when they are involved in activities such as excursions and sports meetings. The lower prices of technology such as laptop computers, personal digital assistants such as palm pilots and WAP-enabled mobile phones mean that it is increasingly possible for a teacher on an excursion to quickly access details of a student's home phone number, or possibly even medical information, in the event of an emergency.

In the face of rapidly changing technology Taylor points out that one problem with the power of modern technologies is the power of modern technologies. The timeframe of power increase means that most senior administrators in education have almost no formal training in information theory. Modern tools have been developed that have front ends that are predicated on ease of use and intuitive design that makes it possible for an educator to easily create an application that returns growing amounts of inconsistent and incorrect information. This is then used to inform the management process. It is vital that these information workers are made aware of the fundamentals of information processing and the onus must fall on the SIS developer to accommodate these shortfalls of end users to be dealt with by the system employed (Taylor, 2001).

The new messages these new technologies and media make possible can dramatically improve institutional (and instructional) outcomes in the 21st century school, but to successfully embrace such an evolution of education practice depends on careful design of the interface between learning communities and tools of institutional management.

5. THE FUTURE FROM NATIONAL PERSPECTIVES

The national government in developed countries directly controls (to a greater or lesser extent), the education system of the nation. The national policies concerning education and the future of the education system must therefore form the basis of any development in its schools management and administration systems. A sample of the most developed countries in terms of SISs have surprisingly convergent perspectives on education development directions which presumably is prompted by current trends towards globalisation. For example the views of the UK government on educational management requirements are characteristic of those in the majority of other westernised countries. The UK government is committed to taking advantage of the electronic age. Initiatives cover the full range of government activity - the aim is to enable the 'e-citizen' to become a reality well before 2010. The UK Department for Education and Employment Information Management Strategy for schools sets out some immediate targets for education management including the easy and transparent exchange of information between schools, local authorities and government. Electronic data transfer will be normal and natural. It is clear that systems will change rapidly during the next few years. The challenge is to focus divergent developments on areas where they can make a real difference to pupils' education. Management systems are not important in themselves - they are tools in a much larger picture. Their use will only be successful if it supports the national agenda in delivering improved education standards. The overall performance of a school, or of a national year-group, may be recorded on information management systems and processed or presented in a variety of ways. The statistics will show rising or falling standards, which will trigger different responses, but, to be effective, these responses will have to influence the learning of individual pupils. Statistics can inform those outside of the process and information can provide cues for positive intervention on the part of the teacher, but the teaching and learning environment needs something more.

One immediate way in which information management systems will help is in reducing the amount of time pupils 'waste' in the education system. Pupils characteristically 'lose time' when transferring between schools, largely due to a lack of information in the receiving school, causing incoming pupils to be treated as 'blank slates' until they have proved otherwise. In the future learning information, which will include specific results from detailed learning activities, will be transferred between schools and colleges with each student. It will be integrated into the receiving system to provide an immediate and accurate basis for progression. This loss of opportunity and lack of progress also occurs in conventional school environments where pupils often make poor use of their time. They are frequently frustrated, either because they are obliged to progress too slowly or because they need more time to assimilate the subject matter. Information management can make a difference, indeed the only difference that ultimately matters, if it becomes learning management and embraces the direction and support of pupils' educational experiences. There are significant academic gains to be made if the learning can be interactively managed so that the work is genuinely tailored to pupils' needs.

This learning management, at pupil level, will require new generations of hardware and software. Education needs to be proactive in specifying new systems requirements rather than accepting, as given, the current market direction. Pupils should have individual access to robust, user-friendly, input/output devices, which are linked to school and wider networks. These should be considered in terms much wider than keyboards and screens and must include a full range of tools maximising pupil involvement and meeting the changing needs of pupils at different stages of education development. Future software should utilise concepts and research findings from a wide range of sources. Years of educational research, and many more years of teachers' experience, is unused because there have, until now, been no effective ways of putting this experience to use. Educational software designers must have the capacity to access, learn from and incorporate this knowledge and expertise to maximise information feedback rather than data feedback to the teacher rather than, as at present, reproduce old systems in electronic form (Whitehead, 2000).

Education has traditionally been regarded in the United States as the concern of local authorities and the Constitution does not confer any responsibility for education upon the Federal Government. However, a different approach has started to emerge in the last few years and government has begun systematically laying down minimum standards and common objectives for all schools thus creating a general frame of reference. These guidelines set down methods of monitoring and investigation that will have to be incorporated into school administration and management systems. The government suggests that all education systems will in the future seek compromises between the need for nationwide definition of objectives and the need to leave scope for the local level initiative. The greater scope left for local initiative, the greater will be the need to define a flexible frame of reference within which that initiative operates. Only a reorganisation involving differentiation of practices and the introduction of new learning and management tools will make it possible to successfully deal with these changes. (Delacote, 1998).

The social environment for education in Japan has changed substantially in moving towards and into the 21st century. Diverse and new views of values and civilization will be demanded in order to create a truly affluent future for humanity and to encourage harmonious development of science, humankind, society and the environment. Educationalists, whose intellectual activities play an important role in efforts to lead the development of society, will need to consider not only the quantity of knowledge but also the comprehensive "intelligence" from various points of view. Education will be urged to advance its structural reform to further strengthen intellectual activities in preparation for the new era of "intelligence" restructuring. These national issues will need to be taken into account by SIS developers who must accommodate the reforms in their system development in order to meet the social expectations in the early 21st century. It will be necessary to further promote education reform on the basis of the progress made in the last decade. To meet the social expectation and needs, institutions of education as a whole will need to promote diversification and individualization based upon their autonomy, in order to secure the ultimate quality of graduates, enhance international currency and commonality and recognise the institutions' social responsibility.

In Finland the new national information strategy (SITRA, 1998) outlines the changes in the national operational environment and the overall development of the Finnish information society. Finland is progressing towards a knowledge-based society. In the information society, knowledge forms the foundation for education and culture and constitutes the single most important production factor. Information and communications technology significantly promotes interaction and exchange between individuals, business enterprises, and other organisations, the utilisation of information and the provision of services and access to them. The rapid development of information and communication technologies and new media such as mobile communicators, electronic books, and digital radio and television create new tools to incorporate into SIS for the ever diversifying educational needs of the population. Traditional media will also continue to be important. Finland considers itself to be one of the leading countries in information society development, providing a fruitful experimental field for technological, social, cultural and pedagogical innovations. Therefore the Ministry of Education intend to improve its strategic lead in the development of the SIS and curricula IT fields and co-ordinate its projects in accordance with the national strategy. Finland's abundance of information technology hardware, its leading position in terms of internet connections and mobile phones, and the relatively free competition in the telecommunication market coupled with reasonably priced telecommunication connections are strengths that will assist in this process. Finland's position has been further reinforced by economic and political integration with the European Union.

The Finnish Government is aware that the weakness of information society development is the fact that it is focused on technology rather than people. An overemphasis on technological solutions threatens to overpower immediate social intercourse (SITRA, 1998). These kinds of views have only recently gained prominence, and the situation in Finland is no exception. There are several problems, ranging from poor work ergonomy to anxiety triggered by the flood of information and all must be dealt with in the future.

6.   THE INTERNATIONAL PERSPECTIVE

The international perspective produces additional pressure at national level for enhanced educational standards. This will in turn produce the need for better information to set targets, assess improvements and ensure accountability. Future SISs will be expected to support this pressure for continual improvement. For national economies to compete in the global marketplace, the imperative for the twenty-first century is therefore to educate the majority of its citizens to a high enough level to participate successfully in the information economy. Human capital is the new currency of the world economy, and this places an enormous burden on schools to deliver to international as well as national community objectives. This was discussed in some detail at the G8 Summit in 1999 where Heads of State and

Government of eight major democracies and the President of the European Commission exchanged ideas and forward-looking solutions to the challenges of the future in many areas facing their nations and the international community (G8 Communiqué, 1999). Education was high on their agenda. They determined that flexibility and change, more than ever, would define the new century and there would be a demand for mobility. While today, a passport and a ticket allow people to travel anywhere in the world, in the future, the alternative mobility will be education and lifelong learning based on electronic communication. The first factor to be taken into account is globalisation. This is a complex process involving rapid and increasing flows of ideas, capital, technology, goods and services around the world and has already brought profound change to our societies. It has cast us together as never before. The view of the G8 Heads of State was that greater openness and dynamism have contributed to the widespread improvement of living standards and a significant reduction in poverty. Integration has helped to create jobs by stimulating efficiency, opportunity and growth. The information revolution and greater exposure to each other's cultures and values have strengthened the democratic impulse and the fight for human rights and fundamental freedoms while spurring creativity and innovation. At the same time, however, globalisation has been accompanied by a greater risk of dislocation and financial uncertainty for some workers, families and communities across the world. The challenge they concluded is to seize the opportunities globalisation affords while addressing its risks to respond to concerns about a lack of control over its effects.

Basic education, vocational training, academic qualifications, lifelong upgrading of skills and knowledge for the labour market, and support for the development of innovative thinking are considered essential to shape economic and technical progress as society moves towards a knowledge-based society. They also enrich individuals and foster civic responsibility and social inclusion. To this end, G8 supported an increase in exchanges of teachers, administrators and students among the nations of the Eight and with other nations and invited their experts to identify the main obstacles to increased exchanges and to come forward with appropriate proposals before the next Summit. They called upon the United Nations Educational, Scientific and Cultural Organization (UNESCO) to study how different countries were attempting to raise education standards, for example, by looking at best practices in the recruitment, training, compensation and accountability of the teaching profession internationally. The G8 also committed themselves to explore jointly ways to work together and through international institutions to help our own countries as well as developing nations use technology to address learning and development needs, for example, through distance learning (G8 Communiqué, 1999).

As a result of their study UNESCO acknowledged that there was a worldwide resurgence of interest in education concurrent with a trend towards politicisation of education and school management. They concluded that it was seen as the gateway to future economic prosperity and the chosen instrument for combating unemployment. In most countries the pressure for change emanated from people seeking to enhance the contribution of education to employment and the economy. These arguments are given new weight by economic imperative and the extent and urgency with which educational reform is politically advocated to respond to this imperative. This politicisation is amplified in many countries by reduction in government funding and by pressure for accountability in the use of resources available to education. Demands for accountability are not limited to governments; they also emanate from parents, employers and other pressure groups. This in turn has led to a weakening of the social consensus on educational objectives as different groups in society strive to see their viewpoint prevail – eventually through the political process – in what concerns not only the allocation of resources to different sectors of education but also the structure of education systems, the organisation of the school and even the curricula and the teaching methods, matters over which educationalists traditionally in the twentieth century held a monopoly (Carnoy, 2000).

7. SOFTWARE VENDORS' VIEWS OF THE FUTURE

The developers and vendors of software provide another perspective of the future SIS. Three major SIS software vendors have contributed their concepts and proposals for their system developments in the 21st century, two from the UK and one from New Zealand.

SIMS is the most widely used School Administration and Management software in England (see chapter 2). The company feels that internet is the future for communication and data transfer. A web based front-end will be particularly important in allowing parental access to children's data over the internet from home internet connectivity devices ranging from PC's to television top boxes. They intend to develop remote working particularly for examination and assessment and teachers will also be able to do the majority of their work on portables rather than on the networked system.

They predicted that within five years they will be using applications servers and server farms. Central processing power will be an efficient utilisation of resources that can be exploited more fully as data transmission rates and bandwidths increase. Pay per use systems are likely to flourish in this environment. They will use wireless technology in schools for data transmission and although the technology at present has some limitations, they think these will be resolved quite soon. Video transmission will become the norm when data transmission rates (currently at 11MB/sec) become available at 50MB/sec. In future emphasis will be put on value added functionality in system interaction and they feel that the integration of software modules is important. The current modular view of data in SIMS must change with no obviously modular interface in a few years time. Behind this, generic use of modules will be the preferred route of development. This will provide a backbone for a more flexible package.

Because of SIMS market position of near monopoly, to be seen promoting an open exchange with other software companies is particularly important to them. Published interfaces into which third parties can hook are being developed. SIMS then offers a validation service for the new software before implementation. It is hoped that a much more seamless environment will be achieved in this way particularly with MSOffice. SIMS is hampered in its software development by the necessity to comply with Government dictated school returns. The majority of its development efforts are devoted to this (SIMS, 2000).

West Country Business Systems (WCBS) supplies accounting and administration systems solely in the UK independent school sector. They view the future of the market in the light of schools making increasing use of information systems in the running of the school as a pastoral centre and as a business. All senior managers will have a PC workstation linked via a school wide network to the central administration server. Users will be allowed access to those areas of the central system that are pertinent to their role in the school. Information will be more readily available and will be shared amongst more users to give a better picture on any subject or issue. It is felt that the company's software and services will not impact directly on administration and management practices, but will respond to the demands of the users. As managers make more use of IT in their roles the demands for more information, more quickly and better processing will mean that the software products will develop in response to these new demands. Similarly new service offerings will be designed to help users get the best out of their administration systems.

WCBS identified three technologies for integration in the foreseeable future. The first is internet and email services. Users will be trained in using this technology and software will offer direct links. This will include the ability to email direct from administration records, using the address stored in the record. Routine reports, mailings and bills will be sent electronically. Parents will be able to access current performance information about their children via the school's website, which will allow controlled access to the administration system. Secondly, the use of video-conferencing using telecommunications systems, such as the Web will be used to improve communication between staff, parents and children – particularly in the boarding environment. The links required to establish this type of connection will be embedded in the administration system to make the process as quick and effective as possible. Thirdly WCBS software will be integrated with document management software so that any correspondence, including email, is attached to the pupil record in some way. This will mean that those in authority will be able to view and retrieve any relevant correspondence about a pupil that has taken place within the organisation or with any outside agent. Functionality will develop in two ways. The first will be specific software features requested by users or the market to enhance the systems use or to respond to changes in practice and legislation. The second will be an increasing need to integrate SIS software with Microsoft desktop utilities and their successors. They feel that these products will become the de facto standards for users and there will have to be a ready exchange of data between specialist software and them. It is believed that increased use of optical mark reader, smart card and Web technology for input and output will take place. WCBS software will work with these technologies to avoid multiple entries of data to several systems. There will be one central data store, which will use some or all of these technologies to update data held centrally and to provide it to users. Eventually all user sites will move to a school-wide central system, but it is possible that they may purchase specific functionality in certain areas, e.g., Exam processing from specialist suppliers. WCBS will develop core systems that can be integrated with additional modules from the same of other suppliers where a requirement exists.

WCBS add that the pace of change and uptake within the schools will be greatly influenced by budgetary resources and the ability to recruit and retain the level of IT staff and managers required to implement school-wide, central systems (WCBS, 2000).

In New Zealand, schools strongly value their individuality and independence and MUSAC SIS software development programme is intended to enhance their ability to 'do their own thing' while remaining within the bounds of the requirements of the Ministry. Over the past decade administration software has concentrated on simple functionality - the ability to print lists, to produce timetables and letters to students, to monitor attendance etc. Given that this functionality now exists and is relatively mature, the current move is strongly into the classroom, where teachers are now being provided with software to record student evaluations, to analyse them and to report on them - using a single data entry process. During the next decade, the functionality of this software will evolve as teachers decide on new requirements and new technologies become available. Easy to use software for administrators (particularly principals) to process simple but meaningful reports resulting from the analysis and integration of data relating to various aspects of the school will be developed. This information is then available for management decision-making. To date this information has been available in a variety of ways, some more complex than others, and none of them instantly available to the principal.

Internet access to relevant data will become standard in the near future, allowing administrators to modify data away from the school network. Parents (particularly of foreign students) will also, with suitable viewing rights, be able to access reports relating to their children. Email will become more pervasive. Email is currently used to transfer files to and from customers and agents.

MUSAC feel that they must move ahead at the speed of their customers. As schools work to very tight budgets, they attempt to ensure that they stay a couple of years behind the technology, allowing the enthusiasts among them to beta-test developments. However they will be exploiting new technologies as the need arises. Cordless networks will simplify the process of data management. Voice recognition is arriving in a usable form and, as schools obtain the facility to use it, they intend to incorporate suitable functionality into the software. They are certainly intending to continue their trend to make their software more and more intelligent. They anticipate that their software will become smarter at anticipating individual users needs and common practices as the demands on software continue to expand such as flexible scheduling. Fortunately, software development tools are also expanding their functionality at an amazing rate enabling SIS developers to keep up with the process. On one hand solid-state storage with the advent of 'disks with no moving parts' will become a reality. On the other hand with the advent of reliable telephonic communication between machines, the need for 'disks' will be substantially reduced and the internet will provide the standard method of software distribution (MUSAC, 2000).

In summary, a common feature of the software vendors who contributed to this chapter is their apparent tendency to be reactive rather than proactive in the technology marketplace at the start of the 21st century. They are in a unique position in the software development market because they operate in an environment where their clients need to respond to government initiatives which are not always easily predictable and which limit the flexibility of any development initiative they might otherwise have implemented. National standards are important but in a fast changing society even these goal posts are being continually moved.

8. THE USERS' VIEW

The education community has already assimilated many of the same ideas as the SIS experts who have contributed thus far to the chapter. They recognise the changes in society that are resulting in schools being run more like businesses. They are experiencing the requirement for increased accountability and the problems of excess data versus limited information. School headteachers and managers, when canvased for their views on their institutions in the future, describe them as changing and taking new directions in the future. They reported that previously the data processing staff in a school acted as conduits for information but were relatively unskilled people. Already there is too much data available and the processing required is too complicated for an unskilled person to deal with. In fact they suggested that to reliably discriminate and sift such a volume of data, intelligent data filtering software agents will be needed by the end-users of the information, particularly where the end users are teachers and their time is too important to be used unproductively.

They considered that community wide access to data was becoming more widely accepted with parents and students becoming more demanding. Consumer rights and data protection are two areas that would become increasingly important over the next decade. With ever increasing demands for accountability from schools, more and more data will be required from more and more external organisations. The formats in which the data will be required are diverse and increasing the school users workload. There is a growing realisation nationally that this flood of data can only be handled in common datasets, for example the Common Basic Data Set (CBDS) being developed in the UK (DFEE, 2000) but currently institutions are still being asked to provide data in many different formats. One user reported that his school had to supply budgetary information in four different formats for different levels of government, inspectors and funding bodies. All interviewees agreed that finances and returns had to be standardised to avoid this scenario. They suggested that all data processing software for school returns would have to be centrally produced in future to achieve this. Information rather than data will need to be transferred quickly and efficiently over national networks.

Schools are generally becoming more autonomous and self-governing. They will be run as independent businesses, so performance management assessment will need to be much more rigorous. In addition they will be constrained by government targets set against national and local data which will have to be met as part of their increased accountability. However, central standardisation will play an increasingly important role in this scenario. They felt that for an effective future education system, accountability must stay within the school and the management and administration systems, which have now become indispensable for running the institution, must reflect this.

9. AGENDA FOR THE FUTURE

Davey reminds us that the ancient fundamental of educational management of controlling the process of bringing students into the presence of talented teachers is not relevant to modern educational environments. Education has always been and now must be seen to be a meta process of managing the interactions between learners and learning experiences, wherever they take place. The technologies developed in other industries to handle the move to 'new economy industries' give education a foundation upon which it can build. The challenge is for SIS developers to see their industry outside the context of classrooms and incorporate the fundamentals of education within their theoretical view of the process of educational management (Davey, 2001).

From his experience in the field of education in Japan, Okamoto conjectures that the new millennium will be marked by a combined intelligent, media-oriented, distance-learning phenomenon. A vision of future educational environments is one of each student with his/her own learning site adapted to his/her needs. Collaborative sessions, proposed by the system or demanded by the user would occur when discussions, debates, exchange of information, are required in the learning process. The transition from the learning stage to the working stage should be gradual and smooth, with a return to relevant education whenever needed for instance when the job requirements change, when changing jobs, or simply for personal development. In such systems, rigid testing methods would be replaced with the evaluation of real practices, or practice simulations. The roles of the individuals in the community will change. Individual abilities and strengths will be identified and vocational training will be oriented towards all the roles that individuals will be expected to play in society. Teachers in this society are both producers of information contents, as well as designers of instructional programs that can then be adapted automatically to fit individual needs. Teachers will be guides in key positions in the information network, answering and directing students only when they, or the automatic guidance systems, fail to find the required information (Okamoto, 2001).

Knowledge management will become essential in school management with information collected and distributed for use by managers and teachers with minimal direct input by end users. There will be more emphasis on connecting, manipulating and storing data through the internet and government/corporate networks. It is clear that the availability and requirement for more and more data could create a culture drowning in information. To address this, information portals will be used to distribute data and facilitate knowledge management operations (Davydov, 2000). Information portals will be used as business intelligence portals, to connect users with the information they need; as collaborative processing portals, to connect users to both the necessary information and relevant co-workers; as mission management portals, to provide specialized content to enable teams to perform mission-critical management activities; and as extended services portals, to organize teams of channel partners, for example, managers, administrators and learning communities. Intelligent agents will also become crucial for filtering information stores to compile information profiles. The development of information portals for the education market knowledge management in conjunction with the use of intelligent agents will surely be seen as a priority in SIS development over the first part of the 21st century.

10. CONCLUSION

This chapter has investigated some of the aspects of what the future might bring for SIS. We have looked briefly at how the political, social and economic climate will change the ways in which education is organised and managed in the 21st century and as a result how SIS will develop. We have attempted to predict how emerging technologies might be used in these systems and how they might solve some of the dilemmas posed by the ever-increasing volumes of information. There are many issues to consider in the future use of these technologies in education that have not been mentioned but will tax the discipline of sociology over the next few years. For example changes will occur to the culture and society of the school when new technologies are introduced, 'information technology literacy' will become essential for information interchange and distance education will become the norm. We will also have to consider how new technologies reduce or exacerbate the gap between the haves and the have-nots in the field of education and make sure that they go beyond merely providing access to information but assist everyone in knowledge building. We need to ask if there are ways in which new technologies can help us achieve the goals of society more easily, or more meaningfully, or in ways we were previously unable to do. Sociologists need to become involved alongside computer scientists and educationalists.

REFERENCES

Brusilovsky, P. (1996). Methods and techniques of adaptive hypermedia. *User Modelling and User-Adapted Interaction* 6, 87-129.

Carnoy, M. (2000). *The Right to Education.* Paris: UNESCO Publishing.

Davey, B. (2001). *Private Communication*, Bill Davey, Department of Business Computing, RMIT University, Melbourne, Australia.

Davydov, M. (2000). EIP: The Second Wave Intelligent Enterprise. *ACM TechNews* 3 (4) 58-67.

De Bra, P., Brusilovsky, P. and Houben, G.-J. (1999). Adaptive Hypermedia: From Systems to Framework. *ACM Computing Surveys*, 31(4), 12-18.

Delacote, P. (1998). The United States Federal Government Education Plan. In *U.S. Department of Education Press Release*, http://www.ed.gov/pubs/planrpts.html.

DFEE (2000). *Blunkett and Mowlam report progress on reducing bureaucracy for schools.* Press Notice 2000/0588, 14 December, 2000. Department for Education and Employment Publications, United Kingdom. http://www.dfee.gov.uk/pns.

Franklin, U. (1990). *The Real World of Technology.* Montreal: CNC Publishing.

Fung, A. (2000). http://www.SchoolBiz.com.hk.

Fung, A. (2001). *Private Communication,* Alex C.W. Fung, Hong Kong Baptist University, Kowloon Tong, Hong Kong SAR, China.

G8 Communique (1999). http://www.wdr.de/tv/cologne_summits/g8index.html.

Hogenbirk, P. (2001). *Private Communication*, Pieter Hogenbirk, ICT-manager for secondary education and teacher training, CPS, The Netherlands.

JISC UK (2000). The Technology Changes *JISC Strategy Statement 2001-06*. http://www.jisc.ac.uk/curriss/general/strat_0105/draft_strat.html.

Long, R. (2000). Schooling for the information society: new paradigms of learning and leadership. In *Report on the Sixth International Educational Management and Administration Research Conference*, Cambridge, United Kingdom. http://www.shu.ac.uk/bemas/rpapers.html.

Latour, B. (1986). The Powers of Association: Power, Action and Belief. A new sociology of knowledge? In Law, J. (ed). *Sociological Review monograph, 32*. London: Routledge & Kegan, pp. 264-280.

MUSAC (2000). *Private Communication*, Rory Butler, MUSAC Central, Massey University, Palmerston North, New Zealand.

Okamoto, T. (2001). *Private Communication*, Toshio Okamoto, Artificial Intelligence & Educational Technology Lab., Graduate School of Information Systems, University of Electro-Communications, Tokyo, Japan.

Paiva, A. (1996). Communicating with Learner Modelling Agents, ITS 96 *Workshop on Architectures and Methods for Designing Cost-Effective and Reusable ITSs*, Montreal, June. http://www.cbl.leeds.ac.uk/~amp/MyPapers/its96/its96-ws.html.

Rogers, E. M. (1995). *Diffusion of Innovations*. New York: The Free Press.

SIMS (2000). *Private Communication*, Phil Neal, SIMS Capita Ltd., United Kingdom.

SITRA (1998). http://www.minedu.fi/julkaisut/information.

Synnes, K., Parnes, P., Widen, J., Schefstroem, D. (1999). Net-based Learning for the Next Millennium, In *Proceedings of SCI/ISAS99*, Florida, USA. Illinois: International Institute of Informatics and Systemics.

Tatnall, A. (2000). *Innovation and Change in the Information Systems Curriculum of an Australian University: a Socio-Technical Perspective*. (PhD thesis). Rockhampton: Central Queensland University.

Tatnall, A. (2001). *Private Communication*, Arthur Tatnall, Department of Information Systems, Victoria University of Technology, Melbourne, Australia.

Taylor, R., Peltsverger, B.W., and Vasu, M.L., (1997), The Nature of Virtual Organizations and their Anticipated Social and Psychological Impacts, *Education and Information Technologies 2*, 347-360.

Taylor, R. (2001). *Private Communication*, Raymond Taylor, North Carolina State University, USA.

Vidgen, R. T. & McMaster, T. (1996). Black Boxes, Non-Human Stakeholders and the Translation of IT through Mediation. In Orlikowski et al. (eds.), *Information Technology and Changes in Organizational Work*. London: Chapman & Hall, pp. 250-271.

WCBS (2000). *Private Communication* with Tony Childs. West Country Business Systems Ltd., United Kingdom.

Whitehead, B. (2000). The Changing Role of the Information System in Educational Organisations in the United Kingdom. *Private Communication,* B Whitehead, *DfEE*, London.

Wholeben, B. E. (2001). *Private Communication*, Brent Wholeben, Department of Educational Technology, Research and Assessment, Northern Illinois University, USA.

Woods, P. J. & Warren, J., (1996). Adapting Teaching Strategies in Intelligent Tutoring Systems, ITS 96 *Workshop on Architectures and Methods for Designing Cost-Effective and Reusable ITSs*, Montreal, June. http://advlearn.lrdc.pitt.edu/its-arch/papers/woods.html.

CHAPTER 9

CONCLUSIONS, REFLECTIONS AND THE ROAD AHEAD

Bill Davey[1], Adrie J. Visscher[2] & Phil Wild[3]
[1]Royal Melbourne Institute of Technology, Australia
[2]University of Twente, The Netherlands
[3]Loughborough University, United Kingdom

1. INTRODUCTION

This chapter reflects upon three aspects of school information system developments:

- What stage the field of school information systems has reached.
- Future directions indicated by the knowledge gained from the SIS-development and evaluation research.
- The further research required to optimize SIS-development and implementation.

Section 2 provides a reflection on chapters 2, 3 and 4 which described the developments of three SISs in three different contexts and the issues surrounding the design, development and implementation, and relates this to the in-depth discussion of SIS-design in chapter 6. Section 3 discusses the conclusions that can be drawn from the research and current understanding of SISs as an innovation and the issues which have been found to impinge on the successful implementation of SISs described in chapters 5 and 7 as well as the views of a wide range of experts on the future scenarios for SISs described in chapter 8. Section 4 concludes this chapter with an agenda for future research focusing particularly on how the problems identified so far can be overcome in future SIS-design and implementation processes.

2. ON THE DEVELOPMENT OF COMPUTER-ASSISTED SCHOOL INFORMATION SYSTEMS

The case studies of chapters 2, 3 and 4, together with other literature (Visscher, 1994; Tatnall, 1995), show that there have been two main paths by which a great proportion of current SISs have been developed. To examine the problems and

A.J. Visscher et al. (eds.), Information Technology in Educational Management, 161–175.
© 2001 *Kluwer Academic Publishers. Printed in the Netherlands.*

potentials of future SISs it is useful to look at the characteristics that have arisen due
to these paths.

2.1 Teacher based School Information Systems

First, there is the development of small, school-based systems by teachers which
then grow into a larger system that becomes adopted across a larger range of
schools. We could call this development path "teacher based SISs".

These beginnings have led to SISs that have characteristics of ad hoc choice of
functionality, difficulties in scalability and expandability and replication of paper
based systems. SISs have been built with little logical redesign of existing processes
and have had a strong emphasis on management reporting with few higher level
functions. On the other hand these aspects of the systems were well received by
teachers, particularly when a teacher was used in providing the training, fulfilled
well known application gaps in schools and obviously benefited from the intimate
domain knowledge of the original developers.

Secondly is the development of monolithic systems to achieve a single
governmental purpose. These have often been for wide scale examination systems,
or financial systems and their development path has the characteristics of being
more commercial in nature and involving very little input at a school level. In
chapters 2, 3 and 4 we found that in all three countries detailed in this book, and in
other literature (Visscher, 1994; Tatnall, 1995), systems were imposed on teachers at
the school level, serving few local school purposes, but requiring input of time and
resources from the school to satisfy national education system purposes. These
systems varied, but often included centralized examination systems based on
University entrance, Government auditing of standards, or financial requirements of
educational funding bodies. These aspects of more centralized systems were
characterized by improved planning of functionality and implementation but with
much more narrowly defined functions. They were more robust particularly in terms
of physical and logical security and the existence of formal design documentation.
These particular systems often cut across data gathered in the teacher based systems,
producing data duplication and adding to the complexity of extending and
integrating total systems.

2.2 Barriers to SIS-development

Many of the characteristics of current SISs have been due to a lack of
sophisticated technology in any of the system development paths. Teacher based
systems have been based on inexpensive personal computers. Centralized systems
have more sophisticated technology but have typically been unable to access data in
other school systems, particularly in the early systems, through problems with
communication, standards and compatibility problems. The absence of even a
standard Graphical User Interface forced designers to produce difficult, counter-
intuitive text based systems that were difficult to learn and awkward to use. This
was particularly the case with early version of SIMS and MUSAC when DOS based.

Even SAMS, which was developed into a windows based system, had the multi-windowing facility disabled which made it function in a similar way to the DOS systems.

The other major hurdle for effective SISs has been an absence in the early period of robust design strategies. Teacher based SISs have been successful in that they reflect almost exactly the requirements of schools. This strength of incorporating user requirements by making the user into a developer has intrinsic problems. A system made by a developer without a design strategy becomes difficult to scale, to maintain and to distribute because the underlying programming structure is not robust. Centralised SISs are enduring since the programming was designed robustly. The same rigidity that produces a robust system also means that user requirements are narrowly defined by the original design brief. Systems meet very few needs apart from the single purpose to which they were designed, but contain vast amounts of data that would be valuable to schools. In chapter 6 Tatnall characterized ownership of systems as a problem of current systems. In that chapter we also look at possible categories of systems that could be developed. He concludes "Many current school administrative applications are based around transaction processing and management reporting, but increased use could well be made of decision support and executive information systems."

Implementations of SISs show the classical problems of implementation in a naive site. Training is difficult, acceptance often delayed and users suddenly making system expansion requests as they become aware of the possibilities of technology.

The findings from three of the largest and most stable SISs in the world show that the implementation phase for SISs is particularly difficult (chapters 2, 3, 4). A hint for future developers is that training performed by a teacher was found to be more effective. Tatnall proposes "As it is impossible for even the most forward looking developers to predict all future trends and to cater for the needs of every school, new systems should be built as open systems. They should then come with published systems documentation so that making changes is possible for individual schools."

2.3   The Future for SIS-development

School information systems have, in general, been developed with an emphasis on replacing paper based systems. As the computer literacy of the education profession becomes more universal SISs will be based more on the educational needs of schools. Evaluations of all SISs in this book have shown a gap between system functionality and important potential uses of SISs in schools. There is also a very small amount of functionality that could be described as decision-support or executive information system level. In current SISs systems developers will need to ensure that user requirements elicitation is done properly and that the inability of users to imagine uses of technology does not effectively constrict the choices they make.

The new technologies having the most effect on SISs of the future are universal communications between computers, mobile and distributed computing, and improved design techniques such as object orientation and iterative methodologies. Chapter 8 more fully describes the possibilities of applications of technology to future SISs. It is proper here to say that developers will have more technology choices each year and the use of technologies will effect development outcomes. These technologies include hardware, software and design methodologies (Davey & Reyes, 1998). At the moment the most pervasive of these technologies is the internet and emerging web standards and tools such as XML. Developers will be able to leverage these technologies to produce SISs that provide information much more closely related to the decision-making needs of schools than has previously been available.

2.4 Development of the Next Stage of SISs

Recent improvements to the SAMS, SIMS and MUSAC have been in a similar vein and give clues to the directions new SISs must explore. Three of the major developers of SISs conclude:

- The data is now being turned into useful information which is accessible to teachers (chapter 2).
- Policy and planning must not merely reflect an unfettered embrace of technology. Such policy and planning, should rest on an understanding of the educational potential of information (chapter 3).
- However, the designs of the future will be much broader in scope and more accommodating than they are now of the inherent complexity, sophistication and subtlety of professional life and work in educational institutions (chapter 6).

We have a different environment, both in the technologies available to the developer and in the sophistication of the various clients of SISs.

2.5 Determining What Technologies are Applicable to SISs

In almost all industries the early introduction of computers saw a phenomenon that Tatnall calls the 'creation of need'. A computer exists, so how can we use it? The education industry has been no different and in the development of many SISs the task performed can be seen as one where a computer is useful rather than one which is useful for the school or the local and national education system. The emergence of new technologies (discussed in chapter 8) should assist in changing this pattern. There are so many new technologies (the web, mobile computing, wireless communications, natural language to name a few) that there is always a variety of ways of solving any information requirement problem. The challenge for SIS-developers is then to choose between technologies and determine the best one. In chapter 6 we saw the process of logical design before physical design. That is, from user requirements determine what must be done, and only then determine how it will be done. The choice of technology moves to a point after the solution, rather than driving the production of solutions looking for a problem.

2.6 Moving beyond the Replication of Paper based Systems to support for Management

In chapter 6 Tatnall identifies a number of levels of information systems, from transaction processing systems to executive information systems. The case studies in chapters 2, 3 and 4 show systems that have migrated from one end of this spectrum towards the other. Early systems seek to replace current paper based transaction processing systems with more efficient electronic systems. To move beyond the first step is to determine what it is that the 'education executive' needs as decision support. What are the information requirements of educational decision-makers? The work of Frank and Fulmer (1998) give us many ideas as to the possible directions of this type of support. All the developers represented in this book have also alluded to the need for additional types of information:

- No one really asked the fundamental question "what does the school really need to support management and administrative structures" (chapter 2).
- Some opined that front-line teachers should be involved in aspects of systems development in order to produce a system that would far more likely benefit the schools, teachers and students. They also stressed that such systems must reflect and support the operating rhythms of the school, allowing more flexibility in daily operations (chapter 3).
- The schools constantly challenge the developers to provide them with the systems they need (chapter 4).

2.7 Incorporating New Development Methodologies that ensure Robust, Scalable, Expandable Systems

The final word about new developments in SISs must be professionalism. Many SISs are an amalgamation of components built for distinct purposes. Most SISs have outgrown their original design specifications to the extent that they no longer reflect the original design structure. Although all systems have accommodated additional functionality this does not mean that they are now robust, nor that they have been designed for extension. Some current SISs are written in microcomputer packages such as Microsoft Access. These packages are not scalable. Microsoft Access has limits such as a practical maximum of 50 users. Systems created in personal computer oriented databases have few features to allow tuning when a database becomes large and so when an application is scaled from a few thousand records to very large data sets the original application no longer performs in any useful way. That scalability has not been designed into even some of the most common SISs in use shows that there is much scope for redesign using logical modelling from the point of specifying user requirements to the finished system. Literature abounds that tells us how to design robust, extensible, reliable and provable systems (Athey et al., 1991; Day & Zmud, 1991; Finegan, 1994; Kendall & Kendall, 1992; Tatnall et al., 2000). The new generation of SIS-developers must take into account good design principles, not just at the code level, but through the whole development cycle. The case studies in this book recognize this as the next step in their systems developments:

- Some SIMS modules were not well quality controlled before shipping and SIMS needed to keep pace with developments in education. There was a need for more flexibility in all modules particularly in user-assigned fields and more presentation options, even at a basic level of font styles, for example.
- Realizing those opportunities, it makes good management sense to design and develop a common, computer-based system that provides core functionality in a manner that will allow for flexibility in implementation while maintaining integrity of data and database structure.

3. EFFECTIVE SIS-USAGE AND THE FUTURE

Over a decade of evaluation and learning about SISs is presented in chapter 5. The social environment of a school has proved hard to change to take advantage of new technologies. A small number of SIS-developers, both from within schools and outside schools, have tried to implement a vision of helping teachers, school managerial and support staff to do their job more effectively. The positive effects of SISs must eventually be based on the improved education of pupils through better decision-making and use of resources. This, in turn, reflects the need for additional and better information that is the underlying aim of developing SISs now that the technology is readily available.

3.1 Research and the Variables

The research described in chapter 5 clearly highlights the large number of variables that are at play in such an environment (chapter 5, Figures 1 and 2). Anything less than a thorough and formal design process, and well thought through implementation procedures, will be doomed to fail, or at best be only partially successful in the gains to teachers and schools. Traditionally teachers have had a large amount of autonomy in what they do. This means that any top down approach to implementing SISs will be resisted. User participation is identified as a key component to success that will contribute to user-acceptance. Much of the research has focused on features of the schools as organisations together with aspects of a 'user acceptance audit' which had been found to work well in identifying problems in the implementation of information systems in industry and commerce (Wild, 1996).

The variable groups, which have been identified as being pertinent to the school environment, can clearly be clustered into fundamental but related categories which will impinge on the success or otherwise of the SIS (chapter 5, Figure 2). The overall intended outcome of investments in SISs is the 'Use of SIS'. This is dependent on the 'SIS Quality', the 'Implementation Process' and the 'School Organisation Features'. By using the SIS there are benefits to the school, teachers, pupils and parents (and national governments through increased educational standards) but there are also potential unintended effects. These mainly relate to the changing nature of the work, organisational processes and human relations. The 'Design Process' has an over-arching influence on all the other clusters of variables.

These identified variable groups, and subsequently the research questionnaire in the Appendix, resulted from knowledge and experience gained in small scale research and development carried out in various countries in the 1980s and early 1990s (see for example Fung 1988; Visscher, 1988; Wild et al., 1992; Nolan et al., 1996). In addition, the more general literature on computerised information system development, which until this time had been concentrated in industry and commerce, provided clear pointers towards the criteria leading to success or failure of those environments. The outcome has been the theoretical framework that has been added to over the years as knowledge has grown and experience shared. The framework can be used to guide us in the identification of flaws in design and implementation. This led to a large scale evaluation of SISs in Hong Kong, The Netherlands and the United Kingdom which all used the same questionnaire with locally required adaptations. The result is more knowledge on what works and what factors limit the use of SIS. A key finding is that use of SIS in schools is limited compared to the full potential.

3.2 Reflections on Successes and Continuing Problems

The results of the large-scale evaluations have helped to point to the factors that can be classed as imperative for the successful implementation of SISs (chapter 7). There are some successes, with teachers starting to accept the SIS as an integral part of the school infrastructure as they realise that such systems can save time in administrative functions. However, what is obvious from the research is that there is, as yet, little impact on decision-making processes and the SIS-functions that could contribute to decision-support are little used. Even at a simpler level of basic record keeping and administration it is wrong to assume that sophisticated and high quality SISs will automatically succeed. The important cluster of variables is within the implementation processes and particularly those that can be said to be 'people factors'. Nolan (1996) reported that MUSAC was successfully implemented in schools that already knew how to handle people within a changing environment. In turn this forms a link between the implementation process and the school organisation features and suggests that the shortfall in the more advanced use of SISs concerns school managers' limited knowledge of how to carry out the change process. Therefore, first, the research has highlighted that the future direction of support for implementation is not simply on how to use the SIS, and the technology of the SIS but also on the management processes of implementing change and a more holistic understanding of the school as an organisation.

Secondly, the research has pointed to serious issues on information management. SIS is good at providing data and can successfully process the data to provide immediately usable information, although this processing is still in its infancy in most SISs currently available. However, school managers are not being trained in how to influence the data processing, or how to use the additional data now available to them. There was evidence of this inherent limitation of managers throughout the 1980s which has been widely reported and discussed in chapter 7. The research in schools is now showing that these findings have not had impact on the training of school managers, including teachers as classroom managers, during the growth period of SISs. Both teachers and managers have to take many decisions on the basis of ad hoc information immediately available. This means that they are not yet in the habit of assessing what wider sources of information are now available with the aid of SISs, either because they have not had training in what is available, or the user perception of the nature of the information, its accessibility and relevance has not been well developed. This might also be due to a lack of retraining as newer and better SISs are installed in schools, when it is assumed that staff will automatically know about the enhanced features. The research is therefore indicating that more attention needs to be given in the future to what information is needed, the ease of access, and the ease of processing to a subset with interpretation. More selective information would then be more manageable by teachers and school managers in a fast changing environment like a school classroom. There is evidence in the United Kingdom that this need has been identified at Government level. A new post at the recently opened National College for School Leadership requires someone "to develop a vision of how successful school leaders of the future will exploit ICT to raise standards, improve learning and increase school effectiveness" (Times Higher Education Supplement, 2001). There is also now a requirement on teachers to use information provided by SISs to set targets for improvement of standards at pupil, class and school level. This is requiring SIS-developers to reactively include such features into the systems, including in-built and annually updated comparisons with national averages and other schools classed as similar on various criteria. All this can move schools and teachers forward in the problem areas that have been identified by the research provided the issue of relevant training, clearly identified as a cause of limited use, is addressed. The work of Visscher and Branderhorst (2001) is of particular relevance to the future design of training programmes to promote more effective use of SIS.

4.   THE AGENDA FOR FUTURE RESEARCH ON COMPUTER-ASSISTED SCHOOL INFORMATION SYSTEMS

In the 1980s the first analyses with respect to school information systems were published in the scientific literature. This often concerned enthusiastic descriptions of the type of support a school information system offered, or/and analyses of problems to be solved in this area (e.g., Bird, 1984; Essink & Visscher, 1989; Gustafson, 1985; Visscher, Spuck & Bozeman, 1991; Visscher & Vloon, 1986).

In the early nineties the first exploratory studies could be observed (Fung, 1992 & 1995; Nolan, 1995; Wild, 1995). Most of this research concerned one shot, small scale (often case study) research in which user perceptions formed the basis for general statements on the introduction and usage of school information systems.

Gradually, this changed as we approached the end of the previous century. At that time, large scale, empirical investigations of SIS-implementation based on an elaborated theoretical framework were carried out in a number of countries (cf.

Visscher & Bloemen, 1999; Visscher, Fung & Wild, 1999; Wild & Smith, 2001). The studies provided the first empirical basis for the design and introduction of systems supporting the management of educational institutions.

Recently, the first investigation has been set up according the 'golden standard of educational research': an experiment in which school managers have been allocated to experimental and control groups in an a-select (at random) manner. The goal of the study is to research the effectiveness of a carefully designed training course to promote managerial SIS-usage (Visscher & Branderhorst, 2001).

Now that we have entered the 21st century and developments in this field are continuing it seems important to formulate an agenda for research on IT in educational management for the next five to ten years.

In general, much more high quality, empirical research is needed to expand our understanding of effective strategies for the design and implementation of SISs and, by that, to improve the practice of management in education. This requires more *large scale research* based on random samples from the population of interest.

The need for large scale research does not mean that case studies are redundant. The problem however is that they do not provide insight into 'the general picture'. In other words, the data found in one case study can differ diametrically from the next case study. Especially in the case of innovative contexts like that of SISs, case studies can help in getting a grasp of what happens in practice and which variables are worthy of study. However, it should not be forgotten that they never could be more than first explorations that should always be followed by large scale tests of associations between variables. Too often these tests are not carried out, and the case study data are treated as if they allow general conclusions.

Ideally, future research is not one shot research but monitors system implementation and its impact *longitudinally*. Data collected at various stages of SIS-implementation will inform us more accurately on how SISs of a certain nature are being received by practitioners over time and which adaptations in SISs and user support are associated with possible changes in SIS-usage.

If possible, the research should not be based solely on user perceptions of the characteristics and quality of SISs, but also on the process of their implementation, the nature of the schools they are introduced into, the extent of system usage and its effects. In some respects user perceptions are very important. For instance, the degree to which users appreciate a specific information system will influence their intensity of SIS-usage. However, in general, user perceptions are very unreliable as reality and perceptions can differ enormously. We, therefore, need more reliable measurements of the nature of SISs, innovation processes, user behaviors, and its effects (in case of the latter pre-test post-test comparisons are needed).

Experimental studies are therefore needed since they are the only way to unequivocally determine the effectiveness of proposed strategies. Correlation research can help us in finding the factors that are associated with, for example, effective SIS-usage. However, they cannot inform us about cause and effect (e.g., about the variables causing effective SIS-usage). Experimental research is much more powerful here and can for instance be valuable in evaluating the quality of approaches for the design of SISs and for improving SIS-implementation (e.g., strategies to improve school managers' SIS-usage). Experimental research is not easily accomplished. In some cases it may even be impossible for practical or other reasons. However, through a raised awareness of its importance for expanding our body of knowledge, and a determination to carry out this type of investigation, much more can be done than at present.

In addition to summative evaluations to judge the quality/effectiveness of an evaluand (the entity being evaluated), *formative evaluation* should be included with the specific aim of improving the evaluand. This is especially important in design processes (when evaluand adaptation is still relatively easy) and prevents the waste of capital due to the poor quality and under-utilization of the outcomes of the design. Timely and systematic evaluations of the 'merit' (the intrinsic, context-independent quality) and 'worth' (the extrinsic quality) for one or more individual/groups of evaluands can increase the probability of successful design and implementation considerably. The body of knowledge in this field is enormous. Maslowski and Visscher (1999) present the evaluation techniques that can be used in the various stages of design and development of computer applications for the administration and management of educational institutions. They also point to reasons why we often fail to apply this know-how and as a consequence develop sub-optimal systems and strategies. As a result, many resources are wasted. It is recognized that it will not be easy to formatively evaluate an evaluand in all stages of development. However, if designers and implementers are more aware of the importance of formative evaluation they will probably feel more inclined to explicitly reserve resources for it and hence reduce the under-utilization of this formative stage of design improvement.

Let us now focus on the questions that need to be answered in future research. The Visscher model presented in chapter 5, showing the variable clusters relevant for the usage of SISs as well as their interrelationships, can serve as a basis for composing our research agenda. The model points to five important questions that are now discussed in detail.

4.1 Which are the (Dis)Advantages of Alternative Strategies for School Information System Design?

In the chapters 1 and 5 it was explained that the design of a SIS is a matter of making choices. Choices, for example, concerning how the information analysis, as a basis for designing the architecture and contents of the SIS, will be carried out, the degree of user participation in the design of SISs, and the way in which the 'worth' and 'merit' of SIS-prototypes will be evaluated.

Some design strategies are labeled as 'quick and dirty' ones, others are considered to be more profound. Although it is likely that the latter will lead to more sophisticated and high-quality SISs than the former, an empirical proof of this assumption is lacking. Moreover, more refined information on the pros and cons of (elements of) alternative design approaches is needed. The ideal strategy as proposed by Tatnall in chapter 6 may for instance not be feasible under all circumstances because of lack of resources (money, time). An interesting question is what the results are of cheaper, less time-consuming variants of Tatnall's strategy. In other words, what are the crucial elements of his plea and which elements can, if the theoretically ideal strategy is not feasible, be neglected without dramatic negative effects?

Ideally, this research question is answered via experiments in which experts evaluate the intrinsic quality of school information systems resulting from deliberately chosen alternative design approaches. Data on the extrinsic quality of these information systems can be collected via user judgements with respect to the degree to which they appreciate the systems, think they receive support from the SISs, the SISs are user-friendly etc.

If the proposed type of research is not feasible (for instance due to lack of resources for building SIS-variants) then retrospective, ex post facto research may be more realistic. The contexts in which existing SISs have been designed, as well as the characteristics of the followed design strategies, and the resulting SISs (based on the aforementioned quality criteria) should then be analyzed carefully.

4.2 What are the Features of High Quality School Information Systems?

SISs are being developed all over the world without exchanging much information on their structure or the support that they provide. Developers can benefit enormously from each other by exchanging this type of information more, as they can use it in the design or redesign of their SISs. It will also help in fully utilizing the potential of SISs in as many countries, including developing countries, as possible and in preventing the reinvention of the wheel and associated waste of resources. A way of accomplishing this may be the cooperative development of an internationally agreed framework for analyzing the nature of SISs that is applied by a team of experts (e.g., members of Working Group 3.7 of ITEM) who publish their findings in journals and distribute them among those interested.

Additionally, it is important to investigate more empirically which types of SISs are accepted and used most by different types of users (e.g., by school office staff, by school managerial staff) and why the differences occur. Distinctions between types of support have been made in chapter one (updating the database, information retrieval and document production, decision-making support, decision-making, data communication). A key question is therefore what do the most successful SISs provide in efficiency, user-friendliness and how do they do it? Also of importance is the kinds of SIS-generated information valued by users The questionnaire in Appendix A includes various items that can be used to collect information on the perceived SIS-quality (the B-questions).

If information on the intrinsic and extrinsic SIS-quality has been collected systematically the challenge will be to design SISs that at the same time optimize both their intrinsic and extrinsic quality. If we accomplish this we will develop systems that are good and are judged as good by those who use them intensively.

4.3   Which Implementation Process Features prove to be Crucial for Successful
SIS-implementation?

Hopefully the answers to research questions 1 and 2 will clarify how SISs should be designed and developed, and which characteristics the resulting school information systems have.

An intrinsically and extrinsically high quality SIS however does not guarantee its successful implementation. Even in the case of a SIS of a very high technical quality fitting the nature of the target users perfectly it takes a careful implementation process to 'put the new idea into practice' (Fullan, 1982).

The target user group for example needs to be informed about the value added by the SIS as well as about how it can help in executing their work more efficiently and effectively. In addition to the prerequisite of motivating them for system usage, timely support is crucial to keep the change process going in case of problems encountered with SIS-usage. These are just a few examples of factors that most possibly matter. More in depth research should clarify more accurately which aspects of the introduction process influence the intensity of SIS-usage.

Case studies based on an elaborated theoretical framework, followed by large scale, longitudinal, correlation research in which hypotheses are being tested statistically can provide what is needed. This information can inspire the design of strategies for optimizing SIS-utilization (e.g., training strategies) that ask for effectiveness-tests in randomized controlled trials.

4.4   Which Roles do the Organizational Features of Schools play in the Utilization
of SISs?

Some school organizational characteristics more or less apply to most schools, for example a high degree of teacher autonomy, limited policy-development at school level, and the nature of information usage by school managers as described in chapter 7. Other organizational features vary more between schools (e.g., how much managers promote SIS-usage within their schools).

We need to find out to what extent and how these general and school specific organizational characteristics influence SIS-innovations as a basis for adapting our SISs (e.g., 'reporting by exception' to managers as described in chapter 8) and our strategies for implementing them. As such we can increase the probability of higher levels of SIS-usage.

The analysis of the general organizational school features can build on the school management literature for formulating items in general terms. The D-questions in the appendix can serve as a starting point for research on the school organizational features. The literature can also assist in formulating hypotheses on how schools vary and how this variation is associated with variation in SIS-usage. The hypotheses should be tested in large scale research.

The information collected could well lead to proposals for improving the practice of IT in educational management in areas which have been identified so far as lacking, such as developing schools' capacity to use SISs-information for policy-development. The follow up to this would be randomized controlled trials to provide more definitive information about the value of these improvement approaches.

4.5 Which (Un)Intended Effects does SIS-usage Produce?

There is clearly a possibility for a combination of positive, negative, intended and unintended effects from using SIS. Investigation of these effects in reliable and valid ways is very hard. It is understandable that in most studies user perceptions have been used to draw conclusions on the impact of SISs. These studies also focused on the intended changes in efficiency and effectiveness of the operation of schools as a consequence of SIS-usage and on undesirable effects like an increase in monotonous work (e.g., as a result of more data entry work), work fragmentation, and information overload. More reliable and valid pre-test-post-test comparisons (ideally longitudinally) form the only way to obtain an answer to research question 5 that can be used for designing new policies to promote SIS-usage.

The research agenda is ambitious. It is, however, worth trying as the answers to the five research questions will provide further insight into 'what matters' for the successful design and implementation of SISs, and as such will help us to benefit even more from these systems all over the world.

5. CONCLUSIONS

The last two decades have seen a major shift in our knowledge of SISs, from systems that were introduced on the first microcomputers with limited functionality to nation-wide systems with extensive functionality and inter-communication. What the authors and editors of this book have endeavoured to do is pull together the changes, research and perceptions from many sources which have contributed to this change in knowledge. At the start there was a concentration on administrative systems with no links to the research on change management and the related problems and difficulties of IT implementation in an organisation. The early research pulled this together and in the last decade the research of SISs has developed an identity of its own. This has now moved on to SIS researchers finding that the technology in both hardware and software is now capable of doing even more, but the inertia which limits organisational change is most probably what is preventing further progress. The time has therefore now come to go back to the basic research questions posed and investigated in this book and summarised above so that researchers and practitioners can progress the technology and change management together within school organisations. We hope that what is now known and presented here will avoid the wasted resource experienced by the 'pioneers' for those just starting out and will guide those who now need to rethink.

REFERENCES

Athey, T.H., Day, J.C. & Zmud, R.W. (1991). *Computers and End-User Software*. New York: Harper Collins.

Bird, P. (1984). *Microcomputers in school administration*. London: Hutchinson.

Davey, B. & Reyes, G. (1998). Overcoming Resistance to Integration: Using Client-Server Systems and Data Warehousing. In Fulmer, C.L., Barta, B.Z., & Nolan, P. (Eds.), *The Integration of Information for Educational Management*. Whitefield, Maine: Felicity Press/International Federation for Information Processing.

Finegan, A (1994). *Soft Systems Methodology: an Alternative Approach to Knowledge Elicitation in Complex and Poorly Defined Systems*. RMIT Centre for Remote Sensing & Land Information: http://www.csu.edu.au/ci/vol1/Andrew.Finegan/paper.html, 15 Nov. 1998.

Frank, F.P., & Fulmer, C.L. (1998). Classroom-Focused Information Systems: Support for Teaching/Learning Entrepreneurs. In Fulmer, C.L., Nolan, C.J.P. & Barta, B.Z. (Eds.), *The Integration of Information for Educational Management*. Whitefield, Maine: Felicity Press.

Fullan, M. (1982). *The meaning of educational change*. New York; Teachers College Press.

Fung, A.C.W. (1988), Trends and development in computer-aided school administration. *Proceedings of Microcomputers in Education Conference*. Hong Kong, pp. A-20 - A28.

Fung, A.C.W. (1992). *Management of educational innovation: the case of computer-aided administration*. London: University of London, Institute of Education.

Gustafson, T. J. (1985). *Microcomputers and educational administration*. Englewood Cliffs: Prentice Hall.

Kendall, K.E. and Kendall, J.E. (1992). *Systems Analysis and Design* (2nd edition). New Jersey: Prentice Hall.

Maslowski, R. & Visscher, A.J. (1999). Formative evaluation in educational computing research & development. *Journal of Research on Computing in Education,*. 32(2), 239-255.

Nolan, P. C.J. (1995). The development of computer-assisted school administration in New Zealand. In Barta, B., Telem, M. & Gev, Y. *Information Technology in Educational management*. London: Chapman & Hall, pp. 63-78.

Nolan, C.J.P., Ayres, D.A., Dunn, S., & McKinnon, D.H. (1996). Implementing computerized school information systems: Case studies from New Zealand. *International Journal of Educational Research,* Vol. 25, 4, 335-349.

Tatnall, A. & Davey, B. (1995). Executive Information Systems in School Management: a Research Perspective. In Tinsley, J.D. and van Weert, T.J. (Eds.), *World Conference on Computers in Education VI. WCCE'95. Liberating the Learner*. London: Chapman & Hall.

Tatnall, A., Davey, B, Burgess, S., Davison, A. & Fisher, J. (2000). *Management Information Systems – concepts, issues, tools and applications* (2nd edition). Melbourne: Data Publishing.

Times Higher Education Supplement , Jan 19th 2001, National College for School Leadership advertisement, p. 37.

Visscher, A.J. (1988). The computer as an administrative tool: Problems and impact. *Journal of Research on Computing in Education, 21*(1), 28-35.

Visscher, A.J. (1992). *Design and evaluation of a computer-assisted management information system for secondary schools* (Ph. D. dissertation). Enschede: University of Twente, Faculty of Educational Science and Technology.

Visscher, A.J. & Bloemen; P.P.M. (1999). Evaluation of the use of computer-assisted management information systems in Dutch schools. *Journal of Research on Computing in Education*, 32 (1), 172-188.

Visscher, A.J. & Branderhorst, E.M. (2001). How should school managers be trained for managerial school information system usage? In Nolan, P. & Fung A. (Eds.) *Institutional Improvement through IT in Educational Management*. London: Kluwer.

Visscher, A.J., Fung, A. & Wild, P. (1999). The evaluation of the large scale implementation of a computer-assisted management information system in Hong Kong schools. *Studies in Educational Evaluation*, 25, 11-31.

Visscher, A.J., Spuck, D. W. & Bozeman, W. C. (1991). Computer-assisted school administration and management: the state of the art in seven nations. *Journal of Research on Computing in Education*, 24 (1), 1-168.

Visscher, A.J. & Vloon, W. (1986). *Schooladministratie en schoolmanagement m.b.v. de computer* [School administration and school management with computers]. Report for the Dutch Ministry of Education: Enschede: University of Twente.

Wild, P. (1995). The use of task analysis and user acceptability audits in implementing information technology systems in schools. In Barta, B., Telem, M. & Gev, Y. *Information Technology in Educational management*. London: Chapman & Hall, pp. 27- 33.

Wild, P. (1996). An assessment of strategies for information system evaluation: Lessons for education. *International Journal of Educational Research,* 25(4), 361-371.

Wild, P. & Smith, D. (2001). Has a decade of computerisation made a difference in school management? In Nolan, P. & Fung A. (Eds.) *Institutional Improvement through IT in Educational Management*. London: Kluwer.

Wild, P., Scivier, J.E. and Richardson, S.J. (1992). Evaluating Information
Technology Supported Local Management of Schools: The User Acceptability Audit, *Educational Management and Administration,* 20, (1), 41-48.

APPENDIX

SAMS questionnaire

SAMS QUESTIONNAIRE

Alex C.W. Fung, Adrie J. Visscher & Phil Wild

This questionnaire has been designed to be answered by four types of school personnel: the school head, the SAMS-administrator, a teacher, and a secretary/clerk in the school office. Please answer all the questions except those not relevant to your post.

For questions with a scale or check boxes, please mark your choice as illustrated below.

1_____②_____3_____4_____5   Yes ☐   No ☐   Don't know ☑

The bold letter number combinations before a questionnaire question correspond with a variable in Figure 2 in chapter 5.

PERSONAL/SCHOOL DETAILS

1. Name: _____(Mr./Mrs./Ms./Dr.)

2. School Name: _____

    Tel: _____ Fax: _____

3. What is your job title? (*Please tick one box*)
    Principal   ☐
    Vice-principal   ☐
    Computer studies teacher   ☐
    Secretary   ☐
    Clerk   ☐

4. Are you the SAMS Administrator?

    Yes ☐   No ☐

5. As at the end of 1996, what is the SAMS version in use in your school? (*Please tick one box*)

    SAMS 1.3   ☐
    SAMS 1.4   ☐
    SAMS 1.5   ☐
    Don't know   ☐

    Has your system been upgraded now to SAMS 2.0?

    Yes ☐   No ☐   Don't know☐

D1   6. How motivated were you for working with SAMS when it was first introduced into your school?
    1_____2_____3_____4_____5   Don't know☐
    very   unmotivated   neutral   motivated   very
    unmotivated   motivated

7. Did you <u>personally</u> have a choice about whether or not to use SAMS?

    Yes ☐   No ☐   Don't know☐

D2   8. Before installation, did you expect SAMS to help you in your job?

    Yes ☐   No ☐   Don't know☐

9. Have you had any experience of using computers before the introduction of
D3   SAMS to the school?

    At home   1_____2_____3_____4_____5
                 none   a little   some   much   very much

    At work   1_____2_____3_____4_____5
                 none   a little   some   much   very much

E1   10. Have you <u>personally</u> been using the SAMS directly (use the computer system
        yourself)?

    Yes ☐   for _____ months already

    No ☐   **[If you answer "No" to this question, then go to question 13]**

B1   11. Each item on the following list describes one part or feature of the SAMS
        hardware. Rate the performance of each component in terms of your experience
        of using it in your work.

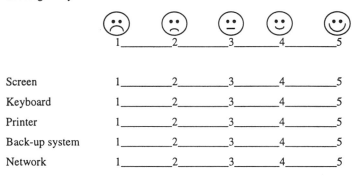

    Screen   1_____2_____3_____4_____5
    Keyboard   1_____2_____3_____4_____5
    Printer   1_____2_____3_____4_____5
    Back-up system   1_____2_____3_____4_____5
    Network   1_____2_____3_____4_____5

12. Can you have a look at this list of features about the SAMS setting/office environment and type of furniture WHERE YOU MAKE USE OF THE SYSTEM. Can you rate them as before?

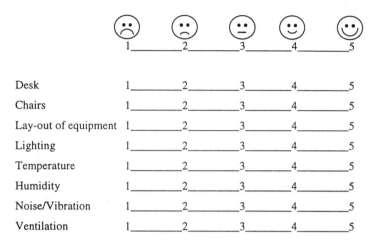

Desk	1_____2_____3_____4_____5
Chairs	1_____2_____3_____4_____5
Lay-out of equipment	1_____2_____3_____4_____5
Lighting	1_____2_____3_____4_____5
Temperature	1_____2_____3_____4_____5
Humidity	1_____2_____3_____4_____5
Noise/Vibration	1_____2_____3_____4_____5
Ventilation	1_____2_____3_____4_____5

TRAINING & SUPPORT

C2 13. How many hours of training have you received in total from a <u>SAMS trainer</u> <u>external to your school</u>? (*Please tick one box*)

0 hour   ☐   **[If you choose 0 hour, please go to question 17]**

5-10 hours   ☐
11-20 hours   ☐
21-30 hours   ☐
>30 hours   ☐

C4

14. How happy are you about the quantity and quality of <u>external</u> training you have received with respect to SAMS?

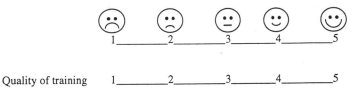

Quality of training   1_____2_____3_____4_____5

C5

15. Please mark on these scales the point which you think best describes the balance of the training you received.

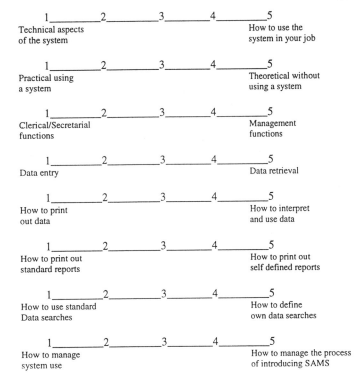

1_____2_____3_____4_____5
Technical aspects   How to use the
of the system   system in your job

1_____2_____3_____4_____5
Practical using   Theoretical without
a system   using a system

1_____2_____3_____4_____5
Clerical/Secretarial   Management
functions   functions

1_____2_____3_____4_____5
Data entry   Data retrieval

1_____2_____3_____4_____5
How to print   How to interpret
out data   and use data

1_____2_____3_____4_____5
How to print out   How to print out
standard reports   self defined reports

1_____2_____3_____4_____5
How to use standard   How to define
Data searches   own data searches

1_____2_____3_____4_____5
How to manage   How to manage the process
system use   of introducing SAMS

16. Who were the SAMS trainers? *(Please tick all that apply)*

       SAMS Training & Research Unit staff   ☐

       Others   ☐

       (please specify _____)

C1   17. How many hours of training have you received in total from internal school staff? *(Please tick one box)*

       0 hour   ☐   **[If you choose 0 hour, please go to question 19]**

       1-4 hours   ☐

       5-10 hours   ☐

       11-20 hours   ☐

       21-30 hours   ☐

       >30 hours   ☐

C3   18. How happy are you about the quantity and quality of <u>internal</u> training you have received with respect to SAMS?

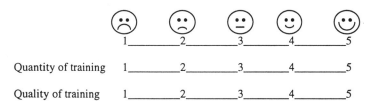

Quantity of training   1_____2_____3_____4_____5

Quality of training   1_____2_____3_____4_____5

C7   19. How happy are you with the ease at which you can get help if you have
           difficulties with SAMS?

           I do not use SAMS   ☐   [If you don't use SAMS, please go to question 21]

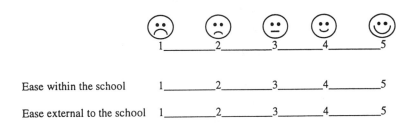

           Ease within the school   1_____2_____3_____4_____5

           Ease external to the school 1_____2_____3_____4_____5

C6   20. If you have a problem with SAMS, how often do you use the following sources
           of help?

                                         1_____2_____3_____4_____5
                                         never   very rarely   rarely   often   very
                                                                                      frequently

           SAMS administrator   1_____2_____3_____4_____5

           SAMS hot line   1_____2_____3_____4_____5

           Colleague within school   1_____2_____3_____4_____5

           Colleague outside school   1_____2_____3_____4_____5

           User manual/guide   1_____2_____3_____4_____5

USE OF SAMS

E1+E2   21. Please indicate how many hours a month on average you use SAMS <u>directly</u> (use the system yourself) and/or <u>indirectly</u> (through the use of printouts provided to you by other staff using the system).

Directly (Hours a month)		Indirectly (Hours a month)	
0 hour	☐	0 hour	☐
-----------------------------		-----------------------------	
1 hour	☐	1 hour	☐
1-4 hours	☐	1-4 hours	☐
5-10 hours	☐	5-10 hours	☐
11-20 hours	☐	11-20 hours	☐
21-30 hours	☐	21-30 hours	☐
>30 hours	☐	>30 hours	☐

[If you neither use SAMS directly NOR indirectly, please go to question 23]

E3   22. The following table contains a list of SAMS modules. Can you enter whether each module has been installed, how much of the data (as a %) necessary for each module has been entered into SAMS and how often you use each module?

SAMS module	Module installed	Data entered	Frequency of use (rating*)
Wordprocessing English	———	———	1 2 3 4 5
Wordprocessing - Chinese	———	———	1 2 3 4 5
Housekeeping	Yes ☐ / No ☐ Don't know ☐	( )% Don't know ☐	1 2 3 4 5
Security	Yes ☐ / No ☐ Don't know ☐	( )% Don't know ☐	1 2 3 4 5
School Management	Yes ☐ / No ☐ Don't know ☐	( )% Don't know ☐	1 2 3 4 5
Student	Yes ☐ / No ☐	( )%	1 2 3 4 5

SAMS module	Module installed	Data entered	Frequency of use (rating*)
	Don't know ☐	Don't know ☐	
Student Assessment	Yes ☐ / No ☐ Don't know ☐	( )% Don't know ☐	1 2 3 4 5
Inter-year Processing	Yes ☐ / No ☐ Don't know ☐	( )% Don't know ☐	1 2 3 4 5
Timetabling	Yes ☐ / No ☐ Don't know ☐	( )% Don't know ☐	1 2 3 4 5
HKEA Processing	Yes ☐ / No ☐ Don't know ☐	( )% Don't know ☐	1 2 3 4 5
Financial Monitoring and Planning (for SMI schools)	Yes ☐ / No ☐ Don't know ☐	( )% Don't know ☐	1 2 3 4 5
Programme Schedule (for SMI schools)	Yes ☐ / No ☐ Don't know ☐	( )% Don't know ☐	1 2 3 4 5
Student Attendance	Yes ☐ / No ☐ Don't know ☐	( )% Don't know ☐	1 2 3 4 5
Staff (core functions)	Yes ☐ / No ☐ Don't know ☐	( )% Don't know ☐	1 2 3 4 5
Communication and Delivery System	Yes ☐ / No ☐ Don't know ☐	( )% Don't know ☐	1 2 3 4 5

* Rating   never   =1
                    every week   =2
                    every month   =3
                    a few times a year =4
                    once a year   =5

D4   23. Which of the following statements, referring to SAMS, do you agree/disagree with?

- SAMS was introduced to improve school administrative efficiency   Agree ☐   Disagree ☐   Don't know ☐

- SAMS was introduced to improve management effectiveness in school   Agree ☐   Disagree ☐   Don't know ☐

- SAMS was introduced to improve administrative effectiveness in school   Agree ☐   Disagree ☐   Don't know ☐

- SAMS was introduced to increase central control by the E.D.   Agree ☐   Disagree ☐   Don't know ☐

- SAMS was introduced to decrease   Agree ☐   Disagree ☐   Don't know ☐

central control by the E.D.

- SAMS was introduced to improve the   Agree ☐   Disagree ☐   Don't know ☐
  education of the pupils

- SAMS was introduced to improve   Agree ☐   Disagree ☐   Don't know ☐
  information flow to/from E.D.

- SAMS was introduced to improve   Agree ☐   Disagree ☐   Don't know ☐
  statistics for strategic planning by E.D.

- SAMS was introduced to provide better   Agree ☐   Disagree ☐   Don't know ☐
  record transfer between school phases

C11 24. Are the goals of introducing SAMS clear to you?

1_____2_____3_____4_____5
Not at   a little   neutral   much   very
all   clear

C12 25. How clear is it to you by which means and activities these goals can be met?

1_____2_____3_____4_____5
Not at   a little   neutral   much   very
all   clear

B2 26. Does SAMS provide the information you need?

1_____2_____3_____4_____5
Not at   a little   some   much   very
all   much

27. To what extent would you like to be able to define the information you want to retrieve?

1_____2_____3_____4_____5
Not at   a little   some   much   very
all   much

B3 28. To what extent does SAMS provide retrieved information in a <u>format</u> which you can easily use?

1_____2_____3_____4_____5
Not at   a little   some   much   very
all   much

29. To what extent would you like to be able to define the <u>format</u> of the retrieved information?

$$1\underline{\hspace{1cm}}2\underline{\hspace{1cm}}3\underline{\hspace{1cm}}4\underline{\hspace{1cm}}5$$

Not at all	a little	some	much	very much

30. List 3 printouts from SAMS that you most frequently retrieve (or have retrieved) <u>for your own use.</u>

1 _____

2 _____

3 _____

None ☐

31. List 3 printouts from SAMS that you most frequently retrieve <u>for others' to use.</u>

1 _____

2 _____

3 _____

None ☐

C8

32. Please mark the following scales which refer to aspects of the introduction and use of SAMS.

The pace of introduction of SAMS in your school was: $1\underline{\hspace{0.5cm}}2\underline{\hspace{0.5cm}}3\underline{\hspace{0.5cm}}4\underline{\hspace{0.5cm}}5$ Don't know ☐

very slow	slow	OK	fast	very fast

C10

The SAMS administrator has encouraged the use of SAMS: $1\underline{\hspace{0.5cm}}2\underline{\hspace{0.5cm}}3\underline{\hspace{0.5cm}}4\underline{\hspace{0.5cm}}5$ Don't know ☐

Not at all	a little	some	much	very much

[Please ignore this question if you are the SAMS Administrator]

C9 The principal has encouraged 1____2____3____4____5 Don't know ☐
the use of SAMS: Not at a little some much very
all much

[Please ignore this question if you are the SAMS Administrator]

[If you don't use SAMS directly, please go to question 39]

B4 33. What are your feelings about the following aspects of SAMS?

☹ ☹ 😐 🙂 😊
1____2____3____4____5

Start up/close down Windows 1____2____3____4____5 Don't know ☐

Start up/close down server 1____2____3____4____5 Don't know ☐

Open/close SAMS 1____2____3____4____5 Don't know ☐

B5 34. What are your feelings about the following data entry options of SAMS?

☹ ☹ 😐 🙂 😊
1____2____3____4____5

Screen format 1____2____3____4____5 Don't know ☐

System terms 1____2____3____4____5 Don't know ☐

Keying in data 1____2____3____4____5 Don't know ☐

Error handling 1____2____3____4____5 Don't know ☐

B6   What are your feelings about the following data retrieval options of SAMS?

Clarity of means   1____2____3____4____5 Don't know ☐

Navigation   1____2____3____4____5 Don't know ☐

B7   What are your feelings about the following output options of SAMS?

On screen
- ease of getting data on 1____2____3____4____5 Don't know ☐
  screen
- clarity of layout   1____2____3____4____5 Don't know ☐

- relevance   1____2____3____4____5 Don't know ☐

Printed
- ease to get print out   1____2____3____4____5 Don't know ☐

- layout   1____2____3____4____5 Don't know ☐

- relevance   1____2____3____4____5 Don't know ☐

B8   35. Does the system always work when you want it to?

Yes ☐   No ☐   Don't know ☐

36. If NO, how often do you have problems?   about _____occasions a month

B9   37. Can you look at the following list of attributes which relate to the retrieved SAMS data.

Please rate each item in relation to your experience of using them.

1____2____3____4____5
very   poor   neutral good very
poor   good

Accuracy of the information   1____2____3____4____5 Don't know ☐

Up to date information   1____2____3____4____5 Don't know ☐

Completeness of information 1____2____3____4____5 Don't know ☐

Ability to provide   1____2____3____4____5 Don't know ☐
management support

Speed of retrieving   1____2____3____4____5 Don't know ☐
information on screen

Speed of printing out   1____2____3____4____5 Don't know ☐
information

B10

38. Please look at the following list of attributes of SAMS and indicate whether you think that they are better or worse than your previous system (manual or computer).

-2____-1____ 0____+1____+2
much worse same better much
worse   better

Data input and storage   -2____-1____ 0____+1____+2 Don't know ☐

Accuracy of the information -2____-1____ 0____+1____+2 Don't know ☐

Relevance of the information -2____-1____ 0____+1____+2 Don't know ☐

Up to date information   -2____-1____ 0____+1____+2 Don't know ☐

Completeness of information -2____-1____ 0____+1____+2 Don't know ☐

Ability to provide information -2____-1____ 0____+1____+2 Don't know ☐
for management support

Speed of retrieving   -2____-1____ 0____+1____+2 Don't know ☐
information on screen

Speed of printing out   -2____-1____ 0____+1____+2 Don't know ☐
Information

Easily available information   -2____-1____ 0____+1____+2 Don't know ☐

F1   39. For the following <u>aspects of your job</u>, please indicate whether SAMS is better
          or worse than your previous system.

-2	-1	0	+1	+2
much worse	worse	same	better	much better

Insight into how the   -2____-1____ 0____+1____+2 Don't know ☐
school functions

Evaluation of school   -2____-1____ 0____+1____+2 Don't know ☐
performance

Utilistion of school   -2____-1____ 0.___+1____+2 Don't know ☐
resources

Information for curriculum   -2____-1____ 0____+1____+2 Don't know ☐
planning

Internal communication with -2____-1____ 0____+1____+2 Don't know ☐
colleagues

Workload   -2____-1____ 0____+1____+2 Don't know ☐

Stress   -2____-1____ 0____+1____+2 Don't know ☐

F2   40. Can you mark the following scales with regard to how SAMS has changed your job?

Monotonous
clerical work
-2____-1____ 0____+1____+2 Don't know ☐
much more   more   same   less   much less

Time needed for
duties
-2____-1____ 0____+1____+2 Don't know ☐
much more   more   same   less   much less

Ease of duties
-2____-1____ 0____+1____+2 Don't know ☐
much more   more   same   easier   much easier
difficult   difficult

Does SAMS help directly
in your job?
-2____-1____ 0____+1____+2 Don't know ☐
not at all   little   some   much   very much

Has SAMS affected your
carreer opportunities?
-2____-1____ 0____+1____+2 Don't know ☐
much worse   worse   same   better   much better

41. As a result of SAMS the quality of teaching and management in your school has become:

F3   In Teaching
-2____-1____ 0____+1____+2 Don't know ☐
much worse   worse   same   better   much better

F4   In Management
-2____-1____ 0____+1____+2 Don't know ☐
much worse   worse   same   better   much better

42. Please indicate which of these figures would best illustrate your feelings if SAMS was withdrawn tomorrow and you returned to your old (computer or manual) system.

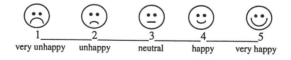

1_____2_____3_____4_____5
very unhappy   unhappy   neutral   happy   very happy

43. Does SAMS do what <u>you</u> expected for the <u>administration</u> of the school?

    Yes ☐ 1   No ☐ 2   Don't know☐ 3

44. Does SAMS do what <u>you</u> expected for the <u>management</u> of the school?

    Yes ☐ 1   No ☐ 2   Don't know☐ 3

F5   45. How motivated are you to work with SAMS <u>now</u> at your school?

1	2	3	4	5
very unmotivated	unmotivated	neutral	motivated	very motivated

QUESTIONS FOR THE PRINCIPAL

46. School type? (*Please tick in the appropriate boxes*)

    Primary – a.m.   ☐
    Primary - p.m.   ☐
    Secondary   ☐
    Government   ☐
    Aided   ☐
    SMI school   ☐

47. How many pupils are there on roll? (*Please tick one box*)

    <500   ☐
    500-750   ☐
    751-1000   ☐
    1001-1250   ☐
    1251-1500   ☐
    >1500   ☐

48. Prior to the installation of SAMS in the school, which of the following systems did you use? (*Please tick one box*)

    Manual system ONLY   ☐
    Other computerised school administration /management system ☐

49. Please indicate how long ago (in months) the following took place in your school:

Site preparation	_____ months ago
Hardware installation	_____ months ago
SAMS package installation	_____ months ago
Data conversion completed	_____ months ago
SAMS in operation	_____ months ago

50. Managerial decisions can be defined as those <u>decisions</u> which directly affect the ethos and running of the school, the work of the teachers, the pupils' curriculum or the work of the individual pupils. Such decisions affect the quality of the services provided.

Please indicate in the following table which lists/reports from SAMS you personally use to support managerial decisions and if you use them the frequency of use.

E4

Reports	Use to support managerial decisions	Frequency of use (rating*)
School calendar	Yes ☐ / No ☐ Don't know ☐	1 2 3 4 5
School place vacancy list	Yes ☐ / No ☐ Don't know ☐	1 2 3 4 5
Departed student list	Yes ☐ / No ☐ Don't know ☐	1 2 3 4 5
Student attainment and annual score statistics	Yes ☐ / No ☐ Don't know ☐	1 2 3 4 5
Student punishment list (by type)	Yes ☐ / No ☐ Don't know ☐	1 2 3 4 5
Student absent/late list	Yes ☐ / No ☐ Don't know ☐	1 2 3 4 5
Class overall score list	Yes ☐ / No ☐ Don't know ☐	1 2 3 4 5
Score statistics list	Yes ☐ / No ☐ Don't know ☐	1 2 3 4 5
Most improved student list	Yes ☐ / No ☐ Don't know ☐	1 2 3 4 5

Student without promotion list	Yes ☐ / No ☐ Don't know ☐	1 2 3 4 5
Vacancy after promotion list	Yes ☐ / No ☐ Don't know ☐	1 2 3 4 5
School and class structure list	Yes ☐ / No ☐ Don't know ☐	1 2 3 4 5
Room detail list	Yes ☐ / No ☐ Don't know ☐	1 2 3 4 5
Class-subject load report	Yes ☐ / No ☐ Don't know ☐	1 2 3 4 5
Teaching load by teachers	Yes ☐ / No ☐ Don't know ☐	1 2 3 4 5
Teaching load by subject	Yes ☐ / No ☐ Don't know ☐	1 2 3 4 5
First warning student list	Yes ☐ / No ☐ Don't know ☐	1 2 3 4 5
Exam result for best subjects	Yes ☐ / No ☐ Don't know ☐	1 2 3 4 5
Analysis of exam subject results	Yes ☐ / No ☐ Don't know ☐	1 2 3 4 5
Longitudinal analysis of exam results	Yes ☐ / No ☐ Don't know ☐	1 2 3 4 5
Other reports not listed above		
1.	Yes ☐ / No ☐	1 2 3 4 5
2.	Yes ☐ / No ☐	1 2 3 4 5
3.	Yes ☐ / No ☐	1 2 3 4 5
4.	Yes ☐ / No ☐	1 2 3 4 5
5.	Yes ☐ / No ☐	1 2 3 4 5
6.	Yes ☐ / No ☐	1 2 3 4 5

* Rating   never   =1
           every week   =2
           every month   =3
           a few times a year   =4
           once a year   =5

51. A 'Management Information System' (MIS) can provide support for management activities, such as storing, manipulating and analysing information or finding out specific information before taking decisions.

The following table contains a list of SAMS modules. Please indicate how often you retrieve information from the modules and whether you use the information for <u>managerial activities</u>.

E4

SAMS module	Use to support managerial activities	Frequency of use (rating*)
Housekeeping	Yes ☐ / No ☐ Don't know ☐	1 2 3 4 5
Security	Yes ☐ / No ☐ Don't know ☐	1 2 3 4 5
School Management	Yes ☐ / No ☐ Don't know ☐	1 2 3 4 5
Student	Yes ☐ / No ☐ Don't know ☐	1 2 3 4 5
Student Assessment	Yes ☐ / No ☐ Don't know ☐	1 2 3 4 5
Inter-year Processing	Yes ☐ / No ☐ Don't know ☐	1 2 3 4 5
Timetabling	Yes ☐ / No ☐ Don't know ☐	1 2 3 4 5
HKEA Processing	Yes ☐ / No ☐ Don't know ☐	1 2 3 4 5
Financial Monitoring and Planning (for SMI schools)	Yes ☐ / No ☐ Don't know ☐	1 2 3 4 5
Programme Schedule (for SMI schools)	Yes ☐ / No ☐ Don't know ☐	1 2 3 4 5
Student Attendance	Yes ☐ / No ☐ Don't know ☐	1 2 3 4 5
Staff (core functions)	Yes ☐ / No ☐ Don't know ☐	1 2 3 4 5
Communication and Delivery System	Yes ☐ / No ☐ Don't know ☐	1 2 3 4 5

* Rating   never   =1
                every week   =2
                every month   =3
                a few times a year   =4
                once a year   =5

52. Please add any further comments you wish to make.

_____

_____

THANK YOU FOR YOUR KIND SUPPORT!